Classics In
Child Development

Classics In
Child Development

Advisory Editors

JUDITH KRIEGER GARDNER
HOWARD GARDNER

Editorial Board

Wayne Dennis
Jerome Kagan
Sheldon White

ASPECTS OF CHILD LIFE
AND EDUCATION · BY G. STANLEY
HALL · AND SOME OF HIS PUPILS

CALIFORNIA SCHOOL OF PROFESSIONAL PSYCHOLOGY

LOS ANGELES

ARNO PRESS

A New York Times Company

New York — 1975

Reprint Edition 1975 by Arno Press Inc.

Reprinted from a copy in
The Newark Public Library

Classics in Child Development
ISBN for complete set: 0-405-06450-0
See last pages of this volume for titles.

Manufactured in the United States of America

———◆———

Library of Congress Cataloging in Publication Data

Hall, Granville Stanley, 1844-1924.
     Aspects of child life and education.

     (Classics in child development)
     Some of the papers have been revised, condensed, or
amplified by T. L. Smith.
     Reprint of the ed. published by Ginn, Boston.
     Includes bibliographies and index.
     CONTENTS: Hall, G. S. The contents of children's
minds.--Smith, T. L. The psychology of daydreams.--
Smith, T. L. and Hall, G. S. Curiosity and interest.
[etc.]
     1. Child study--Addresses, essays, lectures.
I. Smith, Theodate Louise, 1860-1914, ed. II. Title.
III. Series.
BF721.H22 1975   155.4'08   74-21414
ISBN 0-405-06464-0

ASPECTS OF CHILD LIFE

AND EDUCATION · BY G. STANLEY
HALL · AND SOME OF HIS PUPILS

EDITED BY THEODATE L. SMITH, PH.D.

BOSTON, U.S.A.
GINN & COMPANY, PUBLISHERS
The Athenæum Press
1907

The Athenæum Press

GINN & COMPANY · PRO-
PRIETORS · BOSTON · U.S.A.

PREFACE

The papers which constitute this volume have all been printed in my journals, most of them in the *Pedagogical Seminary*, but are here revised, condensed, or amplified, and provided with up-to-date bibliographies on each topic by Dr. Theodate L. Smith, for whose efficiency and careful work I desire to express my heartiest acknowledgments. Material for several other volumes has been gathered and grouped, all of them in the same general field, but each in a different part of it, and with a unity of its own. These may be published later, if the success of this volume warrants the undertaking. For many years the special studies that have emanated from this department of Clark University have been planned with reference to bringing them into ultimate unity in such a way that when published in book form the relations between the different parts of the wide and rapidly extending domain of child study might be exhibited in a systematic way, and their manifold applications, not hitherto apparent to the public, and often not to the individual investigator, might be set forth. Such a series as the above might have borne the collective title of "Chips from a Psycho-Genetic Laboratory."

The papers of this volume have least unity of any in the contemplated series, but are upon topics of most popular and perhaps practical interest. The first paper, "The Contents of Children's Minds on entering School," appeared almost twenty-five years ago, and is often referred to as marking the beginning of child study in America. It was suggested by a somewhat similar test made some years earlier by Professor Lazarus upon a large group of children in Berlin.

The Boston study was made possible by the generosity of Mrs. Pauline Agassiz Shaw, the founder of the kindergarten system of that city, and by the devoted labors of four of the best of her experts, headed by Miss S. E. Wiltse and Miss L. H. Symonds, who under my direction devoted months of careful and conscientious work to collecting the material. This paper has been republished several times in English, and translated in whole or in part into several foreign languages. As here presented, I have enlarged it by incorporating the results of all other similar tests of value that I know of up to date. As children's mental content differs much in different localities, it has often been suggested that some such survey of children just entering school should be undertaken in every community, in order that the teacher may know just what knowledge and ignorance can be assumed as a basis of teaching. This has sometimes been done in such a way as to secure these practical advantages to the teacher, but by methods not accurate enough to give scientific results. A recent official report shows that children who enter the schools of London late tend to surpass those who enter early, because the former, under the educational influences of the street, have acquired a number of facts and concepts which constitute apperception organs that enable them better to assimilate the material of instruction.

The article on " The Psychology of Daydreams " shows how the spontaneous imagination of children often gives us a picture of the purest natural internal growth of the soul. Experiences and tales are not only rehearsed and amplified and sometimes idealized, but images are grouped into new combinations ; and when we consider the favorite themes of childish reverie, and the modifications to which facts are subjected, my own conclusion from the data presented in the original paper, here condensed, is that to explain all these processes we must often go back of events in the individual life of the child and invoke the inherited results of ancestral experience, and that this is true not only for adolescents but for young children. Vaschide [1] well says in substance: " Creative imagination is by no means founded on memory or even sense. Indeed, its richness often seems inversely as these. The ordinary laws of association do not dominate here. Instead of explaining the unknown by the known, the child often reverses this process." Daydreams often seem the expression in semiconsciousness of the actual growth process of the cerebral elements, and this favors the suggestion that we sometimes have here the rehearsals of the experiences of our remote forebears. Archaic laws often rule even where the material digested is made up of the facts of individual life. The full demonstration of this interpretation, which is at variance with most current psychology, and, I think, with the view of the author of this paper, will be forthcoming elsewhere. All agree, however, that reverie, save in the few cases where it threatens to become morbid, is a natural function and should usually be allowed free course.

Curiosity and interest are themes of cardinal moment for both psychology and for pedagogy. The chapter here presented is a contribution to their natural history. Copious as is the recent literature upon these themes, they are still but imperfectly understood. After we have traced the stages of their development in the individual from infancy, and classified their various directions and the objects upon which they focus, there still remains the larger problem as to why they take on specific forms and are often so innately strong. To this question we can only here suggest the general answer that all their outcrops represent the ways in which the soul of the young strives to expand to the dimensions of that of the race, to know what the life of man in his world is and means, and where each person is to find his place and function in it. In

[1] " Recherches experimentales sur l'imagination créatrice chez l'enfant," *IVe Congrès international de Psychologie*, p. 251, Paris, 1900.

the child there is a sacredness about interest, for when mature in the adult it is this impulse that has created the whole domain of knowledge and made man master of nature. To tell just how to feed it is about the whole duty of didactics. "The Story of a Sand Pile" is a very inadequate record of unique and chiefly spontaneous development that seemed to the writer an idyl of recapitulation. I know nothing quite comparable with it, except J. Johnson's "Rudimentary Society among Boys," cited on page 156. The lads of the MacDonogh Institute range over some eight hundred acres, and have spontaneously evolved social, political, and business institutions in a crude way, rudely repeating the evolution of human society. This paper should be read by all who would know what a group of boys can do when left to themselves in the country. To compare such records with Crusoe on his island is well calculated to impress the old adage that truth is stranger than fiction even at its best can be. Such studies take us of the present back to prehistoric times, and enable us to see to-day how primitive society first arose. Some principles here suggested have found their way into the practices of the George Junior Republic. The lesson also should be heeded by those who study the pedagogy of preparing the rising generation for future citizenship. Such and other curricula have not as yet, I fancy, profited as they should by these examples.

It is strange indeed that dolls, which are always and everywhere inseparable from child life, have never before been made a subject of serious study until the paper here presented appeared. Dolls have figured in toy congresses and in several learned accounts of ancient and primitive people, but it remained for Dr. Ellis to show in detail the immense significance they may have for the development of the individual, social, and moral life of the child. For boys they rarely represent babies, and do not always do so for girls, but are often simply adults reduced to the dimensions of the child's mind so that it can take in the details of their form, apparel, and environment at a glance. They also have relations to idols, and nowhere is the fecund fancy of children more rich than in the various forms of play. It still remains to be shown how dolls can best be utilized in the kindergarten and in the primary school, to turn on the full psycho-motor power of this interest and to utilize it in the best way.

Collecting is often not only an instinct but almost a passion with children. Their collections are generally prompted not so much by the instinct to acquire and own as by the love of the activities involved in gathering and in accumulating many similar objects for comparison and for the mere enumeration. Some collections are spontaneously classified and even labeled, and some of them have an intrinsic value apart from their association. Collections vary not only in the kinds of objects sought, which are many, but also with age, sex, environment, motive, and manner of collection, and all these distinctions are suggestive. Imitation plays its part. In younger children it may appear as a blind impulse to hoard. It is extremely educable, and can be turned to valuable account not only to aid interest in school topics but also to secure contributions to local museums. For the most part, however, this zest must be counted as another of the natural powers in the soul, of which the school has not yet learned to take full advantage. Its origin is very obscure and constitutes a most challenging problem. Its nature is undoubtedly extremely complex.

Property and ownership arise from an impulse to extend the dominion of the self over objects in the environment, animate and inanimate. Like the Sammeltrieb, it begins in the animal world. Food, implements, ornaments, and dress are the first forms of property with the child as with the race. With the latter most forms of property seem first communal, and individual ownership arises later, whereas this order, so far as we have yet learned, seems inverse with the child. The school is just beginning to consider its function in regulating and controlling the acquisitive instinct by savings banks. The study here printed, although a slight, is believed to be a real, contribution to a large theme which needs further investigation.

Child fetichists seem a strange recrudescence of a very ancient and widespread psychosis. The very ostensive cases, here collected by Ellis, and those by other writers referred to, show how profoundly significant the phenomena of child life often are, — as keys to unlock the secrets of past stages of human history. In these cases we have within our own nurseries survivals of certain elements of the religion of primitive people the world over for countless generations. Lowly as they now seem they once represented the high-water mark of religious development.

In the last paper I have set down with as much fidelity to fact and detail as I was able certain memories of my own boyhood, the type of which was precisely that contemplated by the founders of our government, but which is now fast passing away. I believe it illustrates the early life of very many, if not a majority, of the boys in this country when life was predominantly rural and farms were small, agricultural machinery undeveloped, and interest in religious and political questions intense. With the decay of this type of farm life certain elements of education, which all agree were valuable, have become obsolete, and they have not yet been completely restored, nor can they be, by any artificial schemes of reverting to the country, although many such have been attempted. Those who may be interested in this article should also refer to another study published elsewhere, which specifies far more in detail many of the items of such an environment and their effects.[1]

[1] See note on "Early Memories," *Pedagogical Seminary*, Dec. 1899, Vol. VI, p. 485.

The child is older than the adult in the sense that its traits existed earlier in the world than those that characterize the mature man or woman. The qualities of the latter were acquired and superposed later, and are by long ages younger and more recent. Studies like those in this little volume may thus be called researches into the archeology of the human soul. If it be true, as I hold, that the most complete knowledge of anything whatever, and especially of all that is vital, is an exhaustive description of its developmental stages from its origin up to the present, we are still very far from having a science of the soul of man. To this science child study has contributed a new method and new results. At every stage its conclusions must be correlated with those derived from the study of the mind of animals and of primitive people. To develop these three lines of investigation, using the results in each to shed light upon those of the other, is a far harder and more complex process than the mere classification or analysis of the adult consciousness, which is but one cross section of the mind at only one of its many stages of unfoldment. The latter studies are valuable just as is the anatomy of the adult body, but genetic studies like these are the embryology of the soul. They reveal the secrets and processes of its making, show its faculties in perspective, and thus bring the manifold elements into proper relations.

G. STANLEY HALL

CLARK UNIVERSITY
WORCESTER, MASSACHUSETTS

CONTENTS

ASPECTS OF CHILD LIFE AND EDUCATION

THE CONTENTS OF CHILDREN'S MINDS ON ENTERING SCHOOL[1]

In October, 1869, the Berlin pedagogical *Verein*[1] issued a circular inviting teachers to investigate the individuality of children on entering the city schools, so far as it was represented by ideas of their environment. Individuality in children, it was said, differed in Berlin not only from that of children in smaller cities or in the country, but surroundings caused marked differences in culture capacity in different wards. Although concepts from the environment were only one important cause of diversity of individuality, this cause once determined, inferences could be drawn to other causes. It was expected that although city children would have an experience of moving things much larger than country children, they would have noticed very little of things at rest; that to names like *forest*, e.g., they, with an experience only with parks, would attach a very different set of concepts from those of the country child. The fact that country children who entered city schools behind city children caught up with them so readily was due to the fact that early school methods as well as matter of instruction were better adapted to country children. Conversation with children in collecting the statistical materials would, it was predicted, tend to interesting and surprising results. When asked what mountain (Berg) they had ever seen, all the girls

[1] Reprinted from *Princeton Review*, Vol. II, pp. 249–272, May, 1883.

in an upper class of a grammar school said *Pfefferberg*, the
name of a beerhouse near by, and for all *Berg* was a place of
amusement. This would cause an entire group of geographical
ideas to miscarry. Others knowing the words *pond* or *lake*
only from artificial ponds or lakes in the park, thought these
words designated water holders, which might or might not
have water in them. A preliminary survey showed that many
children in each city school had never seen important monu-
ments, squares, gardens, etc., near their own home and schoolhouse, and few knew the important features of their city at
large. With the method of geographical instruction in vogue
that begins with the most immediate surroundings and widens
in concentric circles to city, country, fatherland, etc., these
gaps in knowledge made havoc. School walks and excursions,
object-lesson material, as well as the subject-matter of reading,
writing, etc., should be regulated by the results of such inquiry.
This circular, which was accompanied by a list of points for
inquiry, ended by invoking general and hearty personal coöperation. It was not sufficient to have seen a hare, a squirrel, etc.,
but the hare must have been seen running wild, the squirrel
in a tree, sheep grazing, the stork on its nest, the swan swimming, chickens with the hen, the lark must be singing, the
butterfly, snail, lark, etc., must be in a natural environment.
The returns for 13 of the 84 schools of Berlin were worthless.
Other tests suggested but not reported on were colors, knowledge of money, weights, and measures ; how many have seen a
soldier, sailor, peasant, Jew, Moor, or a shoemaker, carpenter,
plasterer, watchmaker, printer, painter, etc., *at work;* how
many knew how bread was made out of grain ; where stockings came from ; how many could repeat correctly a spoken
sentence, say a poem by heart, sing something, repeat a musical
note, had attended a concert, have a cat, dog, or bird, etc.
As an essential object of these inquiries was to distinguish
the concepts which children brought to school from those

acquired there, returns made some weeks or months after the children entered school had little value, yet were worked up with the rest. The very slight interest shown by teachers in making these inquiries was also remarked. As only about one third of a minute for each question to each child was the time taken, there could be no collateral questioning, so that confusion and misunderstanding no doubt invalidated many returns.

The sources of error to be constantly guarded against are errors in counting, imagination, or embarrassment of the children. When the answers were taken in class nearly twice as many children asserted knowledge of the concept as when they were taken in groups of 8 to 10. Nearly half the boys and more than half the girls on entering school had never seen to know by name any one of the following conspicuous objects in Berlin : Lustgarten, Unter den Linden, Wilhelm Platz, Gensdarmenmarkt, or the Brandenburg Gate. From the large number of returns, those from 2238 children just entering school seem to have been pretty complete for 75 questions ; but other returns were usable for a part of the questions, and some for other questions, so that in the tables the number of children is recorded on the uniform basis of 10,000. Arranged in the order of frequency the first Berlin table is as follows:

Dwelling	9026	Moon	6215
Father's business	8945	Swan	6175
Name of father	8517	Butterfly	6028
Firmament	8145	Clouds	5925
Tempest (day)	7873	Fish	5853
Rainbow	7770	Unter den Linden	5590
Sphere	7623	Menagerie	5496
Two	7435	Square	5474
Three	7399	Evening sky	5384
Four	7265	Hasenheide	5121
Hail	7015	Frog	5085
Cube	6957	Circle	4991
Potato field	6323	Snail	4750

Sunset	4625	Palace of King	2886
Meadow	4607	Mushroom	2855
Alexander Platz	4366	Oak	2641
Triangle	4182	Plow	2636
Cornfield	4062	Sleet	2493
Zoölogical Gardens	4057	Moss	2484
Frederick's Grove	3887	Hare	2466
Herd of Sheep	3870	Stralau	2453
Pleasure Garden	3861	Harvest	2368
Forest	3646	Dew	2364
City Hall	3615	Wilhelm Platz	2158
Morning sky	3592	Lake	2078
Squirrel	3579	Arsenal	1957
Brandenburg Gate	3467	Scotch fir	1828
Kreuzberg	3454	Lark	1796
Castle of King	3423	Reed	1702
Village	3374	Willow	1667
Tempest (night)	3347	Whortleberry	1640
Mountain	3248	Birch	1318
Museum	3222	Rummelsberg	1242
Cuckoo	3137	Park for Invalids	1135
Treptow	3065	River	1122
Sunrise	3052	Hazel shrub	907
Gensdarmenmarkt	2909	Botanical Garden	527
Stork	2887		

Thus, e.g., out of 10,000 children, 9026 had the idea of dwellings, while but 527 had any idea of the Botanical Garden. The same returns otherwise presented are as follows :

	Boys	Girls	Children from Families	Children from Kindergarten	Children from Refuges	Children altogether
Number two	7478	7380	7436	8223	7113	7435
Number three	7478	7298	7418	7355	7344	7399
Number four	7279	7247	7224	8258	7067	7265
Triangle	4274	4036	4078	5484	4111	4182
Square	5424	5537	5230	7484	5681	5474
Area of circle	4750	5312	4818	6645	5081	4991
Sphere	7684	7544	7576	8516	7483	7623

	Boys	Girls	Children from Families	Children from Kinder- garten	Children from Refuges	Children alto- gether
Cube	6971	6970	6800	8064	7159	6957
Moon	6043	6438	6067	8000	6144	6215
Sunrise	3410	2590	3194	2710	2633	3052
Sunset	4925	4237	4739	4516	4226	4635
Firmament	8382	7840	8012	8645	8476	8145
Tempest (day) . . .	7613	8209	7776	⸲9226	7760	7873
Tempest (night) . .	3188	3509	3224	4194	3510	3347
Dew	2331	2395	2455	2323	2032	2364
Clouds	6090	5711	5727	6581	6443	5925
Hail	6606	7544	7055	7677	6628	7015
Sleet	2847	2037	2382	2194	3025	2493
Rainbow	7708	7851	7667	⸲9355	7598	7770
Evening sky	5567	5148	5303	6065	5450	5384
Morning sky	3497	3715	3545	4128	3580	3592
Hare	2482	2446	2473	3097	2217	2466
Squirrel	3878	3193	3170	4903	4665	3579
Stork	3212	2467	2897	3290	2702	2887
Swan	6757	5425	5976	7032	6628	6175
Cuckoo	3545	2610	3048	4129	3118	3137
Lark	2220	1249	1739	2258	1848	1796
Frog	5551	4482	4879	6323	5427	5085
Fish	6852	4565	5691	6968	6074	5853
Butterfly	7128	4606	5503	8258	7229	6028
Snail	4877	4585	4612	5484	5012	4750
Birch	1531	1044	1339	1355	1229	1318
Scotch fir	2205	1341	1770	2065	1963	1828
Oak	2625	2661	2776	2451	2194	2641
Willow	2157	1034	1703	1742	1501	1667
Hazel shrub . . .	1055	706	927	1032	762	907
Whortleberry . . .	1792	1443	1564	2645	1570	1640
Sedge (reed) . . .	1840	1525	1655	2581	1570	1702
Mushroom	3204	2405	2539	3419	2610	2855
Moss	2688	2221	2867	3355	1963	2484
Lustgarten	4021	3654	3800	5032	3672	3861
Unter den Linden . .	6122	4993	5436	6129	5982	5590
Wilhelm Platz . .	2696	1464	2345	1935	1524	2158
Alexander Platz . .	4084	4729	4515	3935	3946	4366

	Boys	Girls	Children from Families	Children from Kinder- garten	Children from Refuges	Children alto- gether
Gensdarmenmarkt. .	3450	2221	2915	3032	2841	2909
Brandenburg Gate .	3885	2968	3388	4774	3303	3467
Castle	3465	3367	3333	4192	3510	3423
King's Palace . . .	3180	2508	2788	3613	3002	2886
Museum	3450	2927	2982	3935	3880	3222
Arsenal	2165	1689	1855	2839	2032	1957
City Hall.	3703	3501	3412	5935	3557	3615
Frederick's Grove . .	3600	4258	3915	2710	4203	3887
Menagerie	5964	4893	5261	6516	6028	5496
Zoölogical Garden. .	4346	3685	3727	6323	4503	4057
Botanical Garden . .	452	624	497	1161	416	527
Kreuzberg	4179	2518	3479	4065	3141	3454
Hasenheide	5780	4258	5121	6194	4734	5121
Park	1301	922	964	1355	1709	1135
Treptow	3196	2897	3127	4065	2469	3065
Stralau	2840	1955	2515	2387	2240	2453
Rummelsberg . . .	1459	963	1248	903	1339	1242
Drove of Sheep . .	4005	3695	3739	4323	4203	3870
Cornfield	4322	3726	4012	4194	4203	4062
Potato field	6265	6397	6303	6323	6397	6323
Village	3672	2989	3364	3419	3395	3374
Plow	3283	1801	2570	3290	2656	2636
Harvests	2744	1883	2315	2323	2587	2368
Dwelling	9120	8905	9103	9355	8612	9026
Name of father. . .	8136	9007	8830	8065	7483	8517
Calling of father . .	8652	9324	9194	8968	7991	8945
Mountain.	3402	3050	3067	4645	3441	3248
Forest.	4036	3142	3555	4194	3418	3646
Meadow	5004	4096	4467	4645	5127	4607
Lake	2451	1586	2055	2000	2171	2078
River	1126	1115	1194	968	901	1122

This table shows that out of 10,000 boys, 7478 on entering the Berlin schools have an idea of the number two; out of 10,000 girls, 7380 have it; out of 10,000 children of both sexes indiscriminately, 7436 have it, etc. Here the concepts are arranged in systematic order. Mathematics, 1–8; astronomical, 9–13; meteorological, 13–21; animals, 22–31; plants, 32–40; local geography, 41–61; and miscellaneous. Of three fourths of these concepts as objects more girls are ignorant than boys, and those who have not been in the kindergarten are more ignorant than those who have. Some of these objects were doubtless known but had not acquired a name for the child; others they had seen but had not had their attention called to. It is often said that girls are more likely to excel boys in learning concepts, the more general these concepts are. Perhaps we may also assume that the most common concepts are acquired before those possessed by a few individuals only. The greater the number of concepts in the test lists, the more boys seemed to excel girls. The easy and widely diffused concepts are commonest among girls; the harder and more special or exceptional ones are commonest among boys. The girls clearly excelled only in the following concepts: name and calling of the father, tempest, rainbow, hail, potato field, moon, square, circle, Alexander Platz, Frederick's Grove, morning sky, oak, dew, and Botanical Garden. Of all the children the sphere was known to 76 per cent., the cube to 69 per cent., the square to 54 per cent., the circle to 49 per cent., the triangle to 41 per cent. The girls excel in space concepts and boys in numbers. Girls excel in ideas of family, house, and thunderstorms, children from houses of refuge had more concepts than children from families, and those from kindergartens excelled both. The child's characteristic question, What is that? is so poorly answered at home that he comes to school so poor in concepts that instruction must either operate with words, or use pictures, or go back to nature. Thus text-books and other means of instruction assume a knowledge which the child does not possess, and it is hard to find those which are well adapted to a given population. Thus object lessons, excursions, etc., are suggested as first steps to fill the gaps in the child's knowledge.

The following table shows the relative number of children who knew four Bible stories and four of Grimm's favorite fairy tales.

	Boys	Girls	Children from Families	Children from Kindergarten	Children from Refuges	Children altogether	Per cent. Boys	Per cent. Girls
God	7827	5067	6927	5935	5704	6633	60.7	39.3
Christ	6757	4217	5818	5355	5104	5648	61.6	38.4
Bible stories . .	3743	1453	2727	2258	2979	2744	72.	28.
Prayers and } Songs	5400	4647	5078	5613	4850	5041	53.7	46.6
Schneewittchen .	2173	3009	2436	4387	2263	2538	41.9	58.1
Rothkäppchen .	2427	3664	2800	4581	3025	2967	39.8	60.2
Dornröschen . .	563	1044	661	1871	808	773	35.	65.
Aschenbrödel } Average	1784	2897	2182	3871	2032	2270	38.	61.9
Religious . . .	5852	3846	5138	4790	4659	5021	60.3	39.7
Fairy tales . .	1734	2654	2020	3677	2032	2137	39.5	60.5

Thus girls excel in fairy tales and boys in religious concepts. As the opportunities to learn both would not probably differ much, there seems here a difference of disposition. God and Christ were better learned at home, and the tales best in the kindergarten. Rothkäppchen was better known than God, and Schneewittchen than Christ. More boys could repeat sentences said to them, or sing musical phrases sung to them, or sing a song, than girls. Kindergarten children come from the richer, refuge children from the poorer, class, while parents between these extremes occupy themselves most with their children. The better off the parents, the stiller and less imitative the child, is a law suggested by the statistics of abilities. Not only method but choice and arrangement of the material of instruction depend on the knowledge the child has. Further investigations on narrower and more closely related subjects should be chosen. Investigation of six to twelve closely related points is suggested as the best method, and every teacher could occasionally complete such inventories in his or her room.

In Germany it is more common than in our country to connect songs, poetry, reading and object lessons, instruction in history, geography, botany, geology, and other elementary branches with the immediate locality. A school geography of Leipzig, e.g., begins with the schoolhouse and yard, the street, with cross sections of it to show drainage, gas, etc., and then widens out into the world by concentric circles. Stated holiday walks conducted by teachers for educational purposes and for making collections for the schoolrooms are more common. The psychic peculiarities of different school districts of Berlin seemed to be influenced surprisingly by locality.

In 1879 Dr. K. Lange[1] urged that a six-year-old child has learned already far more than a student learns in his entire university course. "These six years have been full of advancement, like the six days of creation." Concrete conceptions have been accumulated in vast numbers and the teacher must not assume that a *tabula rasa* is before him. Both this and the presumption of too much knowledge would be to build upon sand. Children have experienced and learned far more than they can put into words ; hence again the need of cross questioning. Lange's table on the following page was based on 500 children entering the city schools of Plauen, and 300 entering 21 country schools in outlying districts, and the figures represent the percentages of those having the concept.

---

[1] See " Der Vorstellungskreis unserer sechsjährigen Kleinen," *Allg. Schul-Zeitung*, Bd. 56, pp. 327 et seq. Darmstadt, 1879.

Question or Concept	City Children	Country Children
Sunrise	18	42
Sunset	23	58
Moon and stars	84	82
Appearance and song of the lark	20	70
Fish swimming wild	72	83
Visit to a pond	51	86
Visit to a brook or river	71	82
Visit to high hill or mountain	48	74
Visit to a forest	63	86
Knows an oak	18	57
Seen a corn or wheat field	64	92
Knows how bread comes from grain . . .	28	63
Seen a shoemaker at work	79	80
Seen a carpenter at work	55	62
Seen a mason at work	86	92
Been in a church	50	49
Knows aught of the dear God	51	66

Only 43 per cent. of the city children had ever been to any other town or village, only 18 per cent. had seen the castle near by, and knowledge of colors was as follows, beginning with those best known and ending with the least known: black, white, red, green, blue, yellow. The ignorance of city children shows the utility of school excursions. Girls had seen, heard, and experienced less than boys of all the seventeen subjects of inquiry save the " dear God," of whom they knew more than the boys. Little is told of Lange's methods, or whether or how far they led to a modification of the elementary curriculum.

It was with the advantages of many suggestions and not a few warnings from these attempts that the writer undertook, soon after the opening of the Boston schools in September, 1880, to make out a list of questions suitable for obtaining an inventory of the contents of the minds of children of average intelligence on entering the primary schools of that city.

This was made possible by the liberality of Mrs. Quincy Shaw, who detailed four excellent teachers from her comprehensive system of kindergartens to act as special questioners under the writer's direction, and by the coöperation of Miss L. B. Pingree, their superintendent. All the local and many other of the German questions were not suitable to children here, and the task of selecting those that should be so, though perhaps not involving quite so many perplexing considerations as choosing an equally long list of "normal words," was by no means easy. They must not be too familiar nor too hard and remote, but must give free and easy play to thought and memory. But especially, to yield most practical results, they should lie within the range of what children are commonly supposed or at least desired or expected, by teachers and by those who write primary textbooks and prescribe courses of instruction, to know. Many preliminary half days of questioning small groups of children and receiving suggestions from many sources, and the use of many primers, object-lesson courses, etc., now in use in this country, were necessary before the first provisional list of one hundred and thirty-four questions was printed. The problem first considered was strictly practical, namely, what may Boston children be, by their teachers, assumed to know and have seen when they enter school; although other purposes more psychological shaped other questions used later.

The difficulties and sources of possible error in the use of such questions are many. Not only are children prone to imitate others in their answers without stopping to think and give independent answers of their own, but they often love to seem wise, and, to make themselves interesting, state what seems to interest us without reference to truth, divining the lines of our interest with a subtlety we do not suspect. If absurdities are doubted by the questioner, they are sometimes only the more protested by the children;

the faculties of some are benumbed and perhaps their tongues tied by bashfulness, while others are careless, listless, inattentive, and answer at random. Again, many questioners are brusque, lacking in sympathy or tact, or real interest or patience in the work, or perhaps regard it as trivial or fruitless. These and many other difficulties seemed best minimized by the following method, which was finally settled upon and, with the coöperation of Mr. E. P. Seaver, then superintendent of the Boston schools, put into operation. The four trained and experienced kindergarten teachers were employed by the hour to question the children in groups of three at a time in the dressing room of the school, so as not to interrupt the school work. No constraint was used, and as several hours were necessary to finish each set, changes and rests were often needful, while by frequent correspondence and by meetings with the writer to discuss details and compare results, uniformity of method was sought. The most honest and unembarrassed child's first answer to a direct question, e.g., whether it has seen a cow, sheep, etc., must rarely or never be taken without careful cross questioning, a stated method of which was developed respecting many objects. If the child says it has seen a cow, but when asked its size points to its own finger nail or hand and says, *so big*, as not unfrequently occurs, the inference is that it has at most only seen a picture of a cow, and thinks its size reproduced therein, and accordingly he is set down as deficient on that question. If, however, he is correct as to size, but calls the color blue, does not know that the cow is the source of milk, or that it has horns or hoofs, — several errors of the latter order were generally allowed. A worm may be said to *swim* on the ground, butchers to kill only the bad animals, etc.; but when hams are said to grow on trees or in the ground, or a hill is described as a *lump* of dirt, or wool as growing on hens, as sometimes occurs, deficiency is obvious. Thus many visual and other notions that seem to adults so simple that they must be present to the mind with some completeness or not at all, are in a process of gradual acquisition, element by element, in the mind of a child, so that there must sometimes be confessedly a certain degree of arbitrariness in saying, as, except in cases of peculiar uncertainty, the questioners attempted to do, that the child has the concept or does not have it. Men's first names seemed to have designated single striking qualities, but once applied they become general or specific names according to circumstances. Again, very few children knew that a tree had bark, leaves, trunk, and roots ; but very few indeed had not noticed a tree enough for our " pass." Without specifying further details, it may suffice here to say that the child was given the benefit of every doubt and credited with knowledge wherever its ignorance was not so radical as to make a chaos of what instruction and most primary text-books are wont to assume. It is important also to add that the questioners were requested to report manifest gaps in the child's knowledge *in its own words*, reproducing its syntax, pronunciation, etc.

About sixty teachers besides the four examiners made returns from three or more children each. Many of their returns, however, are incomplete, careless, or show internal contradictions, and can be used only indirectly to control results from the other sources. From more than twice that number two hundred of the Boston children were selected as the basis of the following table. For certain questions and for many statistical purposes this number is much too small to yield very valuable results, but where, as in the majority of cases, the averages of these children taken by fifties have varied less than ten per cent., it is safe to infer that the figures have considerable representative worth, and far more than they could have if the percentages were small. The precautions that were taken to avoid schools where the children come from homes representing extremes of either culture or ignorance, or to balance deviations from a preliminary conjecture averaged in one direction by like deviations in the other, and also to select from each schoolroom with the teacher's aid only children of average capacity, and to dismiss each child found unresponsive or not acquainted with the English language, give to the percentages, it is believed, a worth which, without these and other precautions to this end, only far larger numbers could yield.

The following table shows the general results for a number of those questions which admit of categorical answers, only negative results being recorded; the italicized questions in the "miscellaneous" class being based on only from forty to seventy-five children, the rest on two hundred, or, in a few cases, on two hundred and fifty.

In 1883, shortly after my own tables, as below, were published, Superintendent J. M. Greenwood of Kansas City tested 678 children of the lowest primary class in that city, of whom 47 were colored, with some of my questions. I here print his percentages in the last two columns. In his state, children are admitted to school at six, but his tests were made in March, April, May, or after some seven months or more of school life, and probably at greater age.

Name of the Object of Conception	Per Cent. of Children Ignorant of it		
	In Boston	In Kansas City	
		White	Colored
Beehive	80.	59.4	66.
Crow	77.	47.3	59.
Bluebird	72.5		
Ant	65.5	21.5	19.1
Squirrel	63.	15.	4.2
Snail	62.		
Robin	60.5	30.6	10.6
Sparrow	57.5		

Name of the Object of Conception	Per Cent. of Children Ignorant of it		
	In Boston	In Kansas City	
		White	Colored
Sheep	54.	3.5	
Bee	52.	7.27	4.2
Frog	50.	2.7	
Pig	47.5	1.7	
Chicken	33.5	.5	
Worm	22.	.5	
Butterfly	20.5	.5	
Hen	19.	.1	
Cow	18.5	5.2	
Growing wheat	92.5	23.4	66.
Elm tree	91.5	52.4	89.8
Poplar tree	89.		
Willow	89.		
Growing oats	87.5		
Oak tree	87.	62.2	58.6
Pine	87.	65.6	87.2
Maple	83.	31.2	80.8
Growing moss	81.5	30.7	42.5
Growing strawberries	78.5	26.5	1.1
Growing clover	74.		
Growing beans	71.5		
Growing blueberries	67.5		
Growing blackberries	66.		
Growing corn	65.5		
Chestnut tree	64.		
Planting a seed	63.		
Peaches on a tree	61.		
Growing potatoes	61.		
Growing buttercup	55.5		
Growing rose	54.		
Growing grapes	53.		
Growing dandelion	52.		
Growing cherries	46.		
Growing pears	32.		
Growing apples	21.		

Name of the Object of Conception	In Boston	Per Cent. of Children Ignorant of it In Kansas City White	Colored
Location of the ribs	90.5	13.6	6.4
Location of the lungs	81.	26.	44.6
Location of the heart	80.	18.5	18.1
Location of the wrist	70.5	3.	
Location of the ankles	65.5	14.1	
Location of the waist	52.5	14.	4.2
Location of the hips	45.	14.	4.2
Location of the knuckles	36.	2.9	8.5
Location of the elbows	25.	1.5	
Right and left hand	21.5	1.	10.2
Cheek	18.	.5	
Forehead	15.	.5	
Throat	13.5	1.1	
Knee	7.	1.6	
Stomach	6.	27.2	45.9
Dew	78.	39.1	70.2
The seasons	75.5	31.8	56.1
Hail	73.	13.6	18.1
Rainbow	65.	10.3	2.1
Sunrise	56.5	16.6	
Sunset	53.5	19.5	
Clouds	35.	7.3	
Stars	14.	3.	
Moon	7.	26.	53.
Island	87.5		
Beach	55.5		
Woods	53.5		
River	48.		
Pond	40.		
Hill	28.		
Brook	15.		
Triangle	92.		
Square	56.		
Circle	35.		
Number five	28.5		

NAME OF THE OBJECT OF CONCEPTION	PER CENT. OF CHILDREN IGNORANT OF IT		
	In Boston	In Kansas City White	Colored
Number four	17.		
Number three	8.		
Watchmaker at work	68.	30.1	49.7
File	65.	20.8	36.1
Plow	64.5	13.9	8.5
Spade	62.	7.3	15.
Hoe	61.	5.	10.6
Bricklayer at work	44.5	10.1	2.1
Shoemaker at work	25.	8.7	
Ax	12.	18.4	53.
Green	15.		
Blue	14.		
Yellow	13.5		
Red	9.		
Origin of leathern things	93.4	50.8	72.3
Maxim or proverb	91.5		
Origin of cotton things	90.	35.7	15.
Origin of flour	89.	34.7	57.4
Ability to knit	88.		
Origin of bricks	81.1	33.1	53.
Shape of the world	70.3	46.	47.
Origin of woolen things	69.	55.	44.
Kindergarten	67.5		
Bathing	64.5	13.4	
Story telling	58.	23.6	12.7
Origin of wooden things	55.	19.3	6.4
Origin of butter	50.5	6.7	
Origin of meat (from animals)	48.	8.3	12.7
Sewing	47.5	23.4	
Given musical tone	40.		
Cannot beat time regularly	39.		
Have never saved cents at home	36.	8.2	12.7
Never been in the country	35.5	13.1	19.
Can repeat no verse	28.	20.	42.5
Source of milk	20.5	4.	

Name of the Object of Concept	Per cent. of Ignorance in 150 Girls	Per cent. of Ignorance in 150 Boys	Per cent. of Ignorance in 50 Irish Children	Per cent. of Ignorance in 50 American Children	Per cent. of Ignorance in 64 Kindergarten Children
Beehive	81	75	86	70	61
Ant	59	60	74	38	26
Squirrel	69	50	66	42	43
Snail	69	73	92	72	62
Robin	69	44	64	36	29
Sheep	67	47	62	40	40
Bee	46	32	52	32	26
Frog	53	38	54	35	35
Pig	45	27	38	26	22
Chicken	35	21	32	16	22
Worm	21	17	26	16	9
Butterfly	14	16	26	8	9
Hen	15	14	18	2	14
Cow	18	12	20	6	10
Growing clover	59	68	84	42	29
Growing corn	58	50	60	68	32
Growing potatoes	55	54	62	44	34
Growing buttercup	50	51	66	40	31
Growing rose	48	48	60	42	33
Growing dandelion	44	42	62	34	31
Growing apples	16	16	18	12	5
Ribs	88	92	98	82	68
Ankles	58	52	62	40	38
Waist	53	52	64	32	36
Hips	50	47	72	31	24
Knuckles	27	27	34	12	23
Elbow	19	32	36	16	12
Right from left hand	20	8	14	20	4
Wrist	21	34	44	9	19
Cheek	10	12	14	14	4
Forehead	10	11	12	10	7
Throat	10	18	14	16	14
Knee	4	5	2	10	2

Name of the Object of Concept	Per cent. of Ignorance in 150 girls	Per cent. of Ignorance in 150 boys	Per cent. of Ignorance in 50 Irish Children	Per cent. of Ignorance in 50 American Children	Per cent. of Ignorance in 64 Kindergarten Children
Dew.	64	63	92	52	57
The seasons	59	50	68	48	41
Hail.	75	61	84	52	53
Rainbow	59	61	70	38	38
Sunrise.	71	53	70	36	53
Sunset	47	49	52	32	29
Star	15	10	12	4	7
Island	74	78	84	64	55
Beach	82	49	60	34	32
Woods	46	36	46	32	27
River	38	44	62	12	13
Pond	31	34	42	24	28
Hill	23	22	30	12	19
Number five	26	16	22	24	12
Number four	15	10	16	14	7
Number three	7	6	12	8	0

The first Boston table is based upon about equal numbers of boys and girls, and children of Irish and American parentage greatly predominate; there are 21 Germans, and 19 are divided between 8 other nationalities. 14 per cent. of all examined did not know their age; 6 per cent. were four, 37 per cent. were five, 25 per cent. were six, 12 per cent. were seven, and 2 per cent. were eight years old. The returns were carefully tabulated to determine the influence of age, which seems surprisingly unpronounced, indicating, so far as the small numbers go, a slight value of age *per se* as an index of ripeness for school.

In the second table, which is based on Boston children, only columns 2 and 3 are based upon larger numbers and upon less carefully restricted selections from the aggregate returns. In

34 representative questions out of 49, the boys surpass the girls, as the German boys did in 75 per cent. of the Berlin questions. The girls excel in knowledge of the parts of the body, home and family life, rainbows, in conception of square, circle, and triangle, but not in that of cube, sphere, and pyramid, which is harder and later. Their stories are more imaginative, while their knowledge of things outward and remote, their power to sing and articulate correctly from dictation, their acquaintance with number and animals, is distinctly less than that of the boys. The Berlin report infers that the more common, near, or easy a notion is, the more likely are the girls to excel the boys, and *vice versa.* Save possibly in the knowledge of the parts of the body, our returns do not indicate difference between the sexes. Boys do seem, however, more likely than girls to be ignorant of common things right about them, of which knowledge is wont to be assumed. Column 4 shows that the Irish children tested were behind others on nearly all topics. The Irish girls decidedly outrank the Irish boys, the advantage to the sex being outweighed by the wider knowledge of the boys of other nationalities. Whether, however, the five- and six-year-old Irish boys are not after all so constituted as to surpass their precocious American playmates later in school or adult life, as since Sigismund, many think " slow " children generally do, is one of the most serious questions for the philosophical educator. Column 6 shows in a striking way the advantage of the kindergarten children, without regard to nationality, over all others. Most of the latter tested were from the charity kindergartens, so that superior intelligence of home surroundings can hardly be assumed. Many of them had attended kindergarten but a short time, and the questions were so ordered that the questioners who had a special interest in the kindergarten should not know till near the end of the tests whether or not the children had

ever attended it. On the other hand, a somewhat larger proportion of the children from the kindergarten had been in the country. Yet, on the whole, we seem to have here an illustration of the law that we really see not what is near or impresses the retina, but what the attention is called and held to, and what interests are awakened and words found for. Of nearly thirty primary teachers questioned as to the difference between children from kindergartens and others, four saw no difference, and all the rest thought them better fitted for school work, instancing superior use of language, skill with the hand and slate, quickness, power of observation, singing, number, love of work, neatness, politeness, freedom from the benumbing school bashfulness, or power to draw from dictation. Many thought them at first more restless and talkative.

There are many other details and more or less probable inferences, but the above are the chief. The work was laborious, involving about fifty thousand items in all. These results are, it is believed, to be in some degree the first opening of a field which should be specialized, and in which single concept groups should be subjected to more detailed study with larger numbers of children. One difficulty is to get essential points to test for. If these are not characteristic and typical, all such work is worthless. We believe that not only practical educational conclusions of great scope and importance may be based on or illustrated by such results, but, though many sources of inaccuracy may limit their value, that they are of great importance for anthropology and psychology. It is characteristic of an educated man, says Aristotle in substance, not to require a degree of scientific exactness on any subject greater than that which the subject admits. As scientific methods advance, not only are increasingly complex matters subjected to them, but probabilities (which guide nearly all our acts) more and more remote from mathematical certainty are valued.

Steinthal tells an apposite story of six German gentlemen riding socially in a coupé all day, and as they approached the station where they were to separate, one proposed to tell the vocation of each of the others, who were strangers to him, if they would write without hesitation an answer to the question, What destroys its own offspring? One wrote, Vital force. "You," said the questioner, "are a biologist." Another wrote, War. "You," he said, "are a soldier." Another wrote, Kronos, and was correctly pronounced a philologist; while the publicist revealed himself by writing, Revolution, and the farmer by writing, She bear. This fable teaches the law of apperception. As Don Quixote saw an army in a flock of sheep and a giant in a windmill, as some see all things in the light of politics, others in that of religion, education, etc., so the Aryan races apperceived the clouds as cows and the rain as their milk, the sun as a horse, the lightning as an arrow; and so the children apperceive rain as God pouring down water, thunder as barrels or boards falling, or cannon, heaven as a well-appointed nursery, etc. They bring more or less developed apperceiving organs with them into school, each older and more familiar concept gaining more apperceptive power over the newer concepts and percepts by use. The older impressions are on the lurch, as it were, for the new ones, and mental freedom and all-sidedness depend on the number and strength of these appropriating concepts. If these are very few, as with children, teaching is like pouring water from a big tub into a small, narrow-necked bottle. A teacher who acts upon the now everywhere admitted fallacy that knowledge of the subject is all that is needed in teaching children, pours at random onto more than into the children, talking to rather than with them, and gauging what he gives rather than what they receive. All now agree that the mind can learn only what is related to other things learned before, and that we must start from the knowledge that the children really have and develop this as germs, otherwise we are showing objects that require close scrutiny only to indirect vision, or talking to the blind about color. Alas for the teacher who does not learn more from his children than he can ever hope to teach them! Just in proportion as teachers do this do they cease to be merely mechanical, and acquire interest, perhaps enthusiasm, and surely an all-compensating sense of growth in their work and life.

From the above tables it seems not too much also to infer: (1) That there is next to nothing of pedagogic value, the knowledge of which it is safe to assume at the outset of school life. Hence the need of objects and the danger of books and word cram. Hence many of the best primary teachers in Germany spend from two to four or even six months in talking of objects and drawing them before any beginning of what we till lately have regarded as primary-school work. (2) The best preparation parents can give their children for good school training is to make them acquainted with natural objects, especially with the sights and sounds of the country, and to send them to good and hygienic, as distinct from the most fashionable, kindergartens. (3) Every teacher on starting with a new class or in a new locality, to make sure that his efforts along some lines are not utterly lost, should undertake to explore carefully section by section children's minds with all the tact and ingenuity he can command and acquire, to determine exactly what is already shown; and every normal-school pupil should undertake work of the same kind as an essential part of his training. (4) The concepts which are most common in the children of a given locality are the earliest to be acquired, while the rarer ones are later. This order may in teaching generally be assumed as a natural one, e.g., apples (as appealing directly to the child without mediate process) first and wheat last. This order, however, varies very greatly with every change of environment, so that the results of explorations of children's minds in one place cannot be assumed to be valid for those of another save within comparatively few concept spheres.

The high rate of ignorance indicated in the table may surprise most persons who will be likely to read this report, because the childhood they know will be much above the average of intelligence here sought, and because the few memories of childhood which survive in adult life necessarily bear but slight traces of imperfections and are from many causes illusory. Skeins and spools of thread were said to grow on the sheep's back or on bushes, stockings on trees, butter to come from buttercups, flour to be made of beans, oats to grow on oaks, bread to be swelled yeast, trees to be stuck in the ground by God and to be rootless, meat to be dug from the ground, and potatoes to be picked from the trees. Cheese is squeezed butter, the cow says "bow wow," the pig purrs or burrows, worms are not distinguished from snakes, moss from the "toad's umbrella," bricks from stones, etc. An oak may be known only as an acorn tree or a button tree, a pine only as a needle tree, a bird's nest only as its bed, etc. So that while no one child has all these misconceptions, none are free from them, and thus the liabilities are great that, in this chaos of half-assimilated impressions, half right, half wrong, some lost link may make utter nonsense or mere verbal cram of the most careful instruction, as in the cases of children referred to above, who knew much by rote about a cow, its milk, horns, leather, meat, etc., but yet were sure from the picture book that it was no bigger than a small mouse.

For 86 per cent. of the above questions, the average intelligence of thirty-six country children who were tested ranks higher than that of the city children of the table, and in many items very greatly exceeds it. The subject-matter of primers for the latter is in great part still traditionally of country life;

hence the danger of unwarranted presupposition is considerable. As our methods of teaching grow natural we realize
that city life is unnatural, and that those who grow up without knowing the country are defrauded of that without which
childhood can never be complete or normal. On the whole,
the material of the city is no doubt inferior in pedagogic value
to country experience. A few days in the country at the age
of five or six has raised the level of many a city child's intelligence more than a term or two of school training without could
do. It is there, too, that the foundations of a love of natural
science are best laid. We cannot accept without many careful
qualifications the evolutionary dictum that the child's mental
development should repeat that of the race. Unlike primitive
man, the child has a feeble body and is ever influenced by a
higher culture about him. Yet from the primeval intimacy
with the qualities and habits of plants, with the instincts of
animals, — so like those of children, — with which hawking
and trapping, the riding on instead of some distance behind
horses, etc., made men familiar ; from primitive industries
and tools as first freshly suggested, if we believe Geiger, from
the normal activities of the human organism, especially of
the tool of tools, the hand ; from primitive shelter, cooking,
and clothing, with which anthropological researches make us
familiar, it is certain that not a few educational elements of
great value can be selected and systematized for children, an
increasing number of them, in fact, being already in use for
juvenile games and recreations and for the vacation pastimes
of adults. A country barn, a forest with its gloom and awe,
its vague fears and indefinite sounds, is a great school at this
age. The making of butter, of which some teachers, after hearing so often that it grew inside eggs or on ice, or was made
from buttermilk, think it worth while to make a thimbleful
in a toy churn at school as an object lesson ; more acquaintance with birds, which, as having the most perfect senses,

and most constant motion in several elements, even Leopardi could panegyrize as the only real things of joy in the universe, and which the strange power of flight makes ideal beings with children, and whose nests were sometimes said to *grow* on trees; more knowledge of kitchen chemistry, of foods, their preparation and origin; wide prospects for the eyes — these elements constitute a more pedagogic industrial training for *young* children, because more free and play-like, than sewing, or cooking, or whittling, or special trade schools can, and are besides more hygienic. Many children locate all that is good and imperfectly known in the country, and nearly a dozen volunteered the statement that good people when they die go to the country — even from Boston. It is things that live and, as it were, detach themselves from their background by moving that catch the eye and with it the attention, and the subjects which occupy and interest the city child are mainly in motion and therefore transient, while the country child comes to know objects at rest better. The country child has more solitude, is likely to develop more independence and is less likely to be prematurely caught up into the absorbing activities and throbbing passions of manhood, and becomes more familiar with the experiences of primitive man. The city child knows a little of many more things and so is more liable to superficiality and has a wider field of error. At the same time, it has two great advantages over the country child, in knowing more of human nature and in entering school with a much better developed sense of rhythm and all its important implications. On the whole, however, additional force seems thus given to the argument for excursions, by rail or otherwise, regularly provided for the poorer children whose life conditions are causing the race to degenerate in the great centers of population, unfavorable enough for those with good homes or even for adults.

Words, in connection with rhyme, rhythm, alliteration, cadence, etc., or even without these, simply as sound pictures, often absorb the attention of children and yield them a really æsthetic pleasure either quite independently of their meaning or to the utter bewilderment of it. They hear fancied words in noises and sounds of nature and animals, and are persistent punners. As butterflies make butter or eat it or give it by squeezing, so grasshoppers give grass, bees give beads and beans, kittens grow on the pussy willow, and all honey is from honeysuckles, and even a poplin dress is made of poplar trees. When the cow lows it somehow blows its own horn; crows and scarecrows are confounded; ant has some subtle relationship to aunt; angleworm suggests angle or triangle or ankle; Martie eats "tomarties"; a holiday is a day to "holler" on; Harry O'Neil is nicknamed Harry Oatmeal; isosceles is somehow related to sausages; October suggests knocked over; "I never saw a hawk, but I can hawk and spit too;" "I will not sing do re mi, but do re *you;*" "Miss Eaton will eat us" — these and many more from the questioners' notes; the story of the child who, puzzled by the unfamiliar reflexive use of the verb, came to associate "now I lay me," etc., with a lama; of the child who wondered what kind of a bear was the consecrated cross-eyed bear, as he understood the hymn "The consecrated cross I'd bear"; or of another, who was for years stultified as against a dead blank wall whenever the phrase "answer sought" occurred, suggest to us how, more or less consciously and more or less seriously, a child may be led, in the absence of corrective experience, to the most fantastic and otherwise unaccountable distortions of facts by shadowy word specters or husks.

In many of the expressions quoted the child seems playing with relations once seriously held, and its "fun" to be joy over but lately broken mental fetters. Some at least of the not infrequently quite unintelligible statements or answers may perhaps be thus accounted for. Again, the child more than the adult thinks in pictures, gestures, and inarticulate sounds. The distinction between real and verbal knowledge has been carefully and constantly kept in mind by the questioners. Yet of the objects in the above table, except a very few, like triangle and sparrow, a child may be said to know almost nothing, at least for school purposes, if he has no generally recognized name for them. The far greater danger is the converse, that only the name and not the thing itself will be known. To test for this danger was, with the exceptions presently to be noted, our constant aim, as it is that of true education to obviate it. The danger, however, is after all quite limited here, for the linguistic imperfections of children are far more often shown in combining words than in naming the concrete things they know or do not know. To name an object is a passion with them, for it is to put their own mark upon it, to appropriate it. From the talk, which most children hear and use, to book language is again an immense step. Words *live* only in the ear and mouth, and are pale and corpse-like when addressed to the eye. What we want, and indeed are likely soon to have, are carefully arranged child vocabularies and dictionaries of both verbal forms and meanings, to show teachers just the phonic elements and vocal combinations children have most trouble with, the words they most readily and surely acquire, their number and order in each thought sphere — and the attributes and connotations most liable to confuse them. To that work it is believed the method here employed has already furnished valuable material in protocol soon to be augmented and digested.

To specify a few items more fully, the four color questions were designed to test not color blindness but the power to use color names. The Holmgren worsteds were used, from which the child was asked to pick out, not colors like others to which its attention is directed without naming them, but the color named, to which he has no clew but the name. It did not seem safe to complicate the objects of the latter educational test with the former, so that some of those marked defective in the table may or may not have been color-blind. Excluding colored and Jewish children, both of whom seem to show exceptional percentages, and averaging the sexes, both Magnus and Jeffries found a little over two per cent. of many thousand children color-blind. The children they tested, however, were much older than these, and two or three hundred is far too small a number to warrant us, were it otherwise allowable, in simply subtracting two per cent. and inferring that the remainder were deficient only in knowledge of the color word. Our figures, then, do not bear upon the question whether or not the color sense itself is fully developed before the age of five or six. Again, number cannot be developed to any practical extent without knowledge of the number name. Moreover, as Wundt's careful experiments show, the eye can apprehend but three of the smallest and simplest objects, unless they are arranged in some geometrical order, without taking additional time to count. As the chromatic scale grades musical intervals, or the names we count by graduate the vague sense of more or less, and, later, as visible notes change all musical ideas and possibilities, so figures or number signs almost create arithmetic. A child who seriously says a cat has three or five legs will pick out its own, e.g., the fourth seat, in the fifth row in an empty schoolroom almost every time by happy guessing, and hold up "so many" fingers or blocks, when, if the number name five or six were called for and nothing shown, he would be quite confused. In our tests the number name was sought because it is that which is mainly serviceable for educational purposes. As to the physiological and geographical questions little need be said. Joint, flesh, and vein are often unknown terms, or joint is where the bone is broken, and there are stones in the knees. Within the skin is blood and something hard, perhaps wood. Physical self-consciousness, which is in little danger of becoming morbid at this age, begins with recognition of the hand, then of the foot, because these are the most mobile parts, but has not often reached the face at this age, and blushing is rare; while psychic self-consciousness is commonly only of pain, either internal, as of stomach ache, or peripheral, as of cuts, bruises, etc. The world is square, straight, or flat, and if the other side has been thought of it is all woods or water or ice, or where saved people or Protestants, or anything much heard of but little seen, are; if we go to the edge of the world we come to water or may fall off, or it may be like a house and we live on top. The first notion of a hill may be of some particular pile of sand, perhaps on the molding board, three inches high, or a rubbish heap in the back yard, or a slant where a sled will run alone; but a comprehensive idea of hill with opposite sides, though simpler and easier than most geographical categories, is by no means to be assumed.

If children are pressed to answer questions somewhat beyond their ken, they often reply confusedly and at random, while if others beside them are questioned they can answer well; some are bolder and invent things on the spot if they seem to interest the questioner, while others catch quick subtle suggestions from the form of the question, accent, gesture, feature, etc., so that what seems originality is really mind reading, giving back our very thought, and is sometimes only a direct reproduction, with but little distortion because little apprehension, of what parents or teachers have lately told them. But there are certain elements which every tactful and experienced friend of children learns to distinguish from each of these with considerable accuracy — elements which, from whatever source, spring from deep roots in the childish heart, as distinct from all these as are Grimm's tales from those of some of our weakly juvenile weeklies. These are generally not easily accessible. I could not persuade an old nurse to repeat to me a nonsensical song I half overheard that delighted a two-year-old child, and the brothers Grimm experienced a similar difficulty in making their collections. As many workingmen nail a horseshoe over their door for luck, and many people really prefer to begin nothing important on Friday, who will not confess to a trace of superstition in either case, so children cling to their "old credulities to nature dear," refusing every attempt to gain their full confidence or explore secret tracts in their minds, as a well-developed system of insane illusions may escape the scrutiny of the most skillful alienist. As a reasoning electric light might honestly doubt the existence of such things as shadows because, however near or numerous, they are always hidden from it, so the most intelligent adults quite commonly fail to recognize sides of their own children's souls which can be seen only by strategy. A boy and girl often play under my window as I write, and unconscious words often reveal what is passing in their minds when either is quite alone, and it is often very absurd or else meaningless, but they run away with shame and even blushes if they chance to look up suddenly and catch me listening. Yet who of us has not secret regions of soul to which no friend is ever admitted, and which we ourselves shrink from full consciousness of? Many children half believe the doll feels cold or blows, that it pains flowers to tear or burn them, or that in summer when the tree is alive it makes it ache to pound or chop it. Of 48 children questioned 20 believed sun, moon, or stars to live; 15 thought that a doll, and 16, that flowers, would suffer pain if burned. Children who are accounted dull in school work are more apt to be imaginative and animistic.

The chief field for such fond and often secret childish fancies is the sky. About three fourths of all questioned thought the world a plain, and many described it as round like a dollar, while the sky is like a flattened bowl turned over it. The sky is often *thin*, one might *easily break through;* half the moon may be seen through it, while the other half is this side ; it may be *made of snow,* but is so large that there is *much floor sweeping* to be done in heaven. Some thought *the sun went down at night into the ground* or just behind certain houses, and went across, on, or under the ground to *go up, out of,* or *off the water* in the morning ; but 48 per cent. of all thought that at night it *goes* or *rolls* or *flies,* is *blown* or *walks,* or *God pulls it up* higher out of sight. He *takes it into heaven,* and perhaps *puts it to bed,* and even *takes off its clothes* and puts them on in the morning, or again it *lies under the trees* where the angels *mind it,* or goes through and *shines on the upper side of the sky,* or goes *into* or *behind the moon,* as the moon is behind it in the day. It may *stay where it is,* only we *cannot see it, for it is dark,* or the *dark rains down so,* and it *comes out when it gets light so it can see.* More than half the children questioned conceived the sun as never more than 40 degrees from the zenith, and, naturally enough, city children knew little of the horizon. So the moon (still italicizing where the exact words of the children are given) *comes around when it is a bright night* and people *want to walk,* or *forget to light some lamps ;* it *follows us about* and has nose and eyes, while it *calls the stars into, under,* or *behind* it at night, and they may be *made of bits of it.* Sometimes the moon is *round a month or two,* then it is a *rim,* or a *piece is cut off,* or it is *half stuck* or *half buttoned into* the sky. The stars may be *sparks from fire engines* or houses, or with higher intelligence they are silver, or *God lights them with matches* and *blows them out* or *opens the door* and calls them in in the morning. Only in a single case were any of the heavenly bodies conceived as openings in the sky to let light or glory through, or as eyes of supernatural beings, — a fancy so often ascribed to children and so often found in juvenile literature. Thunder, which, anthropologists tell us, is or represents the highest God to most savage races, was apperceived as God *groaning* or *kicking*, or *rolling barrels about*, or *turning a big handle*, or *grinding snow, walking loud, breaking something, throwing logs, having coal run in, pounding about* with a *big hammer*, *rattling houses, hitting the clouds*, or clouds *bumping* or *clapping* together or *bursting*, or else it was merely *ice sliding off lots of houses*, or *cannon in the city* or sky, hard *rain down the chimney*, or *big rocks pounding*, or *piles of boards falling down*, or very hard rain, hail, or wind. Lightning is God *putting out his finger* or *opening a door*, or *turning a gas quick*, or (very common) *striking many matches at once*, throwing *stones and iron for sparks, setting paper afire*, or it is light going outside and inside the sky, or stars falling. God keeps rain in heaven in a *big sink, rows of buckets*, a *big tub* or *barrels*, and they *run over* or he *lets it down* with a *water hose* through a *sieve*, a *dipper with holes*, or *sprinkles* or *tips* it down or *turns a faucet.* God makes it in heaven out of nothing or out of water, or it gets up by *splashing up*, or he *dips it up off the roof*, or it *rains up off the ground when we don't see it.* The clouds are *close to the sky;* they move because the *earth moves and makes them.* They are *dirty, muddy things*, or *blankets*, or *doors of heaven*, and are made of fog, of *steam that makes the sun go*, of smoke, of *white wool* or *feathers and birds*, or *lace* or *cloth*. In their changing forms very many children, whose very life is fancy, think they see veritable men, or more commonly, because they have so many more forms, animals' faces; and very often God, Santa Claus, angels, etc., are also seen. Closely connected with the above are the religious concepts so common with children. God is a *big*, perhaps *blue man*, very often seen in the sky on or in the clouds, in the church, or even street. He *came in our gate, comes to see us sometimes*. He lives in a *big palace* or a big *brick* or *stone house on the sky*. He makes lamps, babies, dogs, trees, money, etc., and the angels *work for him*. He looks like the priest, Fröbel, papa, etc., and they like to look at him, and a few would like to be God. He *lights the stars so he can see to go on the sidewalk* or *into the church*. Birds, children, Santa Claus, live with him, and most but not all like him better than they do the latter. When people die they just *go*, or are *put in a hole*, or a box or a *black wagon that goes to heaven*, or they *fly up* or are *drawn* or *slung* up into the sky where God *catches* them. They *never can get out of the hole*, and yet all good people somehow get where God is. He *lifts* them up, they *go up on a ladder or rope*, or they carry them up, but *keep their eyes shut so they do not know the way*, or they are *shoved up through a hole*. When children get there they have candy, rocking-horses, guns, and everything in the toy-shop or picture book, play marbles, top, ball, cards, hockey, hear brass bands, have nice clothes, gold watches, and pets, ice cream and soda water, and no school. There are men who died in the war made into angels, and dolls with broken heads go there. Some think they must go through the church to get there, a few thought the horse cars run there, and one said that the *birds that grow on apple trees are drawn up there by the moon*. The bad place is like an *oven* or a *police station*, where it burns, yet is all dark, and folks want to get back, and God *kills* people or *beats them with a cane*. God makes babies in heaven, though the Holy Mother and even Santa Claus make some. He *lets them down or drops them*, and the women or doctors *catch* them, or he leaves them on the sidewalk, or *brings them down a wooden ladder backwards and pulls it up again*, or mamma or the doctor or the nurse *go up and fetch them,* sometimes *in a balloon,* or they *fly down and lose off their wings in some place or other and forget where they came from,* or *jump down to Jesus,* who *gives them around.* They were also often said to be found in flour barrels, and the *flour sticks ever so long you know,* or they *grow in cabbages,* or God *puts them in water,* perhaps *in the sewer,* and the doctor gets them out and *takes them to sick folks that want them,* or the milkman brings them early in the morning, they are dug out of the ground, or bought at the baby store. Sometimes God *puts on a few things* or else *sends them along if he don't forget it;* this shows that no one since Basedow believes in telling children the truth in all things.

Not many children have or can be made to disclose many such ideas as the above, and indeed they seem to be generally already on the ebb at this age, and are sometimes timidly introduced by, *as if, some say,* it is *like,* or *I used to think.* Clear and confident notions on the above topics are the exception and not the rule, yet children have some of them, while some are common to many, indeed to most, children. They represent a drift of consentient infantile philosophy about the universe not without systematic coherence, although intimidated and broken through at every point by fragmentary truths, often only verbal indeed, without insight or realization of a higher order, so that the most diametrical contradictions often subsist peacefully side by side, and yet they are ever forming again at lower levels of age and intelligence. In all that is remote, the real and ideal fade into each other like clouds and mountains in the horizon, or as poetry, which keeps alive the standpoints of an earlier culture, coexists with science. Children are often hardly conscious of these contradictions at all, and the very questions that bring them to mind and invite them to words at the same time often abash the child and produce the first disquieting self-consciousness of the absurdity of his fond fancies that have felt not only life but character in natural objects. Between the products of childish spontaneity, where the unmistakable child's mark is seen, and those of really *happy* suggestion by parents, etc., the distinction is as hard as anywhere along the line between heredity and tradition. It is enough that these fancies are like Galton's composite portraits, resultants in form and shading of the manifold deepest impressions which what is within and what is without have together made upon the child's soul in these spheres of ideas. Those indicated above represent many strata of intelligence up through which the mind is passing very rapidly and with quite radical transformations. Each stratum was once, with but a little elaboration, or is now somewhere, the highest culture, relegated to and arrested in an earlier stage as civilization and educational methods advance. In children belief in the false is as necessary as it is inevitable, for the proper balance of head and heart, and happy the child who has believed or loved only healthy, unaffected, platonic lies like the above, which will be shed with its milk teeth when more solid mental pabulum can be digested. It is possible that the present shall be so attractive and preoccupying that the child never once sends his thoughts to the remote in time and place, and these baby fancies — ever ready to form at a touch, which make the impartation of truth, however carefully put, on these themes impossible before its time; which, when long forgotten, yet often reverberate, if their old chords be struck in adults, to the intensity of fanaticism or even delusion — shall be quite repressed. If so, one of the best elements of education which comes from long experience in laying aside a lower for a higher phase of culture by doubting opportunely, judiciously, and temperately is lost.

De Quincey's[1] pseudopia is thought by Dr. E. H. Clark to be common with children; but although about 40 were

[1] *Collected Writings* (ed. by D. Masson), Vol. XIII, pp. 300–318 and 350–351. A. and C. Black, London, 1897.

asked to describe what they saw with their eyes shut, it is impossible to judge whether they visualize in any such distinctive sense as Mr. Galton has described, or only imagine and remember, often with Homeric circumstance, but with less picturesque vividness. Childish thought is very largely in visual terms ; hence the need of object (*Anschauungs*) lessons, and hence, too, it comes that most of the above questions address the eye without any such intent. If phonic symbols could be made pictorial, as they were originally, and as illustrated primers made them in a third and still remoter sense, the irrational elements in learning to read would be largely obviated. Again, out of 53 children 21 described the tones of certain instruments as colored.[1] The colors, or "photism," thus suggested, though so far as tested, constant from week to week in the same child, had no agreement for different instruments, a drum, e.g., suggesting yellow to one child and black or red to another, and the tone of a fife being described as pale or bright, light or dark colored, intensity and saturation varying greatly with different children. For this and other forms of association or analogies of sensations of a large and not yet explored class so common in children, many data for future study were gathered. This was also the case with their powers of time and tone reproduction, and their common errors in articulation, which have suggested other and more detailed researches, some of which are already in progress.

Each child was asked to name three things right and three things wrong to do, and nearly half could do so. In no case were the two confused, indicating not necessarily intuitive perception, but a general consensus in what is allowed and forbidden children at home, and how much better and more

[1] In the sense of Bleuler and Lehmann. See their treatise, *Zwangmässige Lichtempfindungen durch Schall*, Fues, Leipzig, 1881 ; also, Lazarus's *Das Leben der Seele*, 3. Aufl., p. 131. F. Dummler, Berlin, 1897.

surely they learn to do than to know. Wrong things were specified much more readily and by more children than right things, and also in much greater variety. In about 450 answers 53 wrong acts are specified, while in over 350 answers only 34 different good acts are named. The more frequent answers are to mind and be good, or to disobey, be naughty, lie, and say bad words ; but the answers of the girls differ from the boys in two marked ways : they more often name specific acts and nearly twice as often conventional ones, the former difference being most common in naming right, the latter in naming wrong, things. Boys say it is wrong to steal, fight, kick, break windows, get drunk, stick pins into others, or to "sass," "cuss," or shoot them ; while girls are more apt to say it is wrong not to comb the hair, to get butter on the dress, climb trees, unfold the hands, cry, catch flies, etc. The right things seem, it must be confessed, comparatively very tame and unattractive, and while the genius of an Aristotle could hardly extract categories or infer intuitions by classification from either list, it is very manifest that the lower strata of conscience are dislike of dirt and fear. Pure intuitionalists may like to know that over a dozen children were found who convinced their questioners that they thought they ought not to say bad words if no one heard them, or lie if not found out, etc., or who felt sick at the stomach when they had been bad ; but the soap and water or sand with which their mouths are sometimes washed after bad words in kindergartens, or the red pepper administered at home after lies, may possibly have something to do with the latter phenomenon.

From several hundred drawings, with the name given them by the child written by the teacher, the chief difference inferred is in concentration. Some make faint, hasty lines, representing all the furniture of a room, or sky and stars, or all the objects they can think of, while others concentrate upon a single object. It is a girl *with buttons*, a house *with a keyhole* or steps, a man *with a pipe* or heels or ring made grotesquely prominent. The development of observation and sense of form is best seen in the pictures of men. The earliest and simplest representation is a round head, two eyes, and legs. Later comes mouth, then nose, then hair, then ears. Arms like legs, at first, grow directly from the head, rarely from the legs, and are seldom fingerless, though sometimes it is doubtful whether several arms, or fingers from head and legs without arms, are meant. Of 44 human heads only 9 are in profile. This is one of the many analogies with the rock and cave drawings of primitive man, and suggests how Catlin came to nearly lose his life by "leaving out the other half" in drawing a profile portrait of an Indian chief. Last, as least mobile and thus attracting least attention, comes the body; first round like the head, then elongated, sometimes prodigiously, and sometimes articulated into several compartments, and in three cases divided, the upper part of the figure being in one place and the lower in another. The mind, and not the eye alone, is addressed, for the body is drawn and then the clothes are drawn on it (as the child dresses), diaphanous and only in outline. Most draw living objects, except the kindergarten children, who draw their patterns. More than two thirds of all objects are decidedly in action, and under 18 per cent. are added word pictures or scribbles called the *name* of the objects and made to imitate writing or letters, as children who cannot talk often make gibbering, sputtering sounds to imitate talking. The very earliest pencilings, commonly of three-year-old children, are mere marks to and fro, often nearly in the same line. Of 13 of these, most were *nearly* in the angle described by Javal as corresponding to the earliest combination of finger and fore-arm movements, and not far from the regulation slant of 52° taught in school penmanship.

Each child was asked to tell a verse or story to be recorded verbatim, and nearly half could do so. Children of this age are no longer interested in mere animal noises or rhymes or nonsense words of the "Mother Goose" order, but everything to interest them deeply must have a cat, dog, bird, baby, another child, or possibly parent or teacher in it, must be dramatic and full of action, appeal to the eye as a "chalk talk" or an object lesson, and be copious of details, which need be varied but slightly to make the story as good as new for the twentieth time. A long gradation of abstractions culminates here. First, it is a great lesson for the child to eliminate touch and recognize objects by the eye alone. The first good pictures mentally seen are felt of, turned over with much confusion to find the surface smooth. To abstract from visual terms to words is still harder. Eyes and tongue must work together a long time before the former can be eliminated and stories told of objects first absent, then remote, then before unknown. Children must be far beyond this before they can be interested, e.g., in fairy tales, and stories told interest them far more than if read to them, no matter how apt the language. They are reproduced about as imperfectly as objects are drawn, only a few salient and disconnected points being seized at first, and sentence and sequence coming very slowly after many repetitions. Their own little faults may be woven in or ascribed to animals or even plants in a remote way which they themselves will feel at each stage, and the selfish birdie or the runaway squirrel or flowers as kind words may be referred to in case of need as a reserve moral capital. Why do we never teach maxims and proverbs which, when carefully selected, are found so effective at this age and teach the best morality embodied in the briefest and most impressive way?

Of the 36 per cent. or 72 children of the table who never saved their pennies, 52 spend them for candy, which growing children need, but the adulterations of which are often noxious. Of toys, big things please them best. A recent writer in Austria fears that school savings banks tend to call attention too early to money matters, and to cause its value to be dangerously overrated; but to pass the candy by and drop the cents where they are beyond their control for years is much less pedagogic than to save them until their sum amounts to a total sufficient to buy a larger and more costly, and perhaps more keenly desired, toy.

The next experimental inquiry [1] in the field was also made in quest of a natural basis of the first school instruction. If we look at the developing effect upon the person of the pupil, progress in the upper gymnasial classes is perhaps less than in the first year of school, although, if we regard the quantity of acquisition or its importance, it is much greater. That the matter of instruction is preferred to the development of the person of the pupil is the cause of the memory cram and neglect of pedagogy, which often makes school keeping, as Grimm called it, lower than the work of the day laborer. Herbart, Ziller, and Stoy, however, plead for "educating instruction," and show will to be rooted in the sphere of thought, which should first be moral and religious. Many-sided interest is the root and key of all. Interest may be of knowledge or of perception, and statistical inquiry might seek to determine which class of interests predominate, and whether reproduction was slow, confused, partial, or the reverse. The Berlin tables showed what ideas were lacking, but Lange sought the ideas that were not lacking as a basis of school knowledge. The child's soul is no *tabula rasa*, and very suggestive are papers on the best methods of excursions for city schools, on the educational value and use of home and its environment, and on apperception.

[1] Dr. B. Hartmann, *Die Analyse des Kindlichen Gedankenkreises als die Naturgemässe des ersten Schulunterrichts.* H. Graser, Annaberg, 1890.

Hartmann's tests were made solely, he says, in the interests of the Annaberg schools, to determine the natural basis of the course of study there for the first year or two. The fourteen plainer questions were not enough, and he had not heard of the Boston tests, so those of Berlin were largely his model. His tests were better than all others in one respect, viz., they were repeated five years (1880–1884) on as many groups of children entering school, and they have given rise to analogous tests in other cities, best perhaps in Döbeln. For Hartmann's purpose a large number of questions were needed, and interests of knowledge must be regarded more than those of sympathy or participation. To an Herbartian the former seems earlier and richer, but the ideal of normalizing a sphere of thought is evident. Concepts likely to be wanting in children of that town were excluded in favor of those easily accessible to every child, yet those chosen were not model or normal in the sense that often others as good may have been excluded. The flying, singing lark may be seen every day in spring at Annaberg, and if it has not been noticed, the child may be inert and indifferent, or its senses dull or defective, and this would also be the inference had the swallow been chosen. By this method each locality will find objects especially prominent and peculiar to it. A book by E. Piltz, entitled *Über Naturbeobachtung des Schülers* (1882), and Sigismund's *Die Familie als Schule der Natur* (1856), contain good lists of topics (the former 700 of them) and reports from similar tests. As a manufacturing center of passementerie, and a shire town and retail center, Annaberg has rich and poor, and its prosperity depends on changes in fashions, so that the 265 children entering its schools yearly differ greatly. Some children were very bashful on first entering school, used to only the local dialect which most teachers did not speak, but by beginning with the easiest questions and talking of parents and toys these difficulties were minimized.

Thus answers were often enigmatical, and much cross and indirect questioning was required before the dash which signified knowledge on the point, or the plus sign which signified its absence, could be made. In all 1312 children, 660 boys and 652 girls, were tested, all between 5¾ and 6¾ years old, the tests being made before and after regular school hours by the teacher, who worked with small groups and made them answer individually when possible.

The table below reads as follows : out of 660 boys entering schools in Annaberg from 1881 to 1884, 126, or 19 per cent., had seen a wild hare, etc.

OBJECT	660 Boys	652 Girls	1312 All	PER CENT. Boys	Girls	All
Hare	126	81	207	19	12	16
Squirrel	99	69	168	15	10	13
Flock of sheep	235	198	433	36	30	33
Starling	85	68	153	13	10	12
Goose	272	250	522	41	38	40
Hen	195	178	373	30	27	28
Cuckoo	69	88	157	10	13	12
Lark	76	83	159	12	13	12
Frog	188	126	314	29	19	24
Fish	141	122	263	21	19	20
Bee	75	46	121	11	7	9
Butterfly	287	362	649	44	55	49
Snail	210	201	411	32	31	31
Birch	33	10	43	5	2	3
Pine	145	148	293	22	23	22
Acorn	17	11	28	3	2	2
Cherry tree	83	138	221	13	21	17
Apple tree	208	219	427	31	34	33
Hazelnut	78	42	120	12	6	9
Flowers	322	317	639	49	49	49
Whortleberry	158	193	351	24	29	27
Moss	130	107	237	20	16	18
Mushroom	113	165	278	17	25	21
Sandpit	58	37	95	9	6	7

Object	660 Boys	652 Girls	1312 All	Per Cent. Boys	Girls	All
Quarry	121	105	226	18	16	17
Mine.	41	33	74	6	5	6
Tempest	363	424	787	55	65	59
Fog	186	246	432	28	38	33
Clouds	266	293	559	40	45	42
Hailstones	307	315	622	46	48	47
Rainbow	226	264	490	34	40	37
Evening sky	119	166	285	18	25	22
Sunset	82	77	159	12	12	12
Phases of moon	148	223	371	22	34	28
Starry sky	349	466	815	53	71	62
Clock (time)	27	18	45	4	3	3
Days of week	54	92	146	8	14	11
Seasons	37	64	101	6	10	8
Constellations	4	1	5	1	0	1
Dwelling	543	503	1046	82	77	80
Zürcher Square	346	328	674	52	50	51
Chief market	471	452	923	71	69	70
Buchholzer Street . . .	278	281	559	42	43	43
Real gymnasium	133	164	297	20	25	23
Berg church	210	220	430	32	34	33
Catholic church	231	237	468	35	36	36
Town hall	430	403	833	65	62	63
Post office	297	344	641	45	53	49
Railroad station	418	433	851	63	66	65
Bahls restaurant	167	189	356	25	29	27
Nursery tree	163	180	343	25	27	26
Markus-Röhling (an old mine)	193	267	460	29	41	35
Promenade	228	292	520	35	45	40
Grove	172	253	425	26	39	32
Churchyard	394	469	863	60	72	66
Pöhlberg	217	244	461	33	37	35
Galgenberg	89	89	178	13	13	13
Schreckenberg	117	112	229	18	17	17
Buchheltz	282	329	611	43	50	47
Frohnau	164	226	390	25	35	30
Wiesenbad	121	159	280	18	24	21
Geyersdorf	139	200	339	21	31	26

Object	660 Boys	652 Girls	1312 All	Per Cent. Boys	Per Cent. Girls	Per Cent. All
Valley	51	59	110	8	9	8
River	150	157	307	23	24	23
Bridge	282	258	540	43	39	41
Water mills	152	151	303	23	23	23
Pond.	434	490	924	66	75	70
Meadow.	250	218	468	38	33	36
Cornfield	183	111	294	28	17	22
Potato field	345	358	703	52	55	54
Snow landscape	289	262	551	44	40	42
Village	158	175	333	24	27	25
Soldiers' monument . . .	180	136	316	27	21	24
Fountain	397	394	791	60	60	60
Carriage driving	332	362	694	50	55	53
Road.	300	346	646	45	53	49
Field works	250	181	431	38	28	33
Garden works	213	211	424	32	32	32
Acute-angled triangle . .	62	66	128	9	10	10
Square	101	90	191	15	14	15
Cube.	214	293	507	32	45	39
Circle	280	284	564	42	43	43
Sphere or globe	546	510	1056	83	78	80
Counting from 1 to 10 . .	456	405	861	69	62	66
God	370	401	771	56	61	59
Jesus.	68	142	210	10	22	16
Bible history	7	14	21	1	2	2
Prayers and songs . . .	122	184	306	18	28	23
Divine service	192	223	415	29	34	32
Baptism.	118	228	346	18	35	26
Wedding	70	227	297	11	35	23
Father's name and station .	425	370	795	64	57	61
King.	52	42	94	8	6	7
Coins	450	398	848	68	61	65
Sickness	356	406	762	54	62	58
Fairy tale	32	39	71	5	6	5
Repetition in speaking . .	480	426	906	73	65	69
Recitation	68	62	130	10	9	10
Repetition in singing . .	226	243	469	34	37	36
Singing songs.	102	161	263	15	25	20

The objects it will be observed are here arranged in groups as follows: animals, 1–13; plants, 14–23; minerals, 24–26; events in nature, 27–35; time, 36–39; localities, 40–51; the home landscape, 52–78; mathematical, 79–84; religious, 85–91; social, 92–94; miscellaneous, 95–100. Of the children tested the first year the individual records of a few were followed and given with detail. A boy who passed on 75 out of the 100 showed an excellent record each year. He had a large vocabulary, yet would repeat a story with a fidelity to the words it was told in that was almost servile. He was better in sharp thought than in phantasy. A girl was deficient in all groups and almost zero in some, having only 41 per cent. of the questions, and a boy had but 12 of the 100 usable concepts. The school marks and the carefully kept individuality books in these and other cases corresponded very nearly to the efficiency shown in the preliminary tests. Not only do the latter harmonize with following school years, but Hartmann thinks that from a careful inspection of the results of each group into which the 100 questions fall the mental ability if not the future career of the child can be predicted. What shall be said, he adds, of the waste of the general public school in which all three of these children are taught side by side in the same class?

In this inventory great stress was laid upon the natural setting of each object. The questioners were told that it was not sufficient to have seen, but they must have ridden on the cars, the apple tree must have had apples on it, the butterfly must have been on the flower, the sheep grazing, the frog springing, etc. One of these concepts was known to but 5, and one to 1056 of the 1312 children, and the others were between these extremes. In animals, minerals, and the social group only did boys excel. Girls excelled in 56 and boys in 38 objects. Girls excelled the boys in their marks also in the first, second, and third school year, but less and less, till in the sixth year the boys were distinctly ahead. Again, on entering the usual elementary school each boy had on the average 30.7 of the 100 concepts, and each girl 36.7. At the end of the first school year the boys had an average mark of progress of 3.03, and each girl 2.53. Thus we can form the proportion, $36.7 : 30. 7 = 3.03 : x$, which gives, as the value of its fourth term, 2.535, which varies only 0.005 from the actual mark of the girls. For each of the next three years the deviation is hardly greater. The product of the number of concepts multiplied by the chief school mark in Germany which designates progress comes out about the same in girls' as in boys' classes. Out of the 100 usable concepts the average girl had 32.9, the average boy 30.8. The average Annaberg number, 31.9, is thus small. So valuable were these tests for determining the individuality of the child, for arrangement of the program and for their aid to teachers, that at Easter either the entire hundred, or at least the best thirty, questions are tested each year. These are the following : hare, hen, frog, butterfly, pine tree, flower, tempest, rainbow, moon phases, days of the week, child's home, city hall, railway station, potato field, snow landscape, cube, numbers, work in the field, baptism, coins, sickness, God, Jesus, and localities. In the practice school of the Pedagogical Seminary at Jena each school year begins with this analysis of the children's sphere of thought.

The complete course of study for the first and second school year, based upon his inquest, the author reserves for a later pamphlet, and gives here only an outline of his ideas. Nothing fulfills all the conditions of Herbartian interest at first better than Bible stories ; but only 25 per cent. of the children have usable Bible concepts, and their apperceptive organs are hardly developed enough to make this fruitful. *Genuine* child stories, according to Willmann, must have five marks, viz. : they must be really childlike or simple and full of fancy, they must excite and educate the mental judgment, must be instructive and of permanent worth, they must make a deep unitary impression which shall be a center of future interest. It must thus be popular and classical. Hartmann thanks God that this demand can be met by the Grimm *Märchen*. Since Ziller's first plea for *Märchen* in school nearly a quarter of a century ago the battle about them has raged. Hartmann disagrees with Ziller and Rein in thinking that four of these are enough for the first school year and feed all the Herbartian interests. The *Star Dollars*, which teaches that although all desert the child there is *One* that does not, comes last. Rein is charged with selecting his twelve tales arbitrarily, without the justification which only such a preliminary inquest can give, or else for external reasons, as basis for instruction in natural history, etc. Hartmann's limited use of *Märchen* should not only educate religious and other sentiments, but it should teach to apprehend and to tell again. After this practice for half a year Bible stories should come. The New Testament should precede the Old, and all should center about the Jesus child. To fail of insuring close intimacy with Bible tales in early childhood is, we are told, one of the gravest of all pedagogical errors. The topics of this half year should be the nativity, the visit of the three wise men, Jesus in the temple, the wedding at Cana, the boy at Nain, the entrance to Jerusalem, the arrest of Jesus, his condemnation, death, and burial. This plan has been followed in close connection with the church year in Annaberg, and with the best results. Even for narrative and educational values this has excelled all other material. This matter must be so treated as to evoke the greatest interest and participation, and never at the same part of the year as the *Märchen*. Religious instruction should thus be chief and central. It should select the matter and all it requires without reference to other branches, and in this sense only they should all be subordinate to it. The last sixteen pages are given to an outline or program for each of the forty full school weeks of the German school year. This is divided as narrative matter and object-lesson matter. The first begins with a brief prayer and song, the first *Märchen*, in the third week, and new and longer songs, prayers, and tales, then proverbs and poems with Bible tales the last half year. The second begins with name, place in school, time, school days, movements, with use of slate, sponge, and pencil in the second week, each child's home, street, parents' name, home life, fence, hedge, flowers, animals and birds seen on the way, garden tools, planting and sowing, riddles, drawing, then writing and reckoning, etc. Every object in the table is gone over with detail, as are many more. They draw dog houses, bird cages, mouse traps, spider's web, hat, lamp, stove, moon, star, cat, dish, sled, church, altar, Christmas tree, knife and fork, wine bottle and glass, bed, teacup and pot, hat, cap, gravestone, street lamp, city hall, bookcase, slate, etc.

Recently another census of this kind has been taken. J. Olsen[1] describes a systematic study of 5600 pupils at Varde by the tutorial staff, which began in the year 1898, in order to determine the content of their minds when entering school at the age of six or seven. A series of one hundred ideas, partly of a universal and partly of a local order, was made out and each child was examined singly as to each idea, and the teacher marked on his schedule how many clear concepts of each class the child possessed. The children were of middle and working classes, and the tests were an open-hearted conversation regarded rather as play than as work, at which the most clever ones endeavored to display all their knowledge.

On the following page is the table of results.

[1] Children's Ideas (Denmark), *Paidologist*, Nov., 1900, Vol. II, pp. 128–131.

	Per Cent. Boys	Per Cent. Girls
Hen with her chickens	81	70
Starling	64	62
Beehive	90	54
Stork in his nest	87	85
Leaping frog	90	77
Fish in the water	87	77
Swimming swan	72	77
Ant	90	70
Singing lark	36	8
Creeping snail	54	70
Butterfly in a flower	70	93
Hare in the field	63	30
Blooming cherry	63	48
Apple tree with apples	90	54
Beech in the wood	27	34
Pine in the wood	63	78
Birch in the wood	9	8
Hazel in the wood	9	8
Flower in the field	90	93
Moss in the wood	81	54
Mushroom in the wood	54	61
Gravel pit	9	8
Turf pit	63	22
Flint	54	22
Thunder	72	85
Hail shower	81	93
Father's name	81	93
Residence	100	100
The king	18	0
Coin	100	100
Rope maker	63	45
Joiner	95	52
Church, interior and exterior	54	34
Town hall	72	76
Market place	96	88
Frederick VII (a statue in the market place)	45	14
Leddler Street	100	25
Public school	100	100

	Per Cent. Boys	Per Cent. Girls
College	63	30
Methodist church	54	39
Hospital	81	95
Old cemetery	81	86
New cemetery	88	95
Gas works	81	55
Manege	81	55
Railway station	100	86
Hotel	54	39
Fountain	63	46
Arnebjerg (a grove)	81	100
The grove (a plantation near town)	81	95
Moving clouds	81	46
Rainbow	90	78
Dew	30	46
Dawn	27	0
Evening red	18	8
Sunrise and sunset	36	8
Starry heavens	90	85
Change of the moon	54	23
Quarters of the globe	9	0
Watch	63	98
Days of the week	63	54
The seasons	27	54
Birthday	72	54
Triangle	45	46
Square	72	93
Birch	9	8
Ball	100	100
Cube	18	16
Numbers from 1 to 10	90	85
God	63	70
Christ	27	45
Biblical narratives	36	62
Prayer and psalms	36	62
Church service	27	30
Baptism	9	15
Funeral	54	77

	PER CENT. Boys	PER CENT. Girls
Eiffel Tower	54	23
River	100	100
Bridge	90	86
Meadow	90	62
Valley	18	8
Hill	45	15
Sea	45	23
Plantation	63	38
Heath	90	38
Lake	18	8
Cornfield	72	31
Potato field	90	71
Snow-covered land	72	62
Windmill	100	70
Water mill	36	0
Work in the field	100	47
Work in the garden	100	86
Riding in a carriage	100	86
Riding in the train	100	78
Correct repetition of sounds	90	72
Recitation of verses	30	70
Repetition of singing	36	54
Singing	63	62
Sickness	90	94

From the above we see that girls have on an average fewer clear ideas than boys, save concerning religious matters, funerals, and things which concern the feelings and the seasons. Some of the misconceptions of children were remarkable. Some know moving, but not stationary clouds. Very much that passed under the children's eyes every day was not noticed. School work must be built upon a very poor foundation of clear ideas. The fact that children see objects a hundred times without acquiring consciousness of it suggests that we need to converse with children about the commonest things.

G. STANLEY HALL

THE PSYCHOLOGY OF DAYDREAMS[1]

Perhaps not the least difficult question in connection with the present topic is what mental states shall be included under the term *daydreaming*. The usual definition — " an idle exercise of the imagination during waking hours " — by no means covers the material of the returns, which include nearly every form of mental reproduction from the hypnagogic state, with complete absence of voluntary control, through varying phases in which the initial idea or general trend of the images is voluntarily determined, up to a distinctly purposive picturing of the future with due attention to probable realization. There are, however, certain characteristics which are common to this entire series of phenomena, namely a withdrawal of the attention, more or less complete, from the external senses, and a greater or less degree of mental automatism. Fechner[2] considers that in so far as attention is withdrawn from the senses, their condition is precisely the same as in real sleep, and "*vice versa* the whole sphere of the activity of inner representations may fall asleep." According to this view, the mental life oscillates between sleeping and waking, and there are regions of the brain asleep even in waking states and the distinction between dreams and daydreams is merely one of degree. For convenience in classification, daydreaming may be tentatively defined as including all those reproductive and imaginative mental states in which there is a greater or less degree of automatism in the images which come before the mind. Its limits

[1] Reprinted in abridged form from the *American Journal of Psychology,* Vol. XV, pp. 465–488, October, 1904.
[2] G. T. Fechner, *Elemente der Psychophysik*, Vol. I, p. 440, 2te Aufl. Breitkopf, Leipzig, 1889.

would be, on the one hand, the hypnagogic states which immediately precede sleep, and on the other, states of purposive thinking in which the mind becomes so filled with the subject that its workings tend to become automatic. Some of those who answered the questions attempted definitions, a few specimens of which are here given.

F., 14.[1] Daydreams are the thoughts and wishes which we imagine.

M., 15. Daydreams are dreams about things which are fancied and which have no real foundation.

F., 16. Daydreams are thoughts about what we want the most.

F., 16½. Daydreaming is simply the soul longing for something great.

F., 13. In daydreams, you first start out to think about one thing and then your mind wanders over many things which may or may not be connected with what you first start to think about. It is really going to sleep because you don't work with anything but your brain. You generally have daydreams when everything about you is quiet and you have nobody to talk to. You think, but you don't express your thoughts in words; it 's your brain that is holding a conversation.

The material for the present study was collected in response to a request contained in a syllabus on dreams.

" Ask all who can to write about their daydreams, what they are most often about, where and when they lapse to reverie most often, and if they enjoy it or think it wrong, etc.; and describe one or more in detail."

469 papers were received from normal-school pupils of ages averaging from seventeen to twenty-five, 980 from pupils in the graded schools of ages ranging from seven to sixteen years, 23 from adults, and 3 contributions were received from those who had passed the age of ninety, making a total of 1475 cases. Of these 535 were from girls and 445 from boys in the graded schools. The normal-school material was chiefly from girls, and of the adults slightly over one half were men. Among the entire 1475 cases there were five (3 males and 2 females) who stated positively that they never had daydreams; but of

[1] F. indicates female; M., male; numbers indicate age in years.

these one, a man of twenty-five, described a mental state which would be included in the broader definition of daydreaming, and two others were children who were classed in grades with those several years younger.

The physical characteristics of daydreaming most frequently mentioned were psychic deafness and blindness and muscular relaxation, including that of the eyes. Many children give descriptions of individual instances of this psychic deafness. They fail to hear bells or signals, say that their minds were far away, that the teacher had to speak several times to attract their attention, and one boy graphically describes an occasion on which his teacher threw a piece of chalk at him " to wake him up." A girl of twenty-one writes, "Sometimes I am so interested in my dreams that I do not see or hear anything that is going on around me." Another girl, of seventeen, says, "There are times when I am so far away that I am entirely unconscious of my surroundings until there is some loud noise or my name is called." The "far-away" look of the eyes is repeatedly mentioned and is an external sign of daydreaming which children readily recognize. A child of twelve gives her observations on the difference between hard thinking and daydreaming in these words : "When you do your arithmetic you pucker up your forehead, but when you are daydreaming your eyes look way off." This relaxation of the eye muscles which allows the axes to become parallel, or, according to Donders, actually divergent, is similar to that in actual sleep. Le Conte (9)[1] proved experimentally that in drowsiness and drunkenness the double images are due to divergence of the optic axes, and recognizes this as the absolutely involuntary and passive state of the eye in distinction from the involuntary tonic contraction of the healthy waking state, which holds the lines of regard parallel, and the voluntary state of convergence. It seems probable that both of the involuntary states are represented in

[1] Numbers in the text refer to Bibliography at end of the article.

daydreaming, actual divergence of the axes probably being confined to those mental states which most nearly approach the hypnagogic, while the "far-away" look so often mentioned is due to parallel axes. Besides these cases of more or less complete muscular relaxation there is another class in which daydreaming is an accompaniment of physical activity of a monotonous or automatic character, as walking, sewing, driving, swinging in a hammock, rocking, practicing piano exercises, hoeing, washing dishes, etc. In a few cases bodily automatisms which took the form of an unconscious acting out of the dream were reported, while in others they were quite unconnected with the images of the dream. Mr. Lindley, in his study of the phenomena of mental effort, reached the tentative conclusion that "many automatisms represent processes for the production and maintenance of central nervous energy as well as for the production of the state of attention, and this seems to hold good for states of attention where the object is internal as well as for sensorial states (10).

The conditions mentioned as favoring daydreaming were twilight, moonlight, solitude, soft music, sound of the waves or falling water or any monotonous sound which tends to fatigue the attention, listening to an uninteresting lecture, sermon, or recitation, physical or mental fatigue, watching an open fire and looking at a distant landscape. It will be noted that several of these conditions are favorable for inducing hypnosis. In a large percentage of the cases daydreaming is either directly associated with bodily or mental fatigue, or fatigue is suggested by the conditions mentioned. Many children name the later hours of the school session as the time for daydreaming, and "bedtime, before going to sleep," is a favorite hour for both children and adolescents. There are many indications that daydreaming is often the normal rest of the mind which takes refuge from monotony or fatigue of the attention by this method of relaxation. Voluntary attention is fatiguing even to adults and much more so to children whose control over the finer muscles is but partially developed. Binet (1) in his experiments on the effects of intellectual fatigue found that even for periods of work occupying less than fifteen minutes there was relaxation of the eye muscles, and that for periods exceeding thirty minutes muscular effort, as tested by the ergograph, was diminished. Mosso (12) found that while in some instances the first effect of intellectual fatigue was to increase the energy of the muscles, it was followed by progressive enfeeblement.

Bound up with this question of fatigue is the relation of attention to daydreaming. Mosso considered in his experiments that attention was completely dispersed when, after an effort to make his mind a complete blank, images entirely uncontrolled by will trooped unbidden into his mind. But while this absolutely passive play of association is reported in a few cases, it is by no means the most typical form of daydreaming. From the teacher's point of view, the daydreaming pupil is certainly in a state of inattention, but in far the greater number of cases even voluntary attention is not wholly suspended, for the choice of subject is initially determined, and if the subject of the dream becomes unpleasant it is usually changed or the dream is banished. Instead of complete dispersion of the attention, there is a withdrawal of it from the perception of outward things and a greater or less degree of concentration on the mental content. Usually this attention is of the passive sort, but even this is not always true, if in daydreaming are included those forms of story building which are worked out in logical sequence though possibly quite irrespective of their connection with facts. The tendency of daydreams to become more of the passive type is distinctly increased toward adolescence, and danger of impairment of attention from overindulgence is clearly recognized. This is brought out in the opinions as to the rightness or wrongness of daydreaming, which will be discussed later.

The Content of Daydreams at Different Ages

In reading successively the papers furnished by the different school grades the change and increase in variety of content was very noticeable and there were a sufficient number of papers from the same grade in different localities to bring out differences fairly well. The dreams of the youngest children who could write (7 to 8 years) were almost entirely of play and good times with a sprinkling of the fairy-story type of dream. Memory images are very prominent, and the chief imaginative alteration consists in making the dreamer's self the chief personage of the dream. The particular plays and ideas of a good time vary with the environment, as all classes of children from the rich to the extremely poor are included, but are reducible to a few fundamental interests, namely, plays which involve motor activities and out-of-door life, nature interests, especially in connection with animals, and eating. The plays and games of boys and girls show some divergence, but out-of-door life and activity figure largely in both. Nature interests were especially noticeable in the returns from the Worcester schools and showed a greater variety than in returns from other localities. Images of good things to eat play quite a large part in the consciousness of both boys and girls, figuring in the fairy stories, picnics, excursions, birthday parties and Thanksgiving celebrations, as well as by themselves. The eatables oftenest mentioned were candy, ice cream, cake, and fruit of various kinds. In the returns from very poor children these dreams of eating were pitifully prominent and evidently affected by the physical conditions of ill-nourished bodies, though the interest seems to be a perfectly normal one for children of all classes. The effect of insufficient nutrition on mental states is further brought out in some material[1] from Polish peasant children in which the questions, What is happiness? and

[1] Collected for the University by Madame Anna Grudzinska of Kiev.

What is your greatest wish ? were asked. "To have enough to eat," "Never to be hungry," "To have enough bread," were the typical answers. For girls from eight to ten, the fairy-tale form of daydream predominates over all others. It appears to be a mental device for compassing all desires, and actual experiences and possibilities are often mingled indiscriminately with the wildest impossibilities. Nearly all dreams of being rich and having every desire gratified and the dream of being a princess and living in a palace "with a piano in every room " and having unlimited silk dresses and jewels may be mixed with the wish "to have enough good food every day." The *deus ex machina* in these dreams is most frequently a fairy godmother, though wishing caps or a magic lamp or ring also figure. With boys of this age the fairy-story dream is less common and the form differs from that among girls. An interesting example of this occurred in a grade where the children were evidently all familiar with the story of Aladdin's lamp and the magic carpet. Nearly all of these had daydreams of flying or being transported through the air. Nearly all the girls had preserved the original forms of the stories with slight alterations, but the boys dreamed of all sorts of wonderful flying machines, sometimes mentioning the rate per hour, of trips in a balloon or by means of mechanical wings, of which they were in some cases the inventors. The desire for riches, while quite as widespread among boys as among girls, seems to demand a more logical explanation of its origin than that furnished by a fairy godmother or the turning of a magic ring on the finger. Dreams of finding money in amounts varying from fifty cents to five million dollars occur, or the dream may be projected into the future and acquiring a fortune by possible or impossible means may be imagined, but however improbable the dream there is usually an attempt at logical consistency in it. Typical examples of these dreams are the following :

M., 9. Once I dreamed of finding a fifty-dollar gold piece. The first thing I bought was a bicycle and a riding suit for thirty dollars. And the other twenty dollars I gave to my mother.

F., 10. One of my daydreams was that I could live in a lovely castle. Eat good food, fruit, and vegetables. And be a fairy and have a wand. I could have a hundred houses full of twenty-dollar bills. And ride in a lovely diamond flower team. Have as many dolls as I would wish. And have doll carriages dressed in silk. It would be summer all the time. I could have white silk dresses, pink, blue, and bright gay colors. I could have as many boys and girls to play with me. And I could have storybooks.

M., 9. Once I have thought that when I am a man I should like to be a millionaire and have a house with green grass as far as I could see. And a hundred horses, fine runners. And every day go out on some lake in a canoe and have a man to take care of a canoe better than anybody else. And the best horses in the world and all the things I could think of, I could have.

F., 10. I want to be a king's wife and live in a large castle. And have a great many rooms and in each a nice piano. And have a long silk robe of red, pink, and many other colors. And have a Morris rocking-chair with diamonds and rubies.

These childish dreams of wealth rarely show traces of the commercial instinct. It is always a means rather than an end, and children in whom the commercial instinct is strong are apt to have a much less imaginative type of daydream. They dream, but their mental images are much more closely related to facts. One boy of ten dreamed of playing marbles with another boy and that " he skun all his marbles." Good trades and means of actually earning money also figure in this type of daydreaming where images are usually furnished by the immediate environment and undergo little change. Dreams of wealth characterize the reveries of children of all ages and adolescents, but the vision of wealth ceases to be of the fairy-story type, and the golden palaces, gorgeous jewels and dresses of the childish dreams fade and are replaced by those of a more materialistic character. Wealth is no longer imagined as the gift of a fairy godmother, but as acquired through material agencies. Boys dream of acquiring a fortune by means of some wonderful invention, by going West and discovering a gold mine, or by phenomenal success in business or speculation, but whatever the method, it is always a short and easy process. Girls dream of marrying millionaires, inheriting large fortunes from newly discovered relatives, or of becoming famous actresses, musicians, or authoresses and acquiring wealth along with fame. Frequently there is a strongly altruistic element in these dreams, especially during the early adolescent years. Hospitals are endowed, animal refuges established, public playgrounds fitted up, fresh-air work carried to an extent which quite dwarfs its present proportions, the poor are clothed and fed, and one young philanthropist would "give every boy a bicycle." The part which bicycles play in the consciousness of the American boy, and sometimes of girls also, is astonishingly large. Those who do not possess them dream of having them, and those who have them dream of the good times they have had or expect to have. A boy of eleven writes: "I dream most often of having hundreds of dollars and I go down and order two bicycles and have coaster brakes put on them. Then I bring down my brother and get the bicycles and order bicycle shoes and suits."

Another, of fourteen, writes: "I dream most of riding a bicycle. Once I dreamed that I and some other boys were racing. We had to go around the track three times and I won the race, the other boys coming in a few yards behind, and there were thousands of people looking on."

A few years later automobiles take the place of bicycles, and the desire to own one is widespread though not as universal as in the case of the bicycle.

The following dream so completely sums up the various sports indicated in the "good times" of daydreams that it is given entire.

M., 14½. My daydream is if I had $16,000,000 I would have a couple of red-devil automobiles, a couple of air ships, and a fine big mansion. I would have a couple of hundred nice carriage horses. I would hire a couple of hundred of men to take care of things and keep everything looking swell, and a swell big building for playing indoor-baseball in winter, basket ball, ping pong, Rugby, and all kinds of sports and games. The first thing I would do before I ate my breakfast would be to go out and have a nice swim, and then take a good pair of Arabian horses and take myself out for a ride, and then come back and eat a good breakfast and take one of my red-devil automobiles out for a good ride.

A more modest dream by a boy of the same age is, " I would like to have a snug little cottage by the sea, and have a small yacht and a few rowboats and be able to go out in them whenever I please."

A large part of the daydreaming of the average healthy boy from ten to fifteen appears to be connected with sports and athletics. When tired or not interested in his school work he is apt to take refuge from *ennui* in visions of fishing, gunning, marbles, baseball, swimming, camping, boating. Even when these amusements have little likelihood of becoming realities, he still conjures up visions of what fun it would be if he could have them.

Baseball furnishes the content of many daydreams for boys from twelve to sixteen. The character of the dream varies from reviewing a recent game in all its details or anticipation of games in the near future to dreams of greatness as a famous pitcher in which the applause of admiring multitudes is vividly pictured. In some cases the dream is so vivid that incipient movements connected with the game are made.

M., 13. One day in school I got to thinking what a fine time I would have playing ball after school. I dreamed that I was a fine pitcher in a team and the other boys were glad to let me pitch.

M., 13½. My dreams are mostly about ball games, and I don't enjoy them very much because they make me think I am a whole lot and then when I wake up I 'm nothing but a boy that can't play very well at all.

Dreams of hunting, fishing, swimming, being a cowboy and living on horseback and traveling in unexplored countries are characteristic throughout the teens. Some of these dreams are entirely unconnected with experience, while in others the mental imagery is largely furnished by memories of vacation pleasures. The instinct itself appears to be widely spread and independent of environment, since it is apparently as strong in those who have never been outside a city as in those who have had opportunities for gratifying it. Very few girls have these dreams and they usually take the form of wishing to be a boy so that such things were possible. Girls dream of travel as much as boys, but when details are given they are of comfortable, civilized travel and rarely include elements of adventure. Country life and animals also figure largely, but very few drift beyond the bounds of convention in their imaginings. The chief form in which any inclination toward adventure appeared was in the dream of being a red-cross nurse and going to China or the Philippines.

Dreams of fame and future greatness rarely occur before adolescence. They vary from vague dreams of achieving honors in military or naval service, law, medicine, politics, music, acting, winning social or business success, to the attainment of some coveted school honor, having the highest works, gaining honors at graduation, or being a leader in athletics. To the boy looking forward to college the highest pinnacle of fame seems often to be the attainment of captaincy of a football team. In children the desire for self-recognition and aggrandizement demands immediate fulfillment and is rarely projected beyond the immediate future, while to the adolescent the vague future seems to possess special attraction, and this distinction seems to hold throughout all dreams of the future. A child's vision of future pleasure is usually bounded by "next Saturday" or the nearest vacation, while the adolescent range seems to include past, present, and a boundless future. An apparent exception to this occurs in children's dreams of being grown up, which are very common, but when these are described in detail they almost all prove to be of the fairy-story order and not a real looking forward into the future. The content of these adolescent dreams of future greatness is chiefly dependent upon environment and personal ambitions. Some are a mere expression of desires without expectation of fulfillment, while others show evidence of being a distinct source of inspiration for purposive effort. Several writers state that when tired or discouraged they found in these dreams of future success encouragement and inspiration for further effort.

F., 13. My daydream is mostly about being an actor in an opera company. I dream of being a beautiful singer.

F., 13. Sometimes I dream of being an authoress and travel all over Europe and Asia, writing about the different peoples.

M., 15. Dreams of becoming the champion ball player of the world.

M., 16. Dreams of military greatness and becoming a great general.

M., 19. As I have always wanted to be a lawyer, my air castles have always been of palatial law offices, stump speeches. Congress and the inevitable White House vision looms in the background. Every boy dreams of the presidency. I see myself delivering a powerful speech before some large audience, with roars of applause interrupting. I think it a bad habit and wish I could stop it. It interferes with study and makes me dissatisfied with reality.

M., 18. Dreams of becoming a famous engineer and overcoming great difficulties in problems of construction of bridges and railroads. Never dreams except in leisure time and thinks that he works the harder because of these dreams.

From the age of twelve, the influence of books upon the content of the daydream becomes increasingly important. With the less imaginative, the dream may be merely a reproduction, with slight alterations, of some book recently read, but in other cases the book simply furnishes the raw material out of which the fabric of the dream is woven. Girls put themselves in the place of their favorite heroines and adapt the material of romance, poetry, or travels to their own uses. Their ideals of life are affected by what they read. Some of these dreams of the future are visions of beautiful and useful womanhood, but the trail of the Elsie books, with their morbid religiosity, and the influence of the Duchess and Rhoda Broughton is evident with unfortunate frequency. Boys dream of fighting Indians, having hairbreadth adventures on land and sea, being cowboys, pirates, brigands, or national heroes as the case may be. Detective stories seem to acquire a peculiar charm at about the age of fourteen. The best of these do not apparently exercise any particularly harmful influence and they appeal strongly to the logical instinct which seems to acquire prominence at about this age. But of the baneful effects of the worse class of this literature there is no doubt. Boys become familiar with the details of sin and crime before their moral ideas are fixed. The qualities of courage and hardihood involved in certain forms of crime appeal strongly to their imagination, and many cases of juvenile crimes are directly traceable to literature of this sort. A more common effect is the lowering of ideals and manly honor and pure-mindedness and the taste for emotional excitement which renders other literature tame and uninteresting and destroys interest in school work.

Another type of daydream common in both children and adolescents is the story-making impulse, which in some cases reveals a high type of creative imagination (8). Some children regularly get themselves to sleep by making up stories, the same one sometimes being continued for several nights. The frequency of the continued story was, however, very small, forming in the present collection of data less than one per cent. of those mentioning the story form of dream.

F., 18. My daydreams are in the forms of imaginations in every way remote from my surroundings. They are somewhat in the form of a story whose incidents and scenes are continued from time to time. I have recorded some of my daydreams in the form of stories.

F., 18. My daydreams frequently deal with some adventure in which I am taking an active part. They are like stories and unfold themselves gradually. Since childhood I have been in the habit of putting myself to sleep with these dreams.

Closely akin to the story form of daydream is the imaginary conversation which is sometimes carried on with actual friends and acquaintances, sometimes with strangers casually seen, or with characters in books or history, or in some cases with purely imaginary characters. Some novelists and dramatists have done much of their composing in this form, and these imaginary characters acquire a vivid personality. Lonely children sometimes develop this form of imaginary companionship. Some years ago Dr. G. Stanley Hall collected a number of cases of these imaginary companions, and the records are given with considerable detail. All began at an early age, usually as soon as the child began to talk, and continued for several years, usually until the child began to go to school, or was otherwise brought into contact with children of the same age. One child, a boy, began to play with an imaginary " Gobby " as soon as he could talk, and when nearly five "Gobby" was still his constant companion, but had grown up and had a wife and daughter, who were also playmates. Another child of about the same age had two imaginary playmates, one of whom was responsible for all his bad behavior, and the other played the part of his good genius. His probable behavior could often be inferred by noticing which of his imaginary companions was in evidence at the time. A few years ago, in one of our popular magazines (11), there appeared some letters purporting to be written by a child of eleven to her husband whom she assumed to be somewhere in the world, though she did not know him. Whether these letters are, as they purport to be, the genuine productions of a child, or later reminiscences put into this form for literary effect, they picture with psychological truth the impulse of a lonely and imaginative child to find in an ideal world the sympathy and companionship which was lacking in the outward life.

Daydreams of love and marriage are frequent after the age of seventeen and occasionally earlier than this for girls. Sometimes these are vague dreams of a happy future with a shadowy partner who is to possess all virtues ; sometimes there is a definite picture of a future home and a house is planned and furnished in all details. With girls, unless they are definitely looking forward to marriage, the house planning and furnishing is usually of a luxurious character and without reference to probability. With boys this vision of a home is more apt to be controlled by the possibilities of achievement. Both boys and girls frankly acknowledge dreaming over their friends of the opposite sex, though the more elaborated romances are nearly always woven about comparative strangers or wholly from the stuff of which dreams are made. Many girls imagine themselves in a home with children to whom they give names and even picture the color of their eyes and hair, how they shall be dressed and educated, and the good times they shall have, while the shadowy partner of these joys is rarely visualized or very definitely characterized. A few samples of this type of daydream are given.

F., 18. I dream of being married and having a beautiful home of my own. I picture to myself the arrangement of the rooms. And the prettiest room in it will be a nursery furnished in pink and white and occupied by a curly-headed little boy and girl who will be the dearest children in the world.

F., 17. My daydreams are usually about my future life : if I were married, and had a home of my own, and how cosy I would keep it.

F., 17. Sometimes I dream of meeting my future husband, falling in love with him, etc., and how I would love and care for my children.

F., 20. I do not have much time for dreaming now. I used to imagine the pleasure of having a little home in the country with mother. I know that I ought not to worry, so try to keep those thoughts out of my mind.

F., 20. I nearly always dream of myself as being very famous or at least holding an honored position. I have dreamed of being a teacher, a trained nurse, the head of some great medical institution, or a great speaker. I never dream of being a wife and mother. I cannot say why, but perhaps because I am not a pretty girl, but decidedly homely.

F., 18. There are times occasionally when I think how nice it would be to be married and have a home of my own, and I think of the joy it would be to train up a little child and know that he was your own.

M., 17. My daydreams are sometimes of having a home, a loving wife and children, and the means to keep them in comfort.

M., 21. My daydreams are generally of what I am going to do in the future (of course a certain pretty girl plays an important part).

M., 25. My daydreams are generally made up of plans by means of which I hope to make my sweetheart my happy wife. They are not mere love dreams, but contain all the essential elements that go to make professional life a success. My dreams are of reaching the highest point in my profession and making my wife happy.

The house-planning form of daydream is of frequent occurrence even when not connected with dreams of love or marriage. There are many of both sexes who seem to have a sort of architectural instinct and find recreation in planning not only houses but grounds, and even extend their fancies to landscape gardening and poultry raising.

A more prosaic form of dreaming is that in which the future occupation as a means of livelihood is the content of the dream. With the children of the poor this is influenced by probability at an early age, and the natural instincts for activity and out-of-door life find little play. Both boys and girls of eight or nine look forward to earning money as soon as the legal school years are completed. Those who are able to remain longer in school look forward to nearly every possible range of occupation. The number of occupations mentioned by boys is naturally greater than by girls, but the latter mention nearly every occupation open to women, including teaching, nursing, stenography, bookkeeping, dressmaking, millinery, work in a store, etc. In most cases there were pleasurable anticipations connected with these images of the future, either because of expected enjoyment in the work itself or because of the prospect of earning money, often with desire to benefit others.

Opinions as to the Rightness or Wrongness of Daydreaming

The youngest children who wrote their daydreams (those of the third grade ranging in age from seven to nine) had evidently not thought of a moral aspect of daydreaming and either gave no answer to the question or expressed surprise at its being asked. One child answered, " No one ever told me it was wrong "; and two or three others thought that it was right if the things dreamed about were true, but wrong if they were not. The papers of the children giving this answer showed rather a high degree of imaginative power, and it would be interesting to know whether they ever told their dreams as facts. Several reminiscent papers mention the confusion of fact and fancy in childhood, and one girl of eighteen states that at the age of fourteen her daydreams were so vivid that she sometimes told them as facts. In all grades higher than the third, daydreaming and inattention to lessons seem to have become inseparably associated, and the answer is apt to be of the stereotyped form that daydreaming is wrong in school " because you ought to be attending to your lessons." But in addition to this reply, many children appear to have done some independent thinking and give individual reasons for thinking the indulgence right or wrong. Daydreams are wrong if they are about bad or mean things, wrong " because they make you feel cross when you are interrupted," " because they make you dissatisfied with what you really have," " because it is wrong to wish for what you can't have," " because they waste time." They are *not* wrong " because they are natural," " because they

can't be helped," " because they are about pleasant things."
They are right because they make you happy, make you forget your troubles and worries, and because " they rest the
mind." Typical specimens of the answers given at different
ages are quoted.

M., 11. I do not think it is right to let your mind wander off.
Sometimes my mind will wander off. I will not know what I am doing.
When I try to think, it is very hard to think. Sometimes it will be a
long time before I can think what I am doing.

F., 13. Daydreams are wrong because they make you feel cross when
you are aroused.

M., 11. I think children should try to stop themselves from having daydreams because when you are dreaming like that in school you
might miss a whole lot of lessons.

M., 12. I think it is one wrong thing nature lets us do, because you
might want to do something very bad and sit down and dream away
your time.

F., 15. I think daydreaming is wrong because I have not very much
thinking power and I think they use up a good deal of it.

M., 15. Last year I would sit in school and think of everything but
my lessons. I failed on the final examination.

F., 12½. I think too much daydreaming is not good for anybody, but
when there is nothing else to think about they are very good things to
have, for they keep the mind off dwelling on troubles.

F., 13. I do not think my dreams are wrong, for I hardly ever think
of anything wrong.

M., 13. I think them right because it don't hurt you any to think,
but I think it does in another way : this is in letting your mind go where
it wants to, not taking care of its own business.

M., 14½. I think they are right unless you ought to be doing something else, because then you are not thinking of tricks to do and they
keep you out of mischief.

F., 12½. They always seem right to me because nothing happens like
the things I dream.

F., 15½. I think these dreams are all right because they do not hurt
any one. They are just childish thoughts.

M., 18. I do not think them wrong when I have leisure for them.
When tired I like to let my mind drift away because I think it refreshes
me and stops all the worries I may have.

F., 18. I enjoy daydreaming very much, but I sometimes think it is wrong, for it is apt to make you dissatisfied with your present life.

F., 19. Daydreams are often an inspiration to higher things. They sometimes lead us on to try to reach our ideals.

M., 19. This daydreaming seemed to force itself upon me. I tried hard to resist it because I thought it injurious to my mind. The more I daydream, the harder it is to come back to reality.

Only a small per cent. of children above the fifth grade (10 to 12 years) and adolescents say that daydreaming is right without qualifying the answer in some way. "It is not wrong unless," or "right when it does not interfere," etc. Many adolescents give an unqualified "wrong" in answer to the question, basing their answer upon personal experience. Some state definitely that their power of attention has become so impaired that any work requiring effort or continuity of attention is difficult and irksome. Others, taking a broader view of the subject, consider that while excess is harmful, a moderate indulgence under proper conditions of time and place is restful to the mind and, in some cases, is an inspiration which tends to widen the mental horizon. The insidious tendency of daydreaming to usurp the place of other mental activities is, however, very generally recognized by adolescents and adults, and those who most fully recognize its value as a normal rest and relaxation of the mind, or the soil from which real creative work may spring, appreciate as well the danger that the servant may become the master and mental imagery control the mind even in opposition to an effort of will.

RELATION OF MENTAL IMAGES TO DAYDREAMING

Galton (5) was the first to call attention to the great difference in character of the mental images in different individuals, his investigations showing that while some persons can call up mental pictures which are distinct and vivid in color and outline, others are so deficient in this power that the term *mental image* appears to them a mere figure of speech. Galton found that philosophers and those accustomed to abstract thinking were apt to be deficient in this power, while children were likely to possess it in a high degree. He also found the visualizing power to be somewhat higher in the female sex. Binet (1), following to some extent Galton's method, has gone somewhat farther and made a study of the degree to which mental images are under the control of the will. In addition to his more general investigations, Binet had two subjects (sisters) whom he studied with great care through a series of years and in whom there was a marked difference of type. Both were able to call up visual images, though one did so with greater effort, her images being less complete than those of the other and she had little power to alter or transform them. When, however, the images were allowed to arise spontaneously, as in the more passive forms of daydreaming, there was great variety and richness of imagery. The younger had exceedingly distinct memory images and possessed the power of voluntary control over them in a high degree, altering them quickly and easily in accordance with suggestions made by the experimenter. Her mental imagery was, however, almost entirely lacking in spontaneity, and she seemed unable to comprehend that these images could arise apart from an act of will. Both of these types were abundantly illustrated in the present material. Many children described the succession of mental images which passed through their minds, and said that they came of themselves and could n't be helped. Some described daydreaming as "queer" or "funny" because "you never could tell what was coming next." Others described their daydreams as a definite reproduction of scenes which they had especially enjoyed, or said that they had some favorite daydream which was voluntarily initiated. Still a third form of daydreaming in the broader sense is illustrated by the insistent imagery which appears even in opposition to the will, as

in the case of a boy who said that he did n't enjoy daydreaming because the dream which came oftenest was the repetition,
with all its details, of an accident in which he had seen his
uncle injured.   Dramatic authors sometimes have trouble with
their characters, who persist in behaving in a way quite in opposition to the ideas of their creator.   It is probable that these
insistent ideas, which are usually connected either with some
emotional shock or strain or are an accompaniment of over-
fatigued states, approach very near to the line of morbidity.
The relation of the will to daydreaming, as seen from the children's point of view, is of interest in this connection.   Some say
that daydreaming is not wrong because " you can't help it, and
what you can't help can't be wrong."   Others say that they
" can't help it sometimes," especially if tired or not interested.
One boy says that he can't help it in school, but is never
troubled that way when the subject is baseball.   Many state
that they voluntarily initiate daydreams as a means of passing
the time when lonely or uninterested, or as a refuge from unpleasant actualities.

RELATION OF DAYDREAMING TO THE CREATIVE IMAGINATION

There are a few adults who say that they never daydream,
but their papers show that they have restricted the meaning of
the word to an exercise of the imagination which has no foundation in fact and which has been set aside as a childish mode
of mental action.   In the broader sense of the term it is probable that every normal mind exhibits certain automatisms in its
reproductive activities, whether these be unaltered memory
images or imaginative transformations and combinations which
are a true creative activity.   The richer the content of the
mind, the greater the variety and spontaneity of the daydream
and the greater the possibility that from its automatic working
new and original combinations may arise.   A psychological

study of inventors would probably reveal the fact that many of the great inventions, though sought and worked over for years, have come at last in a flash of insight through the automatic workings of a mind filled with all the possibilities of the subject. Indeed we know this to have been the case with many scientific discoveries ; and the biographies of artists, authors, and scientists emphasize the fact that many of them have been daydreamers in boyhood, but always along with this has coexisted the fact of special interest and activity along some particular line, even though there were deficiencies in other directions. Herbert Spencer (13) has recorded in his autobiography the fact that he was, during his boyhood, "extremely prone to castle building," and that the habit continued even into mature life. This habit, while usually indulged in at bedtime, was frequently a cause of annoying absent-mindedness. In later years he wrote : "I believe that it is a general belief that castle building is detrimental ; but I am by no means sure that this is so. In moderation I regard it as beneficial. It is a play of the constructive imagination, and without constructive imagination there can be no high achievement. I believe that the love I then had for it arose from the spontaneous activity of powers which in future life became instrumental to higher things." Many facts from the biographies of the world's leaders can be adduced in support of this opinion of Spencer's, and it may well be questioned whether too vigorous a pruning and repression of this play of the imagination is good pedagogy and whether a certain amount of this mental recreation is not necessary for mental growth. We know that music, art, and literature are much indebted to the great dreamers. But the mind must first be well stored, and there must be energy for the realization of the dreams. It is never to the idle dreamer that the creative impulse comes. Mozart and Raphael were dreamers, but the harmonies of the one and the visions of the other belong to the world only because their dreams received embodiment by alliance with the drudgery of practical work. Napoleon and Mohammed were, each in his own way, dreamers, but they were also men of action. To Gautama, only after years of mental striving, came the perfect rest and the vision of Nirvana. It is probable that to most artists the vision beautiful comes when the mind is passive and visual images rise unbidden, and literature owes much to that spontaneous play of imagery which is one of the characteristic forms of daydreaming. We do not need to recall that strange fragment of Coleridge's dream, Kubla Khan, to realize that the brains of poets have sometimes worked in an automatic way. The daydream shades by almost imperceptible gradations through hypnagogic states to the dream of sleep, and as those whose mental content is fullest are those who are apt to dream most, so with the daydream. Babies and idiots probably do not daydream, as they have not a sufficient store of mental impressions for reproductive combinations. And among those whose lives are a monotonous round of toil in the bare struggle for existence there are probably few dreams either of the day or night, because little material is furnished by the environment. Experience having bred few images for the fancy to work upon, release from bodily exertion is followed almost immediately by sleep. The effect of monotonous labor in dulling mental images, even in well-stored minds, is noted by those who have spent years in Siberian prisons, even the images of home and friends being no longer recalled with clearness (3).

Enjoyment of daydreaming in itself considered, except in those cases which are either morbid or tend to become so, is universal. The few who say that they do not enjoy it invariably give conscientious scruples in regard to it as the factor which disturbs enjoyment. Children occasionally give some unpleasant consequence resulting from indulgence in daydreaming as a reason for nonenjoyment, but nevertheless do not discontinue the habit. Some say that daydreaming is their greatest pleasure and that they "could not live without it." Even sad dreams are enjoyed, the sadness being of the same nature as that evoked by seeing a tragedy on the stage or reading a book which may be thoroughly pleasurable even though the reader is reduced to tears. Emotions in daydreams of a normal type are all attuned to a low key, due, perhaps, to the relaxation of the muscular and vascular systems. Mosso (10) found experimentally that respiration tends to become periodic, and the pulse is lowered when attention begins to wander in states of drowsiness and in the dreamy states when attention is most completely dispersed. Twilight moods of reverie are typically characterized by the more subdued emotions and by moral and religious aspirations (6). The mood is generally enjoyed, and many say that it rests and helps them.

Morbid Daydreaming

In cases of morbid grief and painful reverie instead of muscular relaxation there is sometimes a partial paralysis and rigidity of the muscles which is apparent in the face and hands, and in the character of the movements when the subject is aroused. These cases of painful reverie are reported chiefly by adults and are sharply distinguished from the enjoyable melancholy and "sweet sadness" of normal reveries. The content is not an imaginary situation, but some actual sorrow or trouble, and the tendency to morbidity is frequently recognized by the subject, and is shunned by an effort to keep the mind occupied with other things. In cases of physical weakness and ill health these reveries tend toward, and in some cases become, obsessive ideas against which the patient struggles in vain, whenever physical weakness prevents constant occupation. Scenes which crush the heart and paralyze effort are re-lived again and again, and the will is powerless to banish these images which the patient may fully realize are leading to mental degeneration. In the entire number of daydreams collected from children only thirteen morbid cases occurred as regards content, though there were a number of cases in which, though there was no morbidity of content, daydreaming had become so excessive and so imperative a habit as to be regarded as a morbid development, very closely approaching the effects upon some hypnotic subjects in the loss of will power. Among the cases of morbid content, two were of snakes. Both subjects were boys, and in one case the cause was stated as due to a fright, which had generated a morbid fear which resulted in images of the object dreaded whenever the mind was allowed to wander uncontrolled. In the other case, no information was given beyond the fact that daydreams were always of snakes and not enjoyed. Two children of thirteen and fourteen dreamed of dying and of the end of the world, and in one of these cases the tendency of the dream to become an imperative idea was marked. Two others habitually have sad daydreams, and in both of these cases the health was reported below normal.

F., $12\frac{1}{2}$. When they are nice and not frighting I enjoy them, but when they are horrible and frighting I do not like them.

F., 13. My dreams are most often different, but about something sad.

M., 14. Daydreams chiefly of snakes, of which he is afraid.

F., 13. When I am sewing or reading I begin to think. I think and think about everything until I think about something I cannot get off my mind. One thing I dream about most is the end of the world. I wonder what will become of the people and how the earth will look and how dreadful it will be.

F., 14. I always think about the past and what if I should die.

F., 19. I am a victim of daydreams to a most annoying degree, insomuch that all efforts at resistance seem futile.

A woman of 39 has met with great loss and sorrow ; sits for hours in the same rigid attitude, with eyes fixed on vacancy. When aroused makes an effort to attend to things about her, but if left alone sinks back into the same attitude. The images of her sorrow are constantly before her mind.

Sir James Crichton Browne[1] inclines to the view that all dreamy mental states have a morbid tendency. He acknowledges that in otherwise healthy minds no harmful consequences either mental or physical can be detected. He quotes various cases in connection with nervous and mental diseases, such as the dreamy state which sometimes forms a distinct aura in epilepsy, and argues that men of genius known to have been subject to these dreamy states have suffered injury and been hampered in their work by them. As an extreme example he quotes the case of John Addington Symonds, the historian of the Renaissance, who suffered from a peculiar dreamy state which he thus describes : " Suddenly in church or in company, when I was reading and always I think when my muscles were at rest, I felt the approach of the mood. Irresistibly it took possession of my mind and will and lasted what seemed an eternity and disappeared in a series of rapid sensations which resembled the waking from an anæsthetic influence. One reason I disliked this state was because I could not describe it to myself. It consisted in a gradual but swiftly progressing obliteration of space, time, sensation, and the multitudinous factors of experience which seem to qualify what we are pleased to call ourself. At last nothing remained but a pure absolute self. The universe became without form and void of content." This description is very closely analogous to those states sometimes experienced in extreme fatigue when, for an instant, the mind seems to stop working and then goes on. It differs from unconsciousness in the fact that the blank is felt, though no effort of memory can recall any mental content. Such states are merely results and symptoms of extreme fatigue, and, unless the fatigue be sufficiently prolonged so that the nervous system loses its normal recuperative power, have apparently no more serious consequences than any other fatigue states. As in the 1080 cases furnished by the graded schools all the children

[1] " Dreamy Mental States," *London Lancet*, July 13, 1895.

present wrote, and, with the few doubtful exceptions already noted, daydreaming was reported by all the children and showed a very small percentage of morbid tendencies, so there seems to be no ground for the assumption of any morbid connection, either mental or physical, with daydreaming *per se* more than with any other mental activity. If morbid cases are sought they are not difficult to find, either in the form of morbidity of content or excessive indulgence, resulting in loss of will power, or cases in which both factors are combined. Ch. Féré cites an interesting case of a man who had been from childhood an inveterate daydreamer to an extent which seriously affected his college course. He had pursued in his dreams a number of fictitious careers, military, marine, engineering, etc., which he seemed to prefer to real life. On leaving college, however, he engaged in an active business career, was happily married, successful in his undertakings, and, having no time for daydreaming, seemed to have overcome the habit. A few years later, however, he began to suffer from insomnia, and at the same time became dissatisfied in regard to his business and household affairs. He took refuge in his former imaginations, and though these were less absorbing than formerly, they gradually became more persistent and finally acquired a fixed form in which he lived an ideal life in a chateau which he gradually elaborated. He acquired an imaginary wife and children and manifested less and less interest in his actual family. He continued nominally to conduct his business, which, however, was really managed by his staff of employees. Finally, on an occasion when some one accosted him by name and wished to confer with him on business he replied, "He is at Chaville," the name of his imaginary chateau. This betrayal of himself in public, however, startled him into a realization of his actual condition, and fearing himself insane he was ready to do anything to banish his ideas, but found that they had become his masters, and that against his will he constantly relapsed into his dreams. After three months of medical treatment with strict supervision night and day to prevent any lapse into dreaming, he recovered. In this case visual images appear to have played an important rôle and the subject was of a strongly visual type. Whether in this case the daydreaming was the cause or result of a diseased mental state is uncertain, but the suppression of the dreams was an important factor in the treatment which resulted in his recovery. As to the danger of daydreaming in a normal individual the following testimony of a man of twenty-six, who has carefully analyzed his own case, is of value. A. B. remembers that as early as the age of eight years he was a dreamer, and says that his daydreaming has been the happiest part of his life, but that " it has made it very hard, sometimes next to impossible, to pay attention to anything dull or abstract. All the will power I can bring to bear only serves to pull my mind back to what it ought to be busy with instead of keeping it steadily focused there. If one could dream up to the limit when one ought to dismiss it entirely and attend to the sterner things of life, I think daydreaming would be a veritable gift from the gods. But it is a curse when the habit becomes so fixed that a man can't pay attention to things which perchance have little natural interest for him."

The tendency of daydreaming to become habitual and excessive is, in the present study, most marked in those who have strong visual imaginations ; yet the power is in itself a mental gift, even though it sometimes prove a dangerous one. The great literary and religious dreamers have usually been men whose visual imagery was exceedingly vivid. Dante, Milton, Mohammed, and Swedenborg were all endowed with the power of visual imagination to an extraordinary degree. Many drugs owe their peculiar fascination to their power of intensifying sensory images and producing dreamy states. The Mexican drug, mescal, the use of which as a religious cult among the southern Indian tribes of the United States has spread in spite of efforts to restrain it, has for its chief mental effect the production of colors and forms of wonderful variety and intensity. The muscular relaxation noted as character- istic of daydreaming is produced by all anæsthetics, and where the oncoming of unconsciousness is not too sudden the mental states preceding are closely analogous to those of daydream- ing. De Quincey, who more vividly than any other writer has depicted the effects of opium, emphasizes the impairment of muscular power and corresponding weakness of will. The effect of nicotine in producing dreamy mental states is too well known to need description, and teachers report that boys who are addicted to cigarette smoking are invariably dreamers and defective in the power of voluntary attention.

In summarizing the results of the present study attention is drawn to the following points :

Daydreaming appears to be a normal and well-nigh univer- sal phenomenon in children and adolescents and may continue throughout life. It is especially characteristic of the years of adolescence.

The content of the daydream is chiefly determined by envi- ronment, though its forms, like those of night dreams, are in- fluenced by age, health, and degree of mental development.

In early childhood daydreams, except in the case of excep- tionally imaginative children, are made up chiefly of memory images, actual experiences or stories being reproduced with little change. This tendency to reproduce memory images un- changed is evidenced not only by the daydreams reported, but is further illustrated by the insistency of children that stories told to them shall be repeated without any change in the de- tails, a fact familiar to every one who has had experience in telling stories to children. The future of childhood is usually a definitely circumscribed and near future, and motor activities and eating figure largely in the content of childish dreams.

With the dawn of adolescence there is a marked increase in the variety and complexity of content, and the range is greatly widened. Dreams of the future are oftenest of the vague future with boundless possibilities. The instinct emotions become an evident factor, and dreams of love are characteristic at this age. Both altruistic and egoistic emotions are greatly intensified.

Though comparatively few daydreams were collected from adults, the content of these indicated a somewhat closer connection with actual life than these of childhood and adolescence. Dreams of the future were more in the form of plans with the possibility of accomplishment either for self or others.

The few cases of the daydreams of old age were almost entirely memories of the remote past, and much time was spent in dreaming. Since daydreaming is closely associated with fatigue states, this appears to be the result which might be expected from mental and physiological conditions.

Though environment exercises an important influence upon the development of the imagination and there is a possibility that it may be dwarfed and starved by repression, much is due to differences of mental endowment, and daydreaming in a marked degree is often associated with high intellectual endowments and creative ability.

Daydreaming, like any other mental activity, may become excessive and pass over into pathological states, and in consequence of the fact that it is usually enjoyable and a passive state, it is peculiarly liable to this source of danger.

Sex differences are especially marked in daydreams, many of them being so characteristically masculine or feminine that the sex of the writer is unmistakable. While this is in part undoubtedly due to environment and conventional training, it also suggests that in the more automatic workings of the mind there may be a fruitful field for the investigation of the question of how far mental differences between men and women are innate and fundamental, and how far they are due to artificial causes.

THEODATE L. SMITH

BIBLIOGRAPHY

1. Binet, Alfred. L'Étude experimentale de l'intelligence. Schleicher frères, Paris, 1903. 309 pages.
2. Binet, Alfred and V. Henri. La fatigue intellectuelle. Schleicher frères, Paris, 1898. 338 pages.
3. Deutsch, Leo. Sixteen Years in Siberia (translated by H. Chisholm). Murray, London, 1903. 338 pages.
4. Fechner, G. T. Elemente der Psychophysik, 2d ed., Vol. I, p. 440. Breitkopf, Leipzig, 1889.
5. Galton, Francis. Inquiries into Human Faculty. Macmillan, London, 1883. 387 pages.
6. Hall, G. Stanley, and Smith, Theodate L. "Reactions to Light and Darkness," *American Journal of Psychology*, Vol. XIV, pp. 21–83, January, 1903.
7. James, William. Psychology: Briefer Course, pp. 302–311, 301–369. H. Holt & Co., New York, 1904. 478 pages.
8. Learoyd, Mabel W. "The Continued Story," *American Journal of Psychology*, Vol. VII, pp. 86–90, October, 1895.
9. Le Conte, J. Sight (International Scientific Series). D. Appleton & Co., New York, 1881.
10. Lindley, E. H. "Motor Phenomena of Mental Effort," *American Journal of Psychology*, pp. 491–517, Vol. VII, July, 1896.
11. Moody, Helen Waterson. "A Child's Letters to her Husband," McClure's Magazine, Vol. XIV, p. 55, 1899.
12. Mosso, Angelo. Fatigue (translated by M. and W. B. Drummond). S. Sonnenschein, London, 1904. 334 pages.
13. Spencer, Herbert. An Autobiography. D. Appleton & Co., New York, 1904. 2 vols.

CURIOSITY AND INTEREST [1]

In the study of the emotions as compared with other activities of the soul, psychology has as yet made little progress. In the older works of the Scotch school and in the Herbartian literature we find elaborate systems of classifying emotions, but of the study of the living emotions in their genesis, development, and relation to other psychic factors, little or nothing. Since the publication of the theories of Lange and James, in 1890, we have had abundant discussion of the theories of emotion and some excellent introspective work, especially upon those emotions which have the greatest bodily resonance. In the study of the expression of emotion Darwin stands almost alone. Experimentally there have been since 1880 various attempts to study the emotions by observation of changes in blood pressure and circulation. The work of Mosso stands foremost in this field, but the plethysmograph has not yet added greatly to our knowledge here. A few monographs on special emotions have been published during the last decade, and there is a considerable body of literature on the pathology of the emotions, but the field to be investigated is wide, and as yet the laborers have been few.

In studying the development of the mental attitude which we call curiosity, we are confronted by difficulties of both definition and analysis. In its fully developed form it is sufficiently easy of recognition, but to determine where and when reflex activities become merged into psychic reactions, which may properly be termed stages in the development of curiosity,

[1] Reprinted in abridged form from *Pedagogical Seminary*, Vol. X, pp. 315–358, September, 1903.

involves us at once in the intricacies of the problems of active and passive attention and the development of the will. The material for the present study was gathered partly in reply to a group of topics contained in a syllabus on "Some Common Traits and Habits," issued in 1895, and partly by a supplementary syllabus of the present year. The data asked for was as follows :

Curiosity and wonder. Prying, spying, inquiring, asking why, what for, or how, persisting in troublesome questions. Describe the first sign of curiosity or wonder in the infant; sample the growth of the instinct by instances up toward maturity, whether manifested toward natural phenomena, facts, or persons seen or read of, mechanisms, motives, religious teaching, treatment by parents and teachers, etc. Cases of breaking open toys to see what is inside, or experimenting " to see what it will do." Later promptings to see the world, know life, travel, read, explore, investigate, etc. What excites chief wonder. Secrecy as a provocative of curiosity. Age of culmination of the chief classes of interest. Utilization and dangers.

Curiosity and interest. I. Give cases of early curiosity or interest shown by infants. State in detail how this was manifested.

II. Give cases of interest or curiosity in children, shown by active observation or experiment.

III. Give instances of destructive curiosity, — toys, etc., destroyed to find out how they were made.

IV. Give cases of interest or curiosity shown by asking questions.

V. Give instances of strong desire to travel. Did the interest in these cases extend to reading books of travel, etc.?

The total number of cases of curiosity received in answer to the syllabi was 1247. These were distributed as follows :

I. Observation		
a. Early stages of staring . . . 163 cases		
b. Active observation . . . . 108 "		
271 " = 21.73 per cent.		
II. Experiments . . . . 78 " 6.25 "		
III. Questions . . . . 477 " 38.25 "		
IV. Inquisitiveness . . . . . . 69 " 5.62 "		
V. Destructive curiosity . . . . . 352 " 28.38 "		
1247		

To these were added the material furnished by the individual child biographies and records kept by mothers. Helen Keller's *Story of My Life* has also furnished some valuable material, and a few facts for comparison have been gleaned from animal psychology. All the material collected is readily classified into the groups given above, with the addition of a group, which for convenience has been called inquisitiveness, and includes the various forms of aimless and misdirected curiosity, peeking, prying, etc.

Ribot distinguishes three stages of curiosity or primitive craving for knowledge, — surprise, wonder, and curiosity ; the first consisting of mere shock, a disadaptation. The second stage, or wonder, is distinguished from the first in that, while surprise is momentary and fleeting, wonder is stable and may persist until worn away by familiarity. The third stage, or attitude of investigation, is that of curiosity proper. But there are indications that a fourth stage, preceding these three, should be recognized in the psychic accompaniment of some early reflexes. Preyer records this first stage of Ribot's as occurring in the fifth week, Mrs. Moore on the 26th day ; Mrs. Hall notes it in the fifth week, and Miss Shinn on the 25th day. It is in each case a light reaction, the first active looking as compared with passive staring, and is described as accompanied by a "dim rudimentary eagerness." But Miss Shinn also records that at about the end of the second week "the baby's gaze no longer wandered altogether helplessly, but rested with a long, contented gaze on bright surfaces which it happened to encounter. It was not active looking, with any power to direct the eyes, but mere staring." In the material collected for the present study 163 cases of this infant staring are reported, nearly one half of which occurred under the age of three months. The earlier ones are all of the same type. Some bright or moving object seems to catch and hold the baby's gaze. There is no turning towards the object, no active looking; the eyes in their wandering, uncoördinated movements are simply arrested, and in many instances it is stated that there is a " contented " or " pleased " look on the baby's face. Light and darkness are distinguished, and moderate light appears to be for normal children a pleasurable sensation. Professor Sully suggests in regard to this first passive staring that " it is conceivable that the eyes, happening to be coördinated opposite some patch of brightness, might maintain this attitude under the stimulus of pleasure." Out of the dim, confused mass of light and shade something, probably a mere patch of brightness, has detached itself, and the physical mechanism of attention is called into play, — a mere reflex, but a reflex whose psychic affective accompaniment, though rudimentary, has in it the germ of future development, the first movement of that intellectual craving which, more than any other endowment, differentiates one man from another in intellectual ability. In this connection a paragraph of Miss Shinn's is so significant that it is here quoted : " It is an important moment that marks the beginning of even a passive power to control the movement of the eyes, and when my grandmother handed down the rule that you should never needlessly interrupt a baby's staring lest you hinder the development of power of attention, she seems to have been psychologically sound." It is now a recognized principle in the education of defective and feeble-minded children that the training of the motor apparatus of attention is the first and fundamental requisite for reaching the dormant psychic activities. Until a certain degree of muscular coördination has been attained, attention cannot be fixed long enough to produce any lasting psychic impressions.

While the infant is acquiring the power to converge the two eyes and move the lid its eye falls a victim to any patch of light upon which it chances to rest. Often the body, or the eye itself, or more frequently the head, gives an involuntary lurch, and then the object of vision is so lost that it seems to cease to exist. Things that are fixated and drop, or move away, appear to vanish mysteriously, whereas these same involuntary movements, on the other hand, may bring new objects so suddenly into the narrow field of vision as to cause a distinct shock or start or other impression of surprise. So purely automatic, and as yet unassociated with touch, are these first optical impressions, that threatening movements toward the eye do not even cause the reflex action of a wink. The light-sense in the human infant is more independent of motor power because of the inability of the newborn infant to move much. Could it coördinate its retinal impressions with motor innervations, this relatively prolonged independence of vision would not occur. In this respect the condition of the feeble-minded child approximates that of the infant before it has acquired the control of its muscular organism. In studying the material collected by the questionnaire method, careful comparison has been made with the data contained in the few continuous records made by scientific observers. Samples of the questionnaire material are here given, and also a few of the points tabulated for comparison from the individual biographies.

Early Stages of Visual Interest

M., 2 weeks. Looked round the room and often stared at one thing quite a while (not active looking).

M., 6 weeks. Examined his hands, turned his fingers over and over.

M., 5 weeks. It was noticed that during the latter part of the second week the eyes lost their aimless look and began to rest upon objects. In the third week the child looked long and steadily at a bright red waist worn by his aunt, and a week later his eyes were always attracted by the striped ribbon of her hat.

M., 8 weeks. His mother held a bright flower up before him. He opened his eyes and mouth very wide, and bounced up and down.

M., 8 weeks. Lying in his aunt's lap, looked at some flowers, reaching out his hand for them.

M., 3 months. Will turn his head and move his eyebrows when he hears a noise.

M., 3 months. Would look steadily at a bright Japanese parasol fastened to the ceiling. Also seemed to look at the fire.

M., 4 months. A lady with a bright green bird in her hat leaned over the cradle. He seemed to notice it and kept looking at it.

M., 5 months. Seemed much attracted by a red dress.

M., 5 months. Hearing a door open tried to raise himself. Failing, he cried. Was lifted up and laughed. Later was laid down without complaint.

M., 5 months. Would sit for a long time and watch the light. Would hold out his hand for a hat or veil.

F., 1 month. Stared intently at a patch of sunlight on the wall for several minutes; looked pleased.

F., 5 weeks. Stared at a lighted lamp, and expression changed when it was removed.

F., 3 weeks. Gazed at a white blanket thrown across the foot of the crib for several minutes. There was a different expression on her face, and her eyes were more widely open than usual.

F., 6 weeks. Occasional coördination of eyes and apparent fixation of gaze since second week, always upon some brightly illuminated surface. In fifth week followed movements of hair brush with the eyes for some time.

It will be noted that with the exception of interest in color there is, for the most part, no greater range of variation than might be expected from individual differences in development. From the 163 cases furnished by the questionnaires, and the six continuous records, the following conclusions have been drawn. The earliest form in which the mechanism of attention develops is in the sight reflex of passive staring, when the baby's gaze is, as it were, caught and held even for a few seconds. This seems to occur in some cases as early as the ninth day, though there are more records of this phenomena from the second week onward. This staring is to be distinguished from the aimless and uncoördinated movements in which, though the eyes may rest upon or seem to follow an object momentarily, there is no continuous fixation and the coördination is purely accidental. The psychic accompaniment of this passive staring is probably the first step by which the baby begins its gropings toward an intellectual life. Whether the stimulus which holds the baby's gaze be pleasure, as Professor Sully suggests, or whether there may enter into it, at times, a vague rudimentary fear, as seems indicated in some of the cases reported, something has stirred in the psychic life, and a distinct step toward the unfolding of dormant powers has been made. The next step is taken when the baby really looks and actively directs its gaze toward the interesting object. This commonly happens about the fourth or fifth week, though a few cases are reported in which the active looking has undoubtedly taken place considerably earlier. In these cases, however, the baby seems to have been equally precocious in other respects. From this time onward, for the next three or four months, sight interests predominate in a baby's life. Of the 163 cases of interest occurring before the sixth month, 139 were visual and only 24 auditory. This, however, does not show superior development of the sense of sight over hearing, as undoubtedly the baby hears and shows decided distaste for loud, harsh, or sudden sounds. The development is largely a psychic one, and the baby finds the sense of sight more useful than that of hearing in acquiring knowledge of his surroundings. While the objects which attract attention are varied, as may be seen from a reference to the samples from the returns, they are reducible to a few groups. All bright or moving objects and anything presenting strong contrast of light and shade, whether in color or black and white, is attractive to a baby.

EXAMPLES OF EARLY VISUAL INTERESTS

M., 5 weeks. Would lie a long time watching red paper flowers dance in the air. They were hung over his cradle.

F., 2 months. Was much interested in a bright red necktie at which she gazed intently, following it with her eyes when the wearer moved.

F., 3 months. Gazed at a lighted lamp as if fascinated by it; became restless when turned away from it and was quieted by being turned toward it.

F., 3 months. Followed a bunch of red roses with her eyes, and when they were taken away gazed after them a long time.

M., 3 months. Was much interested in watching his own hands.

F., 3 months. Sat and stared curiously at her father the first time he kissed her after having shaved off his beard.

M., 4 months. Very much interested in United States flag; reached for it.

F., 4 months. Appeared quite fascinated by hat with bright red flowers. Was also interested in red ball.

F., 5 months. Lay quietly for fifteen minutes watching a glass chandelier which glittered.

F., 6 months. Can almost always be amused with a hand mirror.

F., 6 months. Is interested in faces, especially if spectacles are worn.

M., 13 weeks. Was interested in a bright red ribbon, pulled at it, tried to put it into his mouth, and played with it for some time.

M., 6 months. Finds his grandmother's spectacles a fascinating object.

M., 6 months. Would watch any one who passed him as long as he could. Same child at 9 months would look fixedly at bright flowers.

F., 7 months. Would lie contentedly watching her carriage parasol. It was lined with green and had a fringe which moved.

RECORDS OF EARLY LIGHT INTERESTS

	Mere Sensibility to Light	Passive Staring	Attraction of First Real Looking, Gaze by Motion		Interest in Color	Full Accommodation
Miss Shinn .	1st day	End of 2d week	25th day	1 month	1 year	8 weeks
Preyer . . .	"	11th day	23d day	23d day	23d day	8 weeks
Tiedemann .	"	————	13th day (?)	————	————	
Mrs. Hall. .	"	End of 2d week	28th day	32d day	3d week	8 weeks
Darwin . .	"	9th day	6th week	————	6th week	————
Mrs. Moore .	2d day	————	————	28th day	15th and 20th day	————

Every color except violet was mentioned as attractive, red being mentioned most frequently, but white had almost as many mentions, and the data furnish no positive indication as to whether color, brightness, or contrast was the real stimulus. In the list of red objects which proved attractive are a red lamp, red flowers, red and white necktie, red blanket, red hat, and the American flag ; but it is to be noted that in nearly every case either bright red was mentioned or contrast was involved, as in the United States flag and red and white necktie, or the object was luminous, as the red lamp. The color sense of babies has not yet been experimentally tested, and until it has been, inferences drawn from the apparent attractiveness of colored objects, in which brightness, contrast, and motion may constitute the whole or a part of the stimulus, have little value. Preyer, it is true, mentions his child's interest and pleasure in a rose-colored curtain on the twenty-third day of its life, as a color interest ; but careful and scientific as Preyer's observations usually were, in this case he made no tests to discover whether any surface of equal illumination would not have proved equally pleasing, and Miss Shinn is correct in saying that there is no *proof* of color discrimination or interest within the first year. Hats with nodding flowers of any color, the glitter of spectacles, or the radiance of a lighted lamp, all seem to possess a peculiar fascination for babies, but it is about the human face that interest centers and earliest recognitions cluster. During the first three months it is probable that this interest is due largely to differences in light and shade and to the constant changes produced by motion, recognition by sight being a development of the latter part of the third month, according to the observations which can be classed as really scientific.

But though sight interests so largely predominate during the first four or five months of a baby's life, the other senses are by no means excluded. Sounds are noticed within the first week of life, though oftener as disagreeable than agreeable experiences, the first record of auditory impressions showing that they are often accompanied by a shock which, if not true fear, is at least the basis of what later develops into fear. Preyer's baby listened to the tones of a piano with evident pleasure in his eighth week, and Mrs. Moore's boy lay quietly for twenty minutes on the twentieth day while some one was singing to him, though it is recorded that on the whole his first month was characterized by lack of interest in sound. The earliest manifestations of pleasurable interest in sound seem to be chiefly of an inhibitory nature, the child ceasing to cry or lying still when interested in sound. From the fifth month onward there is a marked rise in auditory interests, and these are, for the most part, mingled with the development of motor activities; the crackling and tearing of paper becomes an absorbing interest; some children love to touch the piano keys and are better satisfied with their own musical attempts than those of others; the ticking of a watch excites active curiosity as to where the sound comes from. Sight interests do not diminish, but they are supplemented by those of hearing and muscular activities, as the baby begins to coördinate things seen, heard, touched, tasted, and smelled. Sully (*Extracts from a Father's Diary*) notes that in the tenth week the sound produced by striking a wine glass excited "an agreeable wonder," though the sound of the piano proved disconcerting. Later the child became fond of it and " evidenced his enjoyment by complete relaxation of the muscles." Inhibitory effects and muscular relaxation are more frequent modes of manifesting pleasure in sound than in sight, where the reaction is often shown by widely opened eyes, movements of the hands and feet, with, later, attempts to grasp the pleasing object, and looks of eagerness and desire. Thus it will be noted that although muscular and skin sensations, including temperature, are those earliest experienced, they do not form the chief centers of interest during the first months of a baby's life; the stage of muscle interest being distinctly later in development than those of sight, and even then sight interests are not subordinated but coördinated with them. This acceleration of sight development beyond that of the senses which genetically precedes it, is undoubtedly due to its greater utility. In the case of hearing, as of sight, the material gathered by the questionnaire has been compared with the continuous records, and examples from both are given. It will be noticed that there is greater variation in the ages at which the different developments occur than in the case of sight. This is, in part, due to the fact that for the first eight weeks, at least, in sight, psychic developments keep pace with certain definite physical factors, which is not the case with hearing, the ability to hear being present from the first week, although the psychic development comes later. It is interest in sound, which is later in development, and not the physical ability to hear. Early sensations of sounds are, in many cases, connected with either unpleasurable or negative-feeling tones. Light sensations, if not too strong, are of a pleasurable kind, while sound frequently causes a shock, or kind of rudimentary fear, and often occasions crying.

RECORDS OF EARLY INTEREST IN SOUND

	Sound First Noticed	First Pleasure in Sound	Turning Head in Direction of Sound
Miss Shinn.	3d day	27th day	3 months
Preyer	4th day	8th week	11th week
Tiedemann	——	40th day	——
Mrs. Hall	3 hours	6th week	21st week
Darwin	——	6th week	49th day
Mrs. Moore	2d day	20th day	30th day

F., 5 months. Would always stop crying to listen to music.

F., 6 months. Turned her head in direction of sounds.

F., 6 months; M., 5 months; F., 5 months; M., 10 months; M., 10 months; F., 1 year. Interested in listening to music.

F., 9 months. Was much delighted with organ music.

M., 7 months. Always cried to be lifted up when he heard any one talking. As soon as he could see, was satisfied.

F., 9 months. Would always amuse herself if allowed to touch the piano keys. Would clap her hands to the rhythm of music.

M., 1 year. At this age he learned to tear paper, and this interest continued for several months.

F., 1 year. Was much interested in a toy that rattled.

M., 1 year. Would sit very still and listen intently to watch.

F., 1 year. Was interested in cornet.

F., 15 months. Tried continually to get her rattle open, shook it, listened, and then tried again.

F., 18 months. Was much interested in ticking of clock.

After these early stages in the development of visual and auditory interests, interest in seeing things done plays a prominent rôle in the baby consciousness, and closely associated with it is the desire to do. The stage of active experimenting fills the second half of the first year. It is the period in which the series of sight, auditory, muscular, and skin sensations coalesce. Of the child at this age Perez writes : " His activity, doubled now by curiosity and stimulated to the highest pitch by emotional sentiments of all sorts, makes him happier and happier, and seems to him so great a necessity that a quarter of an hour of relative inactivity weighs on him as much as a whole day of ennui on a grown-up person." Whatever the development of the baby's time sense may be, Perez is undoubtedly right as to the curiosity and muscular activity which characterize this age. In these months the range of interests is not only greatly increased but individual predilections begin to be apparent. A distinct interest in mechanics is observable in some children as early as the seventh month, — the wheels of a chair or carriage, or the hinges of a door proving a continued source of entertainment. A little later the problem of a lock and key becomes an absorbing interest, the inserting of the key in the lock and trying to turn it holding the attention for astonishingly long periods. Nature interests, too, are shown in these months, the interest in animals, even when accompanied by a certain degree of fear, being marked. Not only living animals, but animal pictures, and later animal stories, are a source of delight, and the joy of outdoor life is plainly manifested by baby coaxing and pleading in sign language long before the development of speech. In Miss Shinn's little niece this interest in animals was almost a passion, developed suddenly just at the close of the first half year, and was unaccompanied by fear. A large dog, which the baby had seen all her life, suddenly roused her desire and she would pay attention to nothing else. " Day after day, for weeks, the little thing was filled with excitement at the sight of the shaggy Muzhik, moving her arms and body, and crying out with what seemed intensest joy and longing. When he came near her excitement increased and she reached out and caught at him." While this case is more marked than is usual in so young a child, the interest in animals seems common to babies in general and continues as a permanent source of pleasure unless interfered with by rousing the fear instinct, which, though it is of frequent occurrence, soon wears off under normal conditions of familiarity with animals.

The stages by which the child passes from passive to active observation and experiment are very gradual, and not only do the different stages overlap in the course of normal development, but we find the rudimentary stages persisting even to adulthood in the case of the uneducated and undeveloped and, perhaps, occasionally manifested by every one under certain conditions of shock or surprise. The inarticulate surprise, the fixed stare, and hanging jaw of the dull-minded youth when brought into new and unaccustomed surroundings are familiar examples of this early manifestation of curiosity persisting beyond its time. Cases of arrested development and imbeciles never outgrow this primitive manifestation. Instead of fully developed, eager, questioning curiosity, there is only the stare of amazement and shock of surprise. This arrest in the development of curiosity is marked in cases of epilepsy and is one of the symptoms of mental degeneration. The patient loses interest in anything new, his attention is hard to gain, and he finally sinks into an apathetic state with " no wants, no desires, no affection," the power of attention completely lost. In the training of the feeble-minded the teacher's chief problem is to rouse interest and curiosity, so that the wandering attention may be held long enough to make a lasting, mental impression.

In the development of normal children active observation begins to play a prominent part toward the close of the first year. No longer content with merely seeing things, the little investigator desires to touch, taste, smell, and handle everything within reach. Curiosity as to the contents of parcels, boxes, bureau drawers, trunks, bags, and pocketbooks seems to be universal. Rummaging through closets, drawers, workbaskets, or writing desks becomes a delight. The mere fact of a closed space seems to exercise a fascination over the childish mind. So widespread and deep-seated is this curiosity and interest in whatever is concealed from view, that we must look for its explanation in the phylogenetic rather than the ontogenetic series. We can trace it far back in the animal line, when undoubtedly its utility lay in the food-seeking impulse, and it is probable that in primitive man, as in animals, the impulse to explore unknown cavities, even though exposing the explorer to danger and coming into conflict with instinctive fears, was, on the whole, an advantage in the struggle for existence. Sixty-nine cases of this active curiosity in regard to parcels and boxes were described, the ages varying from one to seven years, and the larger number of cases occurring between the ages of four and six. At about the same ages interest in discovering why the door bell rang is at its height. With some children this becomes temporarily almost a mania, and all other interests are sacrificed to running to the door or to some position from which the door can be seen.

Active interest in nature, though unfortunately too often repressed by unfavorable surroundings, develops rapidly after the first year. Children of kindergarten age (3 to 6 years) respond readily to any stimulus in this direction, whether of plant or animal life. The desire to touch and handle things at this age is so great that we have numerous instances of seeds regularly dug up to watch their growth, flower buds picked or blown open, and the eyes of puppies and kittens rudely exposed to light before the proper time, as well as numerous other attempts to assist nature in ways which, though detrimental to her processes, are nevertheless inspired by a genuine though mistaken zeal for finding out her ways. The desire to handle things seems to develop concomitantly with the power of locomotion, and so necessary to the child's development is it that we can but sympathize with the little fellow who, after encountering repeated prohibition, inquired tearfully, " What can I touch ? " even though the artificial conditions of social environment demand the restraint of this eager spirit of investigation. But though repression in some directions may be a necessity, good pedagogy demands that some outlet for this instinctive desire, which is at the root of all intellectual advancement, be provided. As an educational experiment, both Mrs. Moore and Mrs. Hogan found that diverting the attention to some object equally as desirable as the forbidden one proved far more effective than direct prohibition. In the former case the object was soon forgotten and there was little tendency to recur to it, while direct prohibition seemed to impress it upon the memory, and constant repetition was necessary until the prohibition was sufficiently impressed for eager desire to yield to force of circumstances, though the small investigators were quite incapable of understanding why the denied object should be unattainable. So wide is the range of interests which come under the classification of active observation that a complete representation of the material would prove tedious to any save specialists, but a few examples are inserted to show the character of the material and the range of ages included in the present study.

ACTIVE OBSERVATION WITH AID OF OTHER SENSES

F., 7 months. Cake basket near her. Upset it apparently out of curiosity.

F., 10 months. Took great interest in examining the frame of a picture which stood on an easel.

F., 1½. When taken up by a lady, began to feel of her bracelet and pin, and to smooth the velvet on her dress.

F., 9½ months. Being put on the floor, crept to the coal scuttle and upset it.

M., 3. Was greatly interested in listening to water rushing through a sewer.

F., 4. Came into the room and saw a box which had not been opened. Would not go out to play, and as soon as others left the room tried to open the box. Failing to open it, she knelt down and smelled of it.

M., 4. When visiting was eager to see the bees. Ran down the walk and pounded on the hives. The bees came out and stung him.

M., 5. Saw a garter snake which he tried to catch. Told his mother he had been trying to get a pretty piece of ribbon for her.

M., 6. Looked at and handled everything he could reach in a depot to see what it was made of. Rubbed his hand all over a sign " No smoking."

M., 6. Curiosity easily aroused about books ; always wants to " see the inside."

M., 6. Was greatly interested in what he saw at a basket factory.

F., Grade III. Got excused from school to see what a toad was doing ; ran all the way back to the toad. He was casting his skin.

F., 8 ; M., 7 ; M., 9. Climbed trees to see the eggs in birds' nests ; rarely destroyed anything.

M., 9. Has a garden which he watches very closely to see when the seeds are sprouting. As soon as they come up he plants others in their places to see them sprout.

M., 9. Would catch and carefully examine insects.

M., 8. Wanted to be allowed to stay at home from school to watch the plumber.

M., 8. On certain afternoons always went to watch the printing of the paper; also liked to watch the veterinary treat a horse which had a lame knee.

M., 10. Was much interested in machinery; very careful in observation, and could put simple apparatus together after taking it apart.

F., 11. Was delighted in examining an old clock which was given to her for a plaything.

M., 13½. Was greatly interested in words; delighted whenever he hears a new one.

F., 12. Was delighted if allowed to go into the kitchen and watch cooking processes.

So closely connected with the stage of active observation that they continually become merged in each other is the experimental stage, the earliest forms of which, in obtaining muscular control of the body, Miss Shinn has so well described. These early experiments with muscle and touch sensations are soon extended to the other senses, and though disagreeable sensations and even pain is a result, these serve as guides for, rather than deterrents from, the spirit of investigation. Experiments in touch, taste, and sound become prominent in the second year, and the latter are frequently carried to an extent which proves trying to the nerves of adults. Active experimenting with taste develops somewhat later. According to Mr. Bell's [1] studies, while ability to carry things to the mouth begins in the fourth month, and some tastes are differentiated at this time, and biting develops along with dentition, active experimenting with taste proper begins in the second year. Children from two to four or five years taste everything. One hundred and eighty-two different articles are mentioned in Mr. Bell's list of objects tasted, including plants, hay, straw, sticks, seeds, paste, cork, rubber, soap, tar, dirt, worms, and insects, in fact anything " that can be carried to the mouth or the mouth to it," quite irrespective of any edible qualities in the objects tasted. Another phase of

[1] Sanford Bell, " Psychology of Foods," *Pedagogical Seminary*, Vol. II, pp. 51–90, March, 1904.

curiosity in regard to taste is the " teasing to taste," which, according to the same authority, reaches its height between the ages of seven and ten. One hundred and twenty-two different articles are mentioned in Mr. Bell's list, the majority of them edibles in some stage of preparation, but uncooked mixtures and medicines of disagreeable flavor also figure largely in the enumeration. Experimenting with mixtures of both foods and drinks is most frequent between the ages of five and ten, and a year or so later comes the stage of adolescent testing, when the desire to try everything new in a bill of fare, to sample new combinations and flavors, appears to be a characteristic of the developmental period.

EXPERIMENTS IN TASTE

M., 14 months. Took a bite of soap. Three weeks later made a second trial, after which he gave up soap as a possible addition to his diet.

M., 3. Began to eat " rat poison " to see what it was ; was interrupted just in time.

F., 4. Wanted to taste horse-radish, and, being refused, tasted it when her mother's back was turned.

F., 4. Was very curious about a box of Paris green and narrowly escaped poisoning.

F., 4, and M., 4½. Tasted grafting wax but did not like the flavor.

F., 4. Ate a raw potato to see how it tasted.

M., 6. Experimented with different things to see if the pig would eat them.

M., 6. Received an Easter egg ; ate it immediately to see how it tasted.

F., 6, and F., 8. My sister and I used to mix up snow with milk and juices to make new drinks.

F., 6. Ate green grapes to see if they would really make her sick, as she had been told.

M., 6. Tasted Tabasco sauce, although he had been warned of the effect.

Another phase of experimental curiosity closely associated with experiments in taste is the smoking craze, which is rife among boys from eight to ten years and appears to begin about a year earlier in girls. Mr. Bell gives a list of seventy-one different substances tested as to their smoking qualities by boys and girls of these ages. Bark of various kinds, spices, seeds, leaves, stems, rattan, cork, in fact almost anything that could be smoked and was easily procurable, is to be found in this list. While it is undoubtedly true that imitation plays a large part in this smoking craze, its root lies in the natural desire of growing children to test new sensations for themselves, and even the unpleasant results consequent upon some of the trials do not prevent further experimentation along the same line.

Up to the age of ten or eleven years there seems to be little tendency to specialize in experiments. In the active, healthy child the desire for knowledge is omnivorous. He experiments not only with his own sensations, but is possessed by a desire to find out how people, animals, and plants will act under certain circumstances. He not only wants to find out what he himself can do, but what others can do, and he wants to know the why of things. His mind is open in every direction, and it is the golden age for arousing the interests that may prove to be lifelong. To repress his activity is to stultify his mind, and sympathy with his interests and an outlet provided for his activity will do more for him at this age than all the codes of discipline ever invented, which fail to recognize that curiosity and activity are normal to his age.

A little consideration of some of the examples which are usually classified as " naughtiness " will show that they are by no means to be entirely set down to intentional misbehavior on the part of the child, and that justice demands an investigation of the child's reason for the act.

F., 2. Showed active interest in closed boxes or bottles; frequently tasted things in bottles until one day she tasted oil of cloves.

F., 2. Was trying to put her fingers in her baby brother's eyes. Said she wanted to know how they felt. " How do they feel, mamma?"

F., 2½. Touched a hot stove to see how it felt.

F., 3. Stuck a pin in her baby sister to see what she would do.

F., 3. Was interested in throwing stones; tried to see how far she could throw.

F., 4–5. Experimented with a mouth organ.

F., 5. Used to scratch pictures of people to see if they had life in them.

M., 4. Found matches a great temptation; always wanted to light them.

M., 4, and M., 5. Were always trying to find out what things were made of.

M., 5. Tried to open the dog's mouth to see what made him bark.

F., 5, and M., 6. Tied a cat's hind legs together to see how she would walk. Several cases of tying up cats' feet in tissue paper.

F., 6, and F., 6½. Cut each other's hair to see how it would look.

F., 6. Was much interested in gardening, but forced open the flower buds because she could not wait for them to open naturally.

F., 5. Dug up the radishes every day to see how they were growing.

F., 5. Seeing tears in her mother's eyes when she was peeling onions, said: "Mamma, the onions must hurt you. Give me an onion and let me find out where the hurt is."

M., 6, and F., 5. Put the dog's head in a paper bag to see what he would do. Several cases of similar experiments with cats.

F., 6. Turned on the gas and said she wanted a fire.

F., 6. Worked very diligently and finally succeeded in taking up enough of a carpet to find out what caused a little hump in one place.

F., 7. Interested in hats. Used to make many new shapes out of paper. Experimented on everything that could be glued.

M., 7, and M., 8. Having seen a steam engine, tried to make one.

F., 8. Dug up a buried canary bird to see how it looked.

M., 8. Was very much interested in a pair of new skates and the way in which they fastened. His next composition was on skating.

F., 6, and M., 7. Were very curious to know how flying felt. Went up a high bank and jumped, flapping their arms.

APPARENT CRUELTY

Under experimental curiosity are to be classed a large number of cases of apparent cruelty, which are due not to any real impulse toward cruelty, but to ignorance and to an impulse which, when properly directed, is the prototype of scientific investigation. When a child of three endangers the life of her pet kitten by putting it into a tub of water, there is, perhaps, scarcely need for the tearful explanation that she wanted " to see if kitty could swim like the swans she saw at the park," to clear her from the charge of cruelty ; but the case is not quite so clear when a boy is found cutting off the leg of a live frog. When, however, an investigation reveals the fact that he has heard that certain lizards reproduce their tails, and wanted to find out whether the frog would " grow a new leg," the case seems to be one of a desire for knowledge rather than intentional cruelty. In each of the appended examples there was an apparently wanton infliction of pain, and yet in no one of them was the motive primarily cruelty.

Cases of Apparent Cruelty

F., 3. Put the kitten's front paws on a very hot stove to see what it would do.

M., 4½. Broke a little chicken's leg and brought it to his mother to learn how to mend it.

M., 8. Cut a crow's tongue to find out whether it would learn to talk. Had been told this was the case.

M., 8 or 9. Shut a squirrel in a dog's kennel to see how long it could live without food. Was much interested in Tanner's fast of forty days, which was the incentive.

M., 6. Cut off a frog's leg to see whether it could hop with one leg. Was not ordinarily a cruel child.

M., 8–12. Broke chickens' legs several times, but always set them. Became a surgeon.

M., 8. Cut off a frog's leg to see if it would grow again.

M., 6. Was found pulling the legs off a fly. Said he wanted to see if the fly could walk on the ceiling without.

M., 8. Dissected a frog to see how it was made (the extent to which this was vivisection is not stated). When reprimanded, said, " Well, suppose another frog was hurt, I thought maybe I could fix its wheels if I knew what was in this one."

Moreover, we find numerous instances of children deliberately exposing themselves to pain to satisfy a desire for knowledge, though probably with the same lack of actual realization of pain as in the case of experiments on animals. The child who ate green grapes to see if they really would make her sick had previously experienced an attack of colic, but the mere memory of pain was not sufficiently vivid to check her desire for experiment. Another child on being told that iron on a very cold day would burn her tongue deliberately tried it ; and a boy of nine exposed himself to whooping cough " to see how it felt." A little girl of five, on observing tears in her mother's eyes as she was peeling onions, remarked, " Mamma, the onions must hurt you. Give me an onion and let me find out where the hurt is." Many cases of what, on first thought, appears to be a shocking callousness in children to the sufferings of others prove upon investigation to be mere inability to appreciate the situation, due to a lack in experience on the child's part of either physical or mental suffering. Most children have, of course, temporary experiences of pain, but childish memories are short, and pain, unless exceptionally sharp or prolonged, is quickly forgotten ; so that the average healthy child has very slight appreciation of illness or suffering, and exhibitions of sympathy are largely imitative. A child who is habitually cruel is an abnormality and will probably be found to have other signs of degeneration, but all the cases above quoted have not cruelty, but a desire for knowledge, however misdirected, for their impelling motive.

QUESTIONS

The development of the questioning phase of curiosity is coincident with that of language, and among all its manifestations the questions of children hold the most prominent place and furnish the most valuable material for study. Though there is a residue of miscellaneous questions which form an exceedingly interesting group, the larger number can be classified under the following groups : questions in regard to (*a*) forces of nature, (*b*) mechanical forces, (*c*) origin of life, (*d*) theology and Bible stories, (*e*) death and heaven, (*f*) questions which are merely inquisitive. These last form but a small group in comparison with the others, less than 5 per cent. of the whole. Under the first group of questions, in regard to nature and natural forces, are included questions in regard to the sun, moon, stars, cloud, rain, fog, wind, thunder and lightning, fire, water, animal and plant life. Of four hundred and sixty-five questions asked by children under the age of ten, if questions on the origin of life be included, over one half were on topics relating to nature and the working of natural forces. Nearly 75 per cent. of these questions relate to causation. To the active imagination of the child all the phenomena of nature furnish material for wonderment, and though he often invents explanations for himself, questions of " what " and " why " are well-nigh universal. Children under seven show a marked tendency to attribute personality to the working of all unknown agencies. Questions often take the form of, "Who made it?" and though this is probably largely due to the fact that children's questions in regard to natural causes are answered by the phrase " God makes it," this does not at all interfere with the child's idea of some intervening agency, more within the limits of his comprehension. Many children show by their questions that they attribute sentience to wind, think that the thunder is caused by some one rolling barrels, and that the flowers and trees have a life of their own. Some of the reminiscent papers describe a state of puzzled wonder, often lasting for years, and which obtained little relief from questions as to how the earth could turn over without tipping people out of their beds, and why the water did n't run out of the wells at night. Some children brood silently for years over questions which they do not themselves originate, but which once put into their minds recur again and again, and when put into articulate form are met only with the unsatisfactory answer, " You are n't old enough to understand it yet." Those who remember their own childish puzzles will also remember the vague feeling of injury which such an answer roused, which, could the child have put it into words, would have probably been expressed in some such form as " Then you should n't have made me think about it in the first place." And good pedagogy is on the side of the child. The active mind of a child can originate enough questions that are, at least, partially within his comprehension and wholly within his interests to furnish the basis of a liberal school curriculum without the addition of insoluble puzzles. Fortunately for the child, the natural tendency to accept things as they appear has a nullifying effect upon this premature instruction in healthy, normal children, but the delicate and neurotic frequently suffer imaginary terrors induced by distorted ideas.

In a recent study of the faults of children[1] it appears that, from the teacher's point of view, the most frequent and troublesome fault in children is inattention and lack of application. Trying enough to the overworked teacher, no doubt, but from the child's point of view there is something to be said in regard to subjects to which he is required to pay attention. A child's attention is chiefly of the passive or involuntary sort, and active or voluntary attention is a later development. It is easy for a child to attend to the things which interest him, but too often he is required to pay attention to things in which he has no interest whatever. Voluntary attention is a much more complex matter and, even in adults, unstable and dependent upon nervous conditions. It is easily fatigued, and to expect a child to continue a voluntary exertion throughout school hours

[1] Norman Triplett, " A Study of the Faults of Children," *Pedagogical Seminary*, Vol. X, pp. 200–238, June, 1903.

without an appeal to his natural interests is irrational. No study of the span of either voluntary or involuntary attention at different ages has yet been made, though some careful observers have taken occasional notes on its development in individual children. Mrs. Hall records that her child paid attention for eight minutes to the rattling of a box on the fifty-third day of his life. The same child, on the sixty-third day, was interested for thirty consecutive minutes in the rattling of a purse of coins. Miss Shinn also notes that, more than once in her fifth month, her little niece spent half an hour at a time in gazing out of the window. Voluntary attention is a complex development involving an effort of will and dependent upon the natural or involuntary attention, and the best educational methods demand a study of children's interests, and an adaptation of the school routine to them, so that full advantage may be taken of the simpler and earlier development.

QUESTIONS IN REGARD TO NATURE

F., 3½. What makes the sun shine? Who puts the stars in the sky at night?

F., 4. If I put a ball on that hill it rolls down, and what I want to know is how God keeps the moon up in the sky?

M., 4½. Asked how the moon got up so high, and said he would n't like to be up on it.

F., 5. What makes the stars twinkle?

F., 5. What do we have a moon for? Why don't it be as bright as the sun? Why don't it be round? How can it be round sometimes? What good is the man? Don't the woman let him go out ever? If I was in the moon could I see you? Why not? Can I go when I die if I want to?

M., 5. Asked if the man in the moon ever went to sleep; why the sun stood still; what made the stars twinkle; how the dew came on the grass; what made the thunder make such a noise; what made the wheels of the clock go round, and what made the pendulum swing.

M., 5. Used to wonder whether the clouds run on the sky or on wheels, and why they did n't fall down.

M., 6. Wanted to know what fog was and what made it?

M., 6. What makes the wind blow? Is some one pushing it along? I should think it would stop when it ran into a house or big tree. Does it know it turns our papers over?

F., 6. Watching a beam of sunlight, said: "Why does it stay so narrow? Why is it on this side of the room in the morning and the other at night?"

M., 6. How can the world turn round and not tip us out of bed? How does the water stay in the wells?

M., 6. On seeing a windmill for the first time, said: "Does the wind make the wheel go round? How does the wind make it go round?"

F., 7. Where does the snow come from? Where does the sun go at night? What makes it thunder and lighten?

F., 7. Was told that the moon was made of green cheese, and was curious to see if it really was.

F., 7. During a thunderstorm, asked: "What is that, thunder? Oh, dear, what good does it do to thunder? Who makes it thunder, anyway? I wonder if it thunders in New York."

F., 7. Seeing plums for the first time, asked: "What are they? Can you eat them? Where did they come from?"

F., 7. What makes the waves roll in? Where does the water come from?

F., 7½. Where do all the worms come from after a shower? Do they rain down?

F., 8. What makes the snow? Why is n't it dirty, like dust?

M., 9. Wanted to know where the rain came from, how it got down, and why it did n't rain all the time.

M., 11. Looking at the river which was very high, exclaimed, "I wonder what made it so high, it has not rained very much."

M., 8. Having had the new moon pointed out to him, wanted to know where the old moon was.

F., 9. What is the end of the world made of? What should I see if I went where the mountains touch the sky? How many stars are there?

M., 9. Why don't nuts fall before the frost comes? What does the frost have to do with it, anyway?

M., 9. Why is the moon different shapes?

QUESTIONS IN REGARD TO ANIMAL LIFE

M., 5. Looking at bears, asked, "Mamma, why do they throw so much bread to bears?" "Because they are hungry, and must have something to eat." "Oh, do they get hungry as we do?"

M., 5. On seeing a Manx cat for the first time, said: "Did a dog bite off her tail in a fight? Did the cat want her tail cut off? Do you think I can make my cat bobtailed?"

M., 4. On seeing a fur boa, asked: "Who killed kitty? Did kitty cry?"

F., 5. Why does kitty have fur?

M., 6. Do fishes go on land to sleep?

F., 6. How do the flies walk upside down?

F., 7. Why do a canary's throat feathers ruffle when he sings? How does he do it?

Nearly twice as many boys as girls, according to the present data, show special interest in mechanics, and the beginning of this interest is shown at a very early age. Mrs. Hogan notes the interest as a persistent one in her boy, at the age of fourteen months, and the five years of the record show that it was continued. Questions are but one phase of the development of this interest, the earlier manifestations being active observation passing into experiment, and very fully developed in the destructive phase of curiosity. Fifty per cent. of the cases of boys' interests and curiosity in all its phases are connected with motion, the desire to find out what makes things go being a powerful incentive to various forms of investigation. Children under three are apt to attribute life to things which have motion, their first experiences being connected with living beings as causal agencies. Many children and animals show fear of mechanical toys, and there is a struggle between this timidity, in the presence of the mysterious and unknown, and curiosity in regard to the moving object. A kitten exhibited, for several weeks, an amusing struggle between evident fear and curiosity whenever a mechanical seal was wound up and turned loose on the carpet. The movements of the seal were somewhat erratic, and the kitten, following at what he probably estimated a safe distance, was occasionally surprised by a sudden turn of the seal, which he invariably avoided by leaping into the air. Whenever the mechanism ran down he smelled of the toy, pushed it about with his paws, and occasionally turned it over, always starting back, however, if he happened to set the wheels in motion. Familiarity finally overcame fear, even when the toy was wound up, but it never proved as attractive an object to chase as a ball, for which the kitten himself supplied the motor power. This attitude seems also to characterize young children, for a baby's early motor interests are in the things which he himself can do, and disappointed friends and relatives have often found their gifts of mechanical toys a failure, simply because they have too far anticipated the natural development, and the toy has proved either a source of fear or failed to excite special interest. In fact, even at a later period, mechanical toys which are too complicated in construction or too delicate to bear investigation, which are apt to be clumsy, soon lose their attractiveness, while something that can be taken to pieces and put together by unskilled fingers, so that it will "go again," may prove a lasting means of amusement and instruction. Kites and tops are as interesting to the children of the present generation as to their fathers, and to the children of the Orient as well as the Occident, because there is something for the operator to do as well as to watch, and curiosity as to just how these toys will behave under certain conditions is kept stimulated by occasional failure, and the necessity for finding a reason therefor. The few examples of questions here given suggest a range of interests which could readily be further stimulated and given an educational impulse which could be utilized in a school curriculum.

Questions showing Mechanical Interests

M., 3. What is inside your watch, auntie, that makes it talk?

M., 4. Watching the walking beam on a steamer, asked: "What makes that thing go up and down? Is it the man?"

F., 4½. Seeing her mother crocheting lace, asked, "Is that the way the lace on my dress is made?" Being answered in the negative, inquired, "Then how was it made?"

M., 7. What makes the trolley go? What does that engine need water for?

F., 7. Always liked to watch the oiling and cleaning of the carriage and asked many questions in regard to it.

M., 7. After seeing a pile driver at work, and visiting a fort, overwhelmed the family with questions in regard to them.

M., 7. How does the steam move engines?

M., 7. Why can't you see the messages on the telegraph wire? How do they go?

F., 7. On seeing an electric car for the first time, asked: "What makes that car go? How can it go without horses?"

M., 7. Why can some people take pianos apart when others must n't?

M., 7. How does pressing the button make the bell ring when it does n't move the wire any?

M., 7½. Asked, "What made the clock run?" When on a ferryboat with his father, asked, "What makes the boat go?"

M., 8. What do all these people want to ride on the boat for?

M., 9. Was very anxious to know how the train ran. When he got out wanted to know how the wheels stayed on the track. Was told that they were grooved and that kept them on. Ran back quickly just as the train was moving off and called, "Wait a minute till I feel it."

M., 9. On seeing a train, asked: "What makes that train go? Why do they ring that bell? Where does that smoke go? Who made that train?"

Origin of Life

The questions relating to the origin of life were asked almost entirely by children between the ages of three and eight, the greater number falling between the ages of five and eight. Very few were reported after this age. This fact is significant and has an important bearing on the question of what teaching should be given to children in this fundamental fact of life. That curiosity on this subject develops in both boys and girls before the age of seven is attested not only by the instances sent in answer to the syllabi (which made no mention of this topic, but asked only for instances of curiosity shown by questions, without suggestions as to subject-matter), but by the personal testimony of a number of teachers of wide experience and many thoughtful mothers to whom personal experience has brought home the importance of the question. That there is really a falling off of curiosity at this age is not probable, and the absence of questions indicates either that the child's requests for information have been evaded, and fanciful and unsatisfactory answers have been given until he has become hopeless of obtaining information from the proper sources, or that curiosity has been satisfied by the teaching of other children in crude and garbled form, and the child is ashamed to ask further questions. The testimony of teachers in regard to conversation overheard among children and a number of answers by adults to the question, " How did your knowledge of the origin of life first come to you ? " have shown that not only is this the case, but that in later years the way in which such knowledge has come is bitterly regretted, because the beauty and sacredness which should belong to all thoughts connected with the coming of new life has for them been sullied, and this is felt as a loss and an injury which no later teaching can ever fully repair. A study of the character of the questions at different ages, here inserted, shows in the earliest years the simple, frank curiosity of childhood. Later ones betray very plainly the false notions acquired from unsatisfactory or untruthful answers which do not explain that for which the eager mind is groping, and, worse even than leaving the puzzle unsolved, plant the seeds of distrust toward parents or teachers.

Questions relating to Origin of Life

F., 3½. Mamma, where did you get me?

F., 5. Where was I when you were a little girl?

M., 5. Where did baby come from? Did God drop baby down from the sky?

M., 6. Was I a speck of dust? Did it have blood in it?

F., 7. How did God send the baby? Did he send an angel down with it? If you had n't been at home, would he have taken it back?

M., 7. Where do doctors get babies from?

M., 7. Who is " Dame Nature "? Did you know she was going to bring you a baby? How did you know whether it was a boy or a girl?

F., 6. Mamma, where do the chickens get their eggs?

F., 7. How did the expressman know where to leave the baby?

M., 7. Where was I before I was born?

M., 7. Where was I when you went to school?

M., 8. Where do little lambs come from? *Do* they come out of old stumps?

F., 8. How did you know baby was coming, and get his clothes ready?

F., 19. When I was twelve years old, suspecting that there was to come to our home a little stranger, and imagining that my mother was occasionally engaged in some secret needlework, I determined to satisfy my curiosity by an investigation. Selecting a time when there would surely be no interruption, I went to her room for proof of my suspicions in the shape of tiny garments. My search was successful, and my curiosity satisfied, but my act was discovered later, and I was reprimanded.

Why, on this subject, on which the child most needs wise and adequate teaching, should he be left to acquire information in stealthy fashion from those totally unprepared to gratify his legitimate and natural curiosity in healthful ways? Too often the information comes from newspaper reports of criminal cases, which are read and discussed by children in the fourth and fifth school grades. Could parents realize what it may mean to a child to have his first knowledge of the origin of life associated with sin, shame, and secrecy, they would be guarded against it as from deadliest poison. One wise and beautiful mother of my acquaintance, whose example is worthy of universal imitation, adopted the principle of answering truthfully, and to the measure of the child's understanding, all spontaneous questions. In a family of five children, each child has known of the coming of the younger ones, and has been allowed to see the dainty garments prepared for the tiny baby who was coming to be a part of the home. This knowledge has been a beautiful secret, too sacred to be shared with any one but "father and mother," but each child has shared in the loving preparations and joyful anticipation of the baby's coming. To the children in that household no false or wrong impressions have ever come. They are safeguarded from evil. To them the coming of new life is surrounded, as it should be, with a sacredness and responsibility born of a pure and wisely given knowledge. In pitiful contrast to this is the stealthily acquired, half-comprehended, and wholly false-in-feeling knowledge of the majority of children in our public schools. Teachers furnish overwhelming evidence that there are few children over eight years old in the public schools who have not some sort of knowledge of the origin of life, and it is, perhaps, sufficient commentary on the kind of knowledge to add that the children regard the subject as something secret and shameful. Unquestionably the home is the place for this kind of instruction, but unfortunately there are too many fathers and mothers who are either unwilling or unfitted to give it, and the educational expert who can devise some scheme for wise and systematic instruction, adapted to the age of the child, and furnishing it with a safeguard against corrupting influences, will do more for the moral welfare of the community by the prevention of evil than any number of crusades against evils already existent. The power of an idea in a child's life is very great, and false and depraved associations may so corrupt and influence the thought of the child that

the baneful effects may linger through life. In regard to
the manner of teaching, Miss Sullivan's perplexities with
Helen Keller [1] and her solution are suggestive. In August,
1887, less than a year and a half after Miss Sullivan first
came to Helen, who was then seven years old, she wrote
the following lines in a letter to a friend: " I do wish things
would stop being born! new puppies, new calves, and new
babies keep Helen's interest in the why and wherefore of
things at white heat. The arrival of a new baby at Ivy Green
the other day was the occasion of a fresh outburst of questions
about the origin of babies and live things in general. 'Where
did Leila get new baby? How did doctor know where to find
baby? Did Leila tell doctor to get very small new baby?
Where did doctor find Guy and Prince (puppies)? Why is
Elizabeth Evelyn's sister?' etc. . . . From the beginning *I
have made it a practice to answer all Helen's questions to the
best of my ability in a way intelligible to her*, and at the same
time truthfully." " Why should I treat these questions differ-
ently?" I asked myself. . . . I took Helen and my Botany,
How Plants Grow, up a tree, where we often go to read or
study, and I told her in simple words the story of plant life.
I reminded her of the corn, beans, and watermelon seed she
had planted in the spring, and told her that the tall corn in
the garden and the beans and watermelon vines had grown
from those seeds. I explained how the earth keeps the seed
warm and moist until the little leaves are strong enough to
push themselves out into the light and air, where they can
breathe and grow and bloom, and make more seeds from
which other baby plants shall grow. I drew an analogy between
plant and animal life, and told her that seeds are eggs as truly
as hens' eggs and birds' eggs, — that the mother hen keeps
her eggs warm and dry until the little chicks come out.

---

[1] Helen Keller, *The Story of My Life*, p. 331. Doubleday, Page & Co., New
York, 1903.

I made her understand that all life comes from an egg. The mother bird lays her eggs in a nest, and keeps them warm until the birdlings are hatched. The mother fish lays her eggs where she knows they will be moist and safe until it is time for the little fish to come out. I told her that she could call the egg the cradle of life. Then I told her that other animals like the dog and cow, and human beings, do not lay their eggs, but nourish their young in their own bodies. I had no difficulty in making clear to her that if plants and animals did n't produce offspring after their kind, they would soon cease to exist, and everything in the world would soon die. But the function of sex I passed over as lightly as possible. I did however try to give her the idea that love is the great continuer of life. The subject was difficult, and my knowledge inadequate, but I am glad I did n't shirk my responsibility; for stumbling, hesitating, and incomplete as my explanation was, it touched deep, responsive chords in the soul of my little pupil, and the readiness with which she comprehended the great facts of physical life confirmed me in the opinion that the child has dormant within him, when he comes into the world, all the experience of the race." If, in the case of this child, blind and deaf since she was eighteen months old, and limited in language to the acquisitions of one year, the problem could be brought within her comprehension to the extent shown above, and touch "the deep, responsive chords," which in all normal children answer so readily to the skillful touch, there surely need be no fear that such instruction cannot be successfully given to children who are not thus limited. The aim in moral education should be to forestall and prevent evil rather than to devise means for its cure after it is already existent.

Very young children, if normal, will never fail to be very curious about the advent of a new infant stranger in their family. Here it would seem that certain provisional answers to their inevitable questions are necessary for years too tender either to understand or to respect reserves that society demands. Their questions, however phrased, call for but little in the way of answer, and it would be mere pedantry and affectation to deluge a three-year-old child with physiological explanations in detail. It is, however, essential that the myth should be such as to give some impression that the mystery is something sweet and sacred, and if we had a complete collection of answers, — the milkman, the stork, the doctor, the gardener, God, the angels, etc., as bringers of the new baby, — we should find very great differences not usually sufficiently recognized and respected. To do this, and to devise a mythic answer that is true to the heart, instincts, and needs of the child in this brief period, is a pedagogical problem still open for solution. Certain it is that these highly sensitized juvenile minds can, by eight years of age, be so told of the modes of fertilizing flowers that some of them will begin to divine analogies with the animal world. The phenomena in the latter probably ought to be taught for the simpler forms first rather than the higher, and the indirect psychic functions of love and the meaning of marriage are modes of approach which may give due sacredness and solemnity to this instruction. Another principle is clear, namely, that information should be personal, given on the right occasion of environment and interest, and that it should be brief and suggestive rather than by dissertations or books that always magnify the topic. The greatest content in the least form is a good law. It seems a grave pedagogical error involving no end of calamity that when interest in sex awakens it should be allowed to develop independently of the ideas of gestation and birth, with which, when it is taught, it should be brought into inseparable unity. In this, as in the theological field, there are generally so many preconceptions to be

removed that it is often hard to distinguish pure and unadul-
terated curiosity from that which is spurious, factitious, or
distorted.

RELIGIOUS CURIOSITY

Closely connected with questions in regard to the origin of
life, and frequently mingled with them, are the theological
and biblical puzzles which assail the childish understanding.
Over and over again come the questions, "Who is God?"
"Who made God?" "Who were God's father and mother?"
"Who came before God?" Often these questions take crude
and bizarre forms that have an irreverent sound to the older
ears, though they are but the efforts of active little brains to
bring the incomprehensible within the limits of experience.

That the story of creation, as given in Genesis, should
arouse in the mind of a child of four or five visions of a sort
of mud-pie process of construction, or that it should picture
God as engaged in baking bread in answer to the petitions
addressed to him, is but one of the natural results of the
literalness of childhood. The child's thought cannot tran-
scend his experience, nor should he, because of this, be
considered as lacking in reverence. His imaginings are certainly no more realistic than those of the early Christian
painters who depicted Eve as actually issuing full grown from
Adam's side. The little philosopher of five who asked, "Does
God make some little boys good and some bad?" was facing
a problem which has puzzled the brains of theologians for
centuries. Frequently it is only through some of these occasional questions that we can get a clue to what is passing in
the child's mind, for with all their frankness children are
often singularly reticent about what they think and feel most
deeply. To any one who is accustomed to being with children,
the following examples will probably seem familiar and suggest a host of similar questions.

M., 4. When shown a picture of the Golden Calf and told that it was worshiped by the people, asked, " Auntie, I wonder if it is all made of gold ? Do the people worship it as we worship God ? Why do the people worship it ? "

M., 4. Mamma, who is God's mother ?

M., 4. Had been gathering shingles and asked, " Mamma, do they play with shingles up in heaven ? "

M., 4. On his first visit to the seashore, asked, " Who made the ocean ? " " God." " Well, who made God ? "

M., 5. Does God make some little boys good and some bad ?

M., 4½. Having been told the story of Christ calling his disciples, asked, " What did they do with the fish ? "

F., 5. If we did n't have any bread, would God give it to us ?

M., 6. " Mamma, does Jesus have an oven up in heaven ? " On being told No, " Well, then, how does he bake our daily bread ? "

M., 6. When Jesus was a baby did he know as much as God ?

M., 9. Had his curiosity aroused in Sunday school and was not contented till the story of Noah had been told over and over.

He had been taught we are all children of Adam and Eve and therefore all brothers, and asked, " Is Ish Armour my brother ? What makes him black ? Am I black ? Why is he black and me white ? "

F., 3½. Was used to hearing God spoken of as Jesus. One day her mother spoke of God. " God, who is God ? " " Jesus is God." " Oh ! is his name God and Jesus too ? "

F., 3½. Did Heavenly Father make your hair ? Did Heavenly Father make that hair that you take off ?

F., 7. Mamma, if I am naughty at night, God can't see me, can he ?

F., 9. If God will keep us, why do we have to pray to him to keep us through the night ?

F., 12. Used to ask how Jonah could come out of a whale's body alive, how Jesus could walk on the sea, etc.

F., ? " Mamma, who made you ? " " God made me." " Who made me ? " " God made you." Some time passed. " Mamma, where does God have his office ? Where does he get so much stuff to make you and me ? What did he make us for ? How did I get down from heaven ? " Not getting satisfaction, she sighed and said, " Does God have an office like other men ? "

F., 7. Could never see why God did not have a beginning once upon a time. She said, " If God made everything and everything had a beginning, when did God begin ? Who made God, and was there another world like this earth ? "

The crudity of some of these ideas is but a natural stage of development and outgrown at a later period, but some childish misconceptions lead to serious results later, and it is a question whether unskillful, even if well-meant, Sunday-school teaching is not responsible for a vast amount of scepticism in later years. The order in which religious truths should be taught, and the form in which they should be presented, is one of the great pedagogical questions which as yet remains unanswered. It is certain that the haphazard teaching which prevails in most Sunday schools has, to say the utmost, very mixed results. Several attempts have been made with deaf and blind children to guard their early ideas from the misconceptions which beset most children in the course of this theological training, and to await the spontaneous awakening of interest in the great problems of life and death. These attempts have been frustrated as far as their scientific import was concerned, partly by the well-meaning but mistaken endeavors of those who did not realize the danger of misconception that might do permanent injury. This happened both in the case of Laura Bridgman and Helen Keller, though fortunately, especially in the latter case, little harm was done, as the form of attempted instruction was unsuited to her comprehension and made but little impression. But when Helen was eight years old, having then been under Miss Sullivan's care for two years, she asked spontaneously, " Where did I come from, and where shall I go when I die ?" The explanations which she was able to understand at this time did not satisfy her ; but two years later the questionings of her active intelligence reached a point where definite religious instruction was demanded, and she was placed under the wise care of Phillips Brooks. At that time she was asking such questions as " Who made the real world ? " and when it had been explained to her as far as possible, asked, " Who made God ? What did God make the new world out of ? Where did he get the soil and the water and the first seeds and animals ? Where is God ? Did you ever see God ? " Probably many of these questions would have come at an earlier age had she not been shut in a world of darkness and silence from the time of her illness, in 1881, till the spring of 1887, when Miss Sullivan opened for her the door of communication with the outer world. But to all children, sooner or later, these questionings come, and the questions themselves are the best guide for tracing the course of the child's thought and finding out its needs. The practical character of childish thinking comes out very plainly in the questions on death and heaven, the question of eating coming up very frequently in this connection.

F., 6. Mamma, do the angels have nothing but angel's food to eat? What shall we have to eat in heaven ?

F., 6. Mamma, where do you go when you die ? Will you go with me ? Will we both be put in the same box ? What will we have to eat ?

DEATH

The attitude of most children toward death, between the ages of three and seven, seems to be chiefly one of curiosity.[1] Occasionally a sensitive child reflects the feeling of those about him, but usually the attitude is one of inquiry. The first experience of death often comes to children in the death of some pet animal, or perhaps from finding the bodies of dead birds or insects. The impression made is not usually a painful one, but curiosity is aroused and numerous questions are asked, and upon the character of the answers given the child's feeling is chiefly dependent.

M., 6. Had an interesting story read to him. In the story the man died. The child went away by himself and said over and over, " Why did he die ? Why did he die ? "

[1] Colin A. Scott, *American Journal of Psychology*, Vol. VIII, p. 93, October, 1896.

F., 4. Saw a man climb an electric wire pole and asked the lady with whom she was, " Addie, will you go to heaven whole ? "

F., 8. Used to wonder what she was, why she was living, whether life was real or only a dream. At one time she half believed that she lived two lives, one by day and one by night, but never had courage to ask anybody about such things. In other matters was always asking " Why ? " and " What for ? "

F., ? Had a strong curiosity about death. She desired to be dead just to see how it felt.

F., 7. Why do people die ? Why do they put them in the ground ? Do they always stay in the ground, or do they go somewhere else ?

The child's interest in death is another great opportunity for moral, religious, and even scientific instruction, which has not only never been met, but perhaps has never been adequately appreciated. Infant curiosity, as we have seen, often focuses on its physical phenomena, and it seems singular that so often there is, at first, no fear. In many cases the birth of terror can be seen in very young children when they first distinguish a corpse from that of a person in normal sleep. Rarely, indeed, would curiosity as to how it feels to die prompt the youngest child to seek to experience death; but often in the history of the race, as in children, heaven is made so attractive as to lessen the love of life and even to counterbalance the fear of death. Perhaps the pains of hell have sometimes been necessary to offset the attractions of heaven in the young, when the latter was made too seductive, so that a little sense of danger, stimulated by awakening qualms of conscience, was needful. One thing is certain, and that is, that death, where taught, should first be presented as the natural and necessary end of a long life, so that the prevailing ideas of it in the young should not be derived from instances of premature, accidental, or tragic death. In this respect, and from this standpoint, the ostensive instance of Jesus, who was killed and did not die a natural death, is often misleading. Death at the end of an ideal old age can be so taught as to make it not only natural but beautiful and attractive, especially at the age of adolescence, when the first realization of it sometimes haunts the soul with great persistence. Youth is not complete without frankly envisaging the great fact that individual life is limited in time, and that the inevitable hour is for all alike. Death, at this age especially, is a muse of great inspiration and can evoke and sustain high ideals. It may be taught as an examination, test, or moral assay. Immortality is biological, and great stress must be laid upon the fact that the good we do will live after us; that one of the best ways to die is, as the Buddhists say, in thinking on our good deeds; and that the soul must be made so virtuous, and the mind so glorious with great ideas, that God, or the universe, cannot afford to have it perish. They should be taught that the sting of death is to die without leaving the world better. Youth can be appealed to powerfully by the thought of leaving a name, a record, a memory, that will be cherished by those who come after; and later the concept that life must be so led that children shall be well-born and perpetuate the race in increasing numbers to the remotest generations can be made of great practical power. If all this is well done, the problem whether the individual consciousness survives in a transcendent world will lose its difficulties and its dangers, both moral and intellectual, and can be met with frankness and left to the domain of hope and faith, where Jesus placed it, with due care to avoid premature theological subtleties.

Perhaps nothing gives a clearer view of the activity of a child's mind, and its various interests, than a list of miscellaneous questions selected on no other basis than that they show thought and observation. The kaleidoscopic picture thus presented is far more than a list of amusing questions at which we may smile and wonder how such ideas ever entered the child's mind, for it reveals the actual workings of the mind in a way not otherwise obtainable. Sometimes, all unconsciously, these questions reveal certain facts of the child's environment in an unmistakable way. A list of all the questions asked by a child during a week or a month would probably furnish material for a very fair guess at the child's interests and surroundings.

F., 2½. Asked if black people were made of black dust.

M., 3. Will the trees all have the same leaves again?

F., 3½. "Seeds are brown, are n't they, mamma?" "Yes." "But the flowers are n't brown. Why are n't they?"

M., 4. Where does the stocking go when a hole comes in it?

M., 4. On being shown his baby brother, asked: "What is he good for, anyway? Can he play ball?"

F., 4½. How do the chickens crow?

F., 5. Wondered why a chair was called a chair and she was called a girl.

F., 6. Are there any fairies now? Did you ever see one?

F., 6. Wanted to know why the minister flung his arms about so much.

F., 6. Asked if she was wound up; wanted to know if she would run down.

M., 5. Papa, why don't your eyesights get mixed when they cross each other?

M., 6. Wanted to know what was inside us to make us laugh.

M., 5. Playing with the cat, asked, "Why can't Titty Tay talk?"

M., 5. Why does my goblet sweat?

M., 5. Shall I be a mamma when I grow up?

M., 6. Looked closely at a sweater and asked, "Where is the buttons on that coat?"

M., 7. On being told that George Washington never told a lie, asked: "What ailed him? Could n't he talk?"

F., 5. Does a hen ever get nervous? Who was the mother of the first horse that ever lived?

F., 6½. Why do the angels never fall down to earth when there is no floor to heaven?

M., 7. Where is to-morrow? What is the highest number you can possibly count?

M., 7. Why does a square piece of wood look round when the lathe is working?

F., 7. Is the tick of the clock round or square? Why did grandpa wind the big clock? How could his winding it up make it go all the week? Did the Lord make it go?

F., 7. What makes my eyes open and close?

M., 8. What makes the old rooster walk different from the old hen?

F., 8. Was eager to know what sleep was, and declared she had never been asleep.

F., 8. Do dogs ever have the headache?

F., 12. Say, pa, when you sneeze, where does the sneeze go to?

M., 12. How can far-off things look near?

M. Why do some people have red hair and some black?

F. What are debts? Do we have debts?

Mere aimless curiosity or inquisitiveness plays but a small part in the incessant questionings of childhood. Every normal child is curious, but the reiterated questions, which often seem tiresome to a busy and tired mother, are prompted by a real desire for information; and the child's point of view was well expressed by the little fellow who, when told he must n't ask so many questions, sighed, " But there's so many things I want to know." Of the more than twelve hundred cases of manifestations of curiosity, only 5.62 per cent. came under the classification of mere inquisitiveness, either in the form of questions or illegitimate peeking and prying shown by actions. Under this heading were classified all cases of aimless prying into what could have no objective interest, and all attempts to find out, by illegitimate peeking and prying, things intentionally concealed or forbidden. In this sense inquisitiveness is not a characteristic of children under five years, and their incessant questioning and investigating is distinctly utilitarian and a developmental process, while inquisitiveness in the specific meaning given above is a perversion of a natural impulse toward a useful end, into what is useless and frequently involves an element of deceit. It is closely connected with defective power of attention, for children whose interests are strong and whose attention is absorbed by these interests are rarely inquisitive in this derogatory meaning of the word. It differs from legitimate curiosity, not in its nature but in its application. The mere fact that anything is concealed or not intended for inspection appears to act as a strong stimulus to some natures, whether or not the object is in itself interesting. Probably the primitive impulse to investigate whatever is concealed is the fundamental element here, and the abnormal development is due chiefly to a lack of inhibition and restraint. In both children and adults it is most frequently associated with neurotic tendencies and frequently with a more or less defective physical development. Manifestations of inquisitiveness are too well known to need illustration. Peeking and prying into parcels, closets, trunks; peeking and listening at keyholes, behind doors, or other places of concealment; desire to know what every one is talking about; efforts to overhear things not intended for them; questions about private affairs of others — are well-known characteristics of the Paul Pry order of person, and as this morbid form of curiosity apparently grows by what it feeds upon, its existence in a child as a marked characteristic should be considered reason for an inquiry into the child's nervous condition. Though occasional exhibitions of this perverted form of curiosity are common enough among normal children, especially before Christmas, when desire to find out what their presents are to be, frequently overcomes the scruples which usually inhibit such manifestations, these occasional lapses, especially where there is a strong temptation from personal interest, are not at all to be considered as symptoms of neuropathic conditions, as in the case of the characteristically inquisitive child.

Echolalia, or the constant repetition of the same question, which becomes so wearisome to the one answering, seems also to have a close connection with nervous fatigue. The questions are asked, not for information, but because, under certain conditions of fatigue, it seems as if certain nervous paths of discharge were established and the repetition became almost automatic.[1] Many of these cases of self-echolalia are reported as occurring toward the close of the day, or on long railway journeys, or when the child is "not quite well" and has been kept in the house for that reason.

Random questions, which are sometimes poured out in an incessant stream, without pausing for answer, are also frequently due to fatigue, and are often a characteristic of feeble-minded children. One child who had sufficient intelligence to act as guide through quite a complicated route of short streets asked disconnected questions constantly during the walk of about twenty minutes. Sometimes an answer was waited for, but in many cases the attention wandered to a new subject before an answer could be given, and the former question was apparently forgotten. The mental condition appeared similar to that of a normal child too fatigued to remember his own questions, but in the one case there is defective development of the nerve cells, and in the other the fatigued nerve cells are capable of recuperation. One child of five years, after a long railway journey, during which she had become very tired and fretful, responded to the effort to amuse her with the frost on the car window by asking the same question in regard to it twenty-two times in half an hour, and every one who has tried the experiment knows the difficulty of holding the attention of a tired child for more than a few minutes at a time. The tendency to echolalia is observable in some forms of delirium, where the same question or sentence is repeated over and over, and the cause, as with the tired child, is to be sought in the fatigued cells of the cortex. Children, undoubtedly, sometimes ask questions merely for the sake of talking and not because of any particular desire for information, and should, of course, be checked

---

[1] T. S. Clouston, *Neuroses of Development*, p. 26. Simpkins, Marshall, Hamilton, Kent & Co., London, 1891.

under such circumstances; yet the boy of six, when asked
" What does make you so tiresome to-day ? " replied far more
aptly than he knew, when he answered, " I 'm not tiresome ;
I 'm tired."

Destructiveness as a phase of curiosity is too frequently
misunderstood, and the child's point of view left out of
account. The *motive* is overlooked, and, considered only on
the side of results, the case is certainly rather bad for the
child. Out of the 1247 cases which furnished the basis for
the present study, 352, or 28.38 per cent., involved destruction
of property, — for the most part toys or the child's own belongings, but in some cases objects of considerable value. The
age at which this overwhelming desire to find out the construction of things reaches its height is between four and
eight. There appears to be little difference between boys and
girls in this impulse to investigation, though the objects
destroyed differ somewhat. The distribution of cases according to objects destroyed is as follows :

	M.	F.
Musical instruments	44 +	22
Clocks and watches	57 +	25
Dolls	12 +	66
Mechanical toys, etc.	20 +	22
Miscellaneous objects, to see what was inside	21 +	31
Thermometers	2 +	2
Miscellaneous	12 +	16
	168 +	184 = 352

As considerable pains has been taken by the observers who
answered the syllabus to find out the child's real motive, and
cases in which this precaution was wanting have been rejected,
the evidence is conclusive that in the 352 cases of which use
has been made, wanton destructiveness or carelessness played
a very small part. Curiosity as to the cause of sound and
motion, and desire to see the inside of things, were the chief

motives which influenced the youthful investigators. They
wanted to find out what made the noise, why dolly opened
and shut her eyes, what made the cow moo, and what was
inside tops, marbles, and thermometers, and grief at the loss
of some valued toy was aggravated by a keen disappointment at non-success in finding the noise of the drum or the
tick of the watch. Cherished dolls were sacrificed to the overwhelming desire to find out what made the eyes move, or why
pressing the body caused a cry. One child cried bitterly
after she had spoiled her doll by poking in its eyes, not
because the doll was ruined, but because, as she tearfully
explained, "Now I can't ever find out what makes dolly shut
her eyes. Won't you buy me another one so I can find out?"
Numerically, at the head of the list of objects destroyed, stand
clocks and watches, many of them toys, though the list is by
no means restricted to these. In the younger children, desire
"to find the tick" is the ruling motive, but this develops into
the larger interest in motion and the desire to find out what
makes the watch go. The injury done is frequently an
unexpected result to the child. So keen and widespread is
this interest in clocks and watches, even when not exhibited
in the destructive form, that the gift of a cheap clock with
permission to take it to pieces affords more pleasure to many
children than any number of costly toys whose mechanism
cannot be investigated.

Several instances were given in the returns, in which old
clocks have proved a source of interest and amusement, and
boys of nine to twelve years, after numerous trials, succeeded
in putting them together after taking them apart, a feat which
certainly has sufficient educational value to compensate for
some failures at readjustment. Mechanical toys, more than
any others, seem to have the shortest existence in the hands
of bright, active children, a fact which suggests that toys so
constructed as to show principles of motion and elementary

physical laws, without involving their own destruction, are an educational need yet to be supplied. Some such, indeed, already exist, but they are far too few and too little known. This destructive form of curiosity, due to normal development of mentally active children, needing guidance, and to be furnished with a proper outlet, but not repressed, is not to be confused with the careless destruction of toys, due to lack of interest, which is unfortunately common in children whose interest and powers of appreciation have been weakened and dissipated by overloading them with toys and diversions until it has bred in them an ennui which has sapped their power of attention and left them incapable of self-entertainment. Healthy children, if allowed to develop under normal conditions, find interests and amusements for themselves, and the child who has been so reared that he wants to be constantly amused, and has no keen desires because they have been too frequently anticipated, has been deprived of one of the rights of childhood. The child who suffers from too many toys is, perhaps, on the whole, more to be pitied than the child who has too few. Destructiveness, when the impelling motive is curiosity, is closely allied to constructiveness, and some of the appended examples mention the transformation which has appeared at a later stage of development.

EXAMPLES OF DESTRUCTIVE CURIOSITY

M., 3. Broke his toy gun to find out what made the noise.

M., 3 years 7 months. Broke a toy cow "to find the moo." Broke a mechanical toy to find out what made it go.

M., 4. Pulled a clock to pieces to find out what made it strike. When twelve years old could put a clock together.

M., 5. Took a toy watch apart to find out what made the hands move.

F., 5. Cut her doll's body open "to see what kind of blood it had." Said it was something like sugar.

F., 6. Broke her doll to see what made it shut its eyes.

F., 8. Had a doll, and one day knocked its eye in. She broke the head to find out what had become of the eye, and then cried as if her heart would break.

M., 8. Took a clock apart and put it together again, though it never struck properly afterwards. Took a wringer apart and put it together again correctly.

M., 8. Broke a tape measure to find out how the tape was drawn in.

M., 4. Had a toy rooster which crowed; broke it to see what made it crow.

F., 8. Had heard that tortoise shell will not burn, but that celluloid will. She collected all the side combs in the house and tested them to find out whether they were tortoise shell.

M., 4. Cut the hair of his sister's doll to see if it would grow again.

M., 8. Dropped a toy engine from third-story window so that it would break and he could find out what was inside it.

F., 6, and M., 7. Each received a large Easter egg. There was a glass at the end to look through. Both broke their eggs to see what was inside.

M., 6. Took a toy steamboat to pieces to find out what made it go. He tried to put it together again but failed.

M., 7, and F., 8. Broke the thermometer by putting it on the stove to see how high the mercury would rise.

M., $5\frac{1}{2}$. Pulled a toy engine apart "to see where the 'choo choo' was."

M., $4\frac{1}{2}$. Had a gong on wheels; made a great effort to see what was inside it. It was iron, and he did not succeed. At last he put it in the road and let a cart go over it.

M., 7. Had a small rubber ball with shot in it. After vainly trying to see what made the noise, took a hatchet and cut it open.

F., 9. Took a music box to pieces; found she could not get it together again.

F., 5. Had a bank in the form of a frog; took it apart to see what became of the pennies that went into its mouth.

M., 5. Took a mouth organ apart to see what made the noise; broke a toy horn for the same reason.

M., 6, and F., 7. Smashed a large colored glass marble to see what was inside.

M., 12. Took a mechanical toy to pieces to see what made it go. After several attempts succeeded in putting it together again.

DESIRE TO TRAVEL

The desire for travel seems well-nigh universal in the American adolescent, only three in the entire number (482) of those answering this question stating that they had never had it. There are but few cases in which a developed form of it occurs before the age of ten. The initiative of this desire is found either in stories told by friends who have traveled or in books. Among juvenile books the *Swiss Family Robinson* has the largest number of mentions by both boys and girls, and *Robinson Crusoe* has the largest number of mentions by boys. When this desire for travel is aroused in those who have the migratory instinct strongly developed, there are a few cases of starting out in search of runaway adventure. These, however, were chiefly children under ten, and nightfall proved a corrective to the spirit of adventure.[1] One case of running away from home at the age of fifteen was stated to have been inspired by this desire for travel, but, on the whole, the influence seems to have been beneficial. In 40 per cent. of the cases, desire to travel led to interest in reading books of travel, and in many cases this led to a love of history and kindred subjects. The influence of a book on the South Sea Islands in determining the career of an imaginative and home-loving child has been vividly described by Pierre Loti in his *Roman d'un enfant.* But while this desire for knowledge of new people, places, and things is so widespread, very few of the cases described in detail show indications of an interest sufficiently absorbing to prove a disturbing influence in the ordinary routine of life. Americans as a nation are accused of a restless desire for change, which is detrimental to the best interests of home life, but the interest in travel, which is one of the phases of curiosity, and most active during the

[1] Cf. L. W. Kline, "Truancy as Related to the Migratory Instinct," *Pedagogical Seminary*, Vol. V, pp. 381–420, January, 1898.

adolescent years, seems to have no necessary connection with the later development of nervous restlessness. It appears rather to be an intellectual development belonging to the age when the desire for new experiences of all kinds is characteristic.

In comparative psychology, though statements that certain *animals are curious* abound, no attempt has been made to trace the development of curiosity in either the ontogenetic or phylogenetic series, except, perhaps, by Romanes, who essayed to group animals at different levels, according to their psychic development, and to correlate these with the different stages of human development. Romanes places insects and spiders on his third level, and it is in this group that he places the first appearance of curiosity, but he gives as an example of insect curiosity the tendency to fly toward any bright light or shining surface. But there seems to be no sufficient reason for attributing this tendency to any psychic impulse, since it is explainable on a purely physiological basis. Even in the human infant we do not attribute the first turning of the eyes toward light to any psychic impulse, but interpret it as a physiological reflex. On the next higher level Romanes places fishes; and here, perhaps, we have some ground for attributing a psychological impulse, though Professor Sanford[1] considers even this somewhat doubtful. "They may, perhaps, possess the beginnings of curiosity, if the luring by light is not a physiological phenomena." Groos quotes Eimer as authority for the statement that some species of lizards are so curious that they may be captured by dangling a noose in front of them. A step higher, and the psychic development becomes unquestionable. We have abundant evidence of curiosity displayed by crows, canaries and parrots, and nightingales. A parrot with which some personal experiments were

[1] E. C. Sanford, "Psychic Life of Fishes," *International Quarterly*, Vol. VII, p. 330, No. 2, 1903.

made never failed to show curiosity in regard to the ticking of a clock. When placed on the mantel he invariably walked around it, examined it on all sides, stretched his neck to see the top of it, tried to look behind, and showed great excitement whenever he happened to get into a position where the tick was most plainly audible. Lloyd Morgan gives instances of curiosity in chicks, but considers their mental attitude as reducible to a simple "what," rather than "why," which involves more complex psychic factors. Cats, dogs, raccoons, goats, horses, cows, and deer all show curiosity in marked degree, and advantage of this fact is taken in hunting the latter by the method of luring by light. Scheitler calls the dog the most curious of animals, and calls attention to the fact that this trait greatly enhances his value as a watchdog, but most students of animals give the monkey precedence over all others in the development of this trait. Thorndike found that the attention of monkeys was very easily distracted, and considers the attention of animals as working always for immediate, practical associations and below the grade of the passive attention in human beings, which in its development is closely connected with the acquisition of a stock of free ideas. Groos considers curiosity the only purely intellectual form of playfulness in the animal world, and says, "It is apparently a special form of experimentation, and its psychologic accompaniment is attention, which is indeed a requisite to the exercise of the most important instincts."

In curiosity, attention loses the purely utilitarian function which it has in connection with the cravings of hunger, desire, and the necessity of avoiding danger, and becomes play. Groos ascribes the primary reason for this sort of playfulness to a necessity for mental exercise. But since the new object may always prove advantageous, it also aids in the preservation of the species. In the higher animals, manifestations of curiosity closely resemble those of the child. One of the monkeys, a

Macacus rhesus, formerly used by Mr. Kinnaman[1] in his experiments, showed his curiosity in an unmistakable way when a closed box, painted black on the inside, was placed in his cage. He immediately came to the end of the cage where it was placed, examined it closely, touched it cautiously, and finally picked it up and tried to open it. It came open rather suddenly and he dropped it and started back. His curiosity soon overcame his timidity, however, and he picked it up again, smelled it, bit it, put his hand, and finally his head, into it. In all this the monkey was closely paralleling the stages of curiosity shown by children, though his attention was less concentrated and he was more easily startled than is the case with children.

The larger aspect of interest and curiosity is almost coextensive with the range of educability; but it is believed that this paper marks a decidedly important advanced step toward a larger synthesis that has so long beckoned students of childhood, namely the determination of intellectual nascent stages. Curiosity is the apparent, now partial, now dominant, motive in many fields where its importance has never been adequately estimated. For instance, Kline[2] and Arnett[3] have shown that the truancy and runaway motives are, in part, due to curiosity to see the world. Partridge[4] has shown that many take their first drink, or, perhaps, even acquire their first experience of intoxication, to see how it tastes or how it feels, respectively. Curiosity is very manifest in the infant stages of acquaintance

[1] A. J. Kinnaman, "Mental Life of Two Macacus Rhesus Monkeys in Captivity," *American Journal of Psychology*, Vol. XIII, pp. 98–148, January, 1902.

[2] "Migratory Impulse," *American Journal of Psychology*, Vol. X, pp. 1–81, October, 1898.

[3] "Origin and Development of Home and the Love of Home," *Pedagogical Seminary*, Vol. IX, pp. 324–365, September, 1902.

[4] "The Psychology of Alcohol," *American Journal of Psychology*, Vol. XI, pp. 318–376, April, 1900.

with its own body.[1] Dawson[2] has given us suggestions for the order of development of interest in the personages and events and sentiments of the Bible. Many studies on the development of language and children show stages of curiosity concerning the form, meaning, or even origin of words. Interesting illustrations of this theme, too, especially as related to association, and causal and other types of reasoning, are shown in the data presented by H. W. Brown.[3] Studies of suggestibility and the quest of certainty, like those by M. H. Small,[4] show many outcrops of the same motive. How essentially attention is dominated by interest or curiosity all the laboratory and other studies of it show. How dangerous is the neglect of natural interest is elsewhere pointed out in the single field of physics.[5]

Important as we deem the results of this study, it is thus really only preliminary to a larger presentation of the characteristic outcrops of interest or the desire to know, which, when determined for successive ages and stages, will be the best and surest norm for ascertaining when all such matter can be taught with greatest economy and with most effectiveness, and will also shed great light upon methods of instruction. All this again shows very clearly how far we already are beyond the arid and abstract formulæ of Herbart. It may be that we shall sometime come to reflect that forcing knowledge upon unwilling minds that are unripe for it is immoral.

---

[1] G. S. Hall, " The Early Sense of Self," *American Journal of Psychology*, Vol. IX, pp. 351–395, April, 1898.

[2] " Children's Interest in the Bible," *Pedagogical Seminary*, Vol. VII, pp. 151–178, July, 1900.

[3] " Thoughts and Reasonings of Children," *Pedagogical Seminary*, Vol. II, pp. 358–396, December, 1893.

[4] *Pedagogical Seminary*, Vol. IV, pp. 176–220, December, 1896; and Vol. V, pp. 313–380, January, 1898.

[5] " High School Physics," *Pedagogical Seminary*, Vol. IX, p. 193.

A question uttered or unexpressed is a prayer for knowledge. The moment when it arises in the soul should be sacred, almost like that of the hour of visitation of the Holy Ghost to the religious teacher. Not to feed every normal curiosity the good teacher will consider recreancy to his duty.

Many questions, no doubt, arise in the average mind but once in an entire lifetime, and if the opportunity which they make is not promptly and effectively utilized, the bud of promise is forever blasted. Perhaps, in the future, education will realize the idea of being guided solely by these chief expressions of psychic need or want. For most of us there comes for a time, most commonly in very early adolescence, an all-sided, disinterested curiosity, which is the basis of liberal education, but which vanishes later and is succeeded by a second growth of interests, which are more and more tinged with utility, professional success, or individual advancement. When such studies as these shall be carried more fully into the later teens, this change from what we may call pure curiosity to that with an alloy of gain or advancement in it will be more clearly seen. Indeed, few people in any community illustrate up to full maturity what man as man most centrally wants to know. One great purpose of education is to so place and to so environ a few individuals that they shall thus illustrate the deeper tendencies of race advancement, so that their interests shall point as truly as the needle to the goal of human destiny. This, we grant, is a very difficult problem, only partially attainable. Even the child's theological interests, as here illustrated, are more or less factitious, and are very different in unknown and non-Christian lands and ages, and due to precocious doctrinal inculcation. They thus rest on a very different foundation, and have a very different culture value from the purely spontaneous interests in the varying phenomena and objects of nature, or even from that in things hidden, or in the mechanical secrets of toys, etc.

In summarizing the results of this study it appears that curiosity develops by gradual stages and is a fundamental factor in the development of attention.

Four stages of development may be recognized:

1. Passive staring, considered as a reflex with psychic accompaniment; manifested in infants as early as the second week of life.

2. Surprise, usually noted in the second month.

3. Wonder, which is observable about the end of the second month, the time when the accommodation of eye takes place.

4. Interrogation or curiosity proper, which begins to be manifested about the fifth month.

These last three stages are those recognized by Ribot.

The chief stimuli of curiosity during the first half year are those of sight. The order in which interest in other sensations develop is hearing, touch and muscle sensations, smell, and taste. These do not successively predominate but overlap, and sight, the first in order, is not subordinated as other interests develop.

Curiosity is manifested by (1) observation, passive and active; (2) experiments; (3) questions; (4) destructiveness; (5) desire to travel.

Aimless curiosity or inquisitiveness is, in normal children, usually a sign of fatigue, and this is also true of echolalia. When chronic, both these manifestations indicate neurotic tendencies associated with defective power of attention and lack of inhibitory control.

Curiosity is the active factor in the development of attention, and lack of it shows either mental deficiency or bad pedagogy.

Animals show the various stages in the development of curiosity, and manifest it by observation (as do human beings), experiment, and destructiveness, though it is probable that, except in the higher animals, the full stage of interrogation is never reached.

THEODATE L. SMITH
G. STANLEY HALL

BIBLIOGRAPHY

Compayré, Gabriel. Intellectual and Moral Development of the Child (translated by Mary E. Wilson). D. Appleton & Co., New York, 1896.

Darwin, Charles. "Biographical Sketch of an Infant Mind," *Mind*, Vol. II, pp. 285–294, July, 1877.

Darwin, Charles. Expression of Emotion in Man and Animals. D. Appleton & Co., New York, 1873. 374 pages.

Darwin, Charles. Descent of Man (2d edition). D. Appleton & Co., New York, 1903. 688 pages.

Groos, Karl. The Play of Animals (translated by Elizabeth L. Baldwin). D. Appleton & Co., New York, 1898. 341 pages.

Hall, Mrs. Winfield S. "The First Five Hundred Days of a Child's Life," *Child Study Monthly*, Vol. II, pp. 330–342, 394–407, 458–473, 522–537, 586–608, 1896–1897.

Hogan, Louise E. A Study of a Child. Harper & Brothers, New York, 1898. 219 pages.

James, William. Principles of Psychology, pp. 383–441. D. Appleton & Co., New York, 1890.

Keller, Helen A. The Story of My Life, pp. 22, 23. Doubleday, Page & Co., New York, 1904. 441 pages.

Moore, Mrs. Kathleen C. Mental Development of a Child, New York, 1896 (150 pages); also *Psychological Review, Monograph Supplements*, Vol. I, No. 3, 1896 (150 pages).

Morgan, C. Lloyd. Introduction to Comparative Psychology. W. Scott, Ltd., London, 1902. 382 pages.

Preyer, Wilhelm. Mind of the Child: Part I, The Senses and Will; Part II, The Development of the Intellect (translated by H. W. Brown). D. Appleton & Co., New York, 1888–1889. 2 vols.

Perez, Bernard. The First Three Years of Childhood. Bardeen, Syracuse and London, 1899. 294 pages.

Ribot, Th. Diseases of the Will (2d edition). Open Court Publishing Company, Chicago, 1896. 137 pages.

Ribot, Th. Psychology of Attention. Open Court Publishing Company, Chicago, 1890. 137 pages.

Ribot, Th. Psychology of the Emotions. W. Scott, Ltd., London, 1897. 455 pages.

Romanes, G. J. Mental Evolution in Animals. D. Appleton & Co., New York, 1900. 411 pages.

Romanes, G. J. Mental Evolution in Man. D. Appleton & Co., New York, 1889. 452 pages.

Shinn, Milicent W. Biography of a Baby. Houghton, Mifflin & Co., Boston and New York, 1900. 247 pages.

Shinn, Milicent W. Notes on the Development of a Child, University of California Studies, Berkeley, California, 1893-1899.

Sully, James. The Human Mind, Vol. II, pp. 122-171. Longmans, Green & Co., New York, 1892.

Sully, James. Studies of Childhood. D. Appleton & Co., New York, 1896. 193 pages.

Stout, G. F. Manual of Psychology, pp. 393-434. Hinds, Noble & Co., New York, 1899. 643 pages.

Thorndike, Edward L. "Mental Life of Monkeys," *Psychological Review, Monograph Supplements*, Vol. III, No. 5, 1901. 57 pages.

Thorndike, Edward L. Animal Intelligence. Macmillan, New York, 1898.

Thorndike, Edward L. "Intelligence of Monkeys," *Popular Science Monthly*, Vol. LIX, pp. 273-279, July, 1901.

Wundt, Wilhelm. Lectures on Human and Animal Psychology (translated by Creighton and Titchener). Macmillan, London and New York, 1894. 454 pages.

THE STORY OF A SAND PILE

The town of B—— is a quiet community of a few score families of farmers, some twenty or thirty miles from Boston. Among the few cottagers who spend the summer months there is the Rev. Dr. A——, a professor at Cambridge, Massachusetts, and widely known as an author. The family consists of Mrs. A—— and two bright, healthy boys, now fourteen and twelve, whom I will here call, respectively, Harry and Jack. Nine summers ago the mother persisted, not without some inconvenience, in having a load of fine clean sand hauled from a distant beach and dumped in the yard for the children to play in. What follows might be called a history of that load of sand, which I will try to sketch in the most literal and unadorned way, as I saw and heard of it, for the sake of its unique educational interest.

The "sand pile" at once became, as every one who has read Fröbel or observed childish play would have expected, the one bright focus of attraction, beside which all other boyish interests gradually paled. Wells and tunnels; hills and roads like those in town; islands and capes and bays with imagined water; rough pictures drawn with sticks; scenes half reproduced in the damp, plastic sand and completed in fancy; mines of ore and coal, and quarries of stone, buried to be rediscovered and carted to imaginary markets, and later a more elaborate half-dug and half-stoned species of cave dwelling or ice house — beyond such constructions the boys probably did not go for the first summer or two. The first and oldest "house," of which tradition survives, was a board pegged up on edge with another slanted against it, under which toys were taken from the nursery to be sheltered from

showers. Next came those made of two bricks and a board.
The parents wisely refrained from suggestions, and left the
hand and fancy of the boys to educate each other under the
tuition of the mysterious play instinct.

One day a small knot of half-rotten wood was found, a part
of which suggested to Harry the eye and head of a horse, and
a horse it at once became, though it had nothing to suggest
tail or legs. In another artificial horse soon attempted these
were represented by roughly whittled projections. Gradually
wooden horses, made in spans for firmer standing on uneven
ground, held together by a kind of Siamese-twins commissure,
to which vehicles could be conveniently attached, were evolved.
These horses were perhaps two inches long, with thread tail and
mane, pin-head eyes, and a mere bulb, like the Darwinian
protuberance on the infolded margin of the human helix, for
an ear. For the last two or three years this form has become
rigidly conventionalized, and horses are reproduced by the
jig saw as the needs of the community require, with Chinese
fidelity to this pattern. Cows and oxen, with the characteristic distinctions in external form strongly accented, were
drawn on paper or pasteboard and then cut or sawed into shape
in wood. Those first made proved too small compared with
later standards of size, and so were called yearlings and calves,
and larger "old steers" and "Vermont spotted cattle" were
made. Pigs and sheep came later, poultry alone being still
unshapely, hens consisting of mere squares of wood of prescribed size.

There is no further record or memory of the stages of
development of this community, for such it soon became by
the gradual addition of half a dozen other congenial boys from
the neighborhood, and I can only describe the buildings,
government, tools, money, trade, laws, men, etc., as I found
them. Nearly a dozen farms are laid out on one main and
several lesser streets, somewhat like those in town, each,

perhaps, five or six feet square, with tiny rows of stone for walls and fences, with pastures and mow lots, and fields planted with real beans, wheat, oats, and corn, which is topped before it has spindled, and with a vase or box for a flower garden. A prominent feature of these farms is at present the gates, which are admirably mortised and hung, and perhaps represent the high-water mark of skill in woodwork. This unique prominence of a single feature on which attention is concentrated is a typical mark of childish production; as a girl or boy is drawn with buttons, or a hat, or a pocket, or a man with a pipe, or a house with a keyhole, etc., strikingly predominant. The view of this Lilliputian settlement from the road is quite picturesque. Houses and barns are perhaps a foot high, and there is a flagpole, painted and sanded at the base to prevent the tiny inhabitants from whittling it, with a joint, and cords to raise and lower the flag, and a peg ladder, the top towering perhaps two feet above the ground. There are pig pens with quite well-carved troughs, and hen yards with wire-net fences, and a very undeveloped system of sewerage, suggested by a disastrous shower and centering in a sunken tomato can.

Great attention has been bestowed on the barns. On one side are stanchions for cows, with stalls for horses and others for yoked cattle, and stairs and lofts for hay, and genuine slanting roofs, and doors that clamp and bar inside against horse thieves. One boy built a cupola and another a windmill, painted in many colors, on his barn, but this fashion did not take. The doors are not large enough for the boys' hands to enter with facility, and so the whole building was made to lift up from its floor on hinges. Hay is cut and dried, and sometimes stored in mows on scaffolds, while poorer hay is stacked out of doors about a skewer for a stack pole. More recently, however, most hay is put up in pressed bales, about one by two inches, for market, or to be kept over for another year. Most other crops that are planted do not come to maturity, and so wheat, beans, corn, oats, etc., are bagged and sold or stored "as if" they had been grown by the seller. In this community, as often in real life in New England, the barn is often far larger, more expensive, and attracts more interest than the house. Only the outsides of the latter are attended to. The youngest boy alone, despite some ridicule for his girlishness, has embellished his house within, and set out moss and planted flower beds and vines without. A young lady visitor thoughtlessly introduced a taste for luxury by painting not only shingles on the roof and bricks into the chimney, but lace curtains into the windows of one house. Another boy proprietor dug and stoned up a well, made a long sweep and hung it with a counterweight in a natural crotch, and made a bucket of a cherry stone.

The adult population of this community are men and women about two and a half inches tall, whittled out of wood. The women stand on a base made by their broad skirts, and the men stand on ground, or on carts, etc., by means of a pin projecting from the feet, by which they can be stuck up anywhere. One or both arms are sometimes made to move, but otherwise they are very roughly manufactured. They have been kept for years, are named Bill Murphy, Charles Stoughton, Peter Dana, etc., from real men in town, and each have families, etc. Each boy represents one of these families, but more particularly the head of it, whose name he takes, and whom he talks both to and for, nasally, as does the original Bill Murphy, etc. In fact, the personality of the boys is strangely merged in that of these little idols or fetiches. If it is heard that the original Farmer Murphy has done anything disreputable, — cheated in a horse trade, for instance, — the other boys reproach or threaten with expulsion the boy who represents the wooden Murphy, greatly to his chagrin. The leg of one wooden man was blown off by a toy cannon accidentally one Fourth of July, and he was given up as dead, but found some months later, and supplied with a new leg by the carpenter doctor. The boys get up at night to bring these men in if they get left out accidentally, keeping them in the house if they catch cold by such exposure, take them along in their pockets if they go to the city or on a pleasure trip, send them in letters and express packages to distant friends, to be returned, in order that they may be said to have been to this or that place. The best man has traveled most, keeps his farm in best order, has the most joints in his body, keeps dressed in the best coat of paint, represents the best farmer in town, and is represented by the best boy. The sentiment toward these little figures is more judicial and paternal than that of little girls for dolls. Their smallness seems to add a charm akin to that of largeness in a doll for girls. If a new boy enters the community, or if accident or general consent or any other cause requires the production of new men, they are still made roughly after the old patterns, and far below the best skill the boys have now acquired in woodwork. Two years ago, when clothes began to be painted on these figures, those who were created as wage workers were painted with overalls. The question at once arose whether these men should be allowed to come into the house with their employers without a change of garments, which involved, of course, a new coat of paint. It was decided that they must live apart by themselves. Thus the introduction of hired men marked the beginning of a system of castes. The boys' own wishes and thoughts are often, especially if of a kind that involves a little self-consciousness or restraint, expressed by saying half seriously that the little figure wishes to do this, or thinks that, etc. Their supposed relation to one another in the high tide of the play spirit dominates the actual relation of the boys to one another, as two little girls who were sisters were overheard saying, " Let's play we are sisters," almost as if the play made that relation more real than the fact.

Prominent among the benefits the " sand-pile " community has brought the boys is the industrial training it has involved, particularly in woodwork. In this respect preparation for the summer is made to enliven the long Cambridge winters. The evolution of the plow, e.g., is as follows : It began as a rough, pointed paddle, then came a pole drawn by the small end with a stiff branch cut long and sharpened, then a rough share, then a metallic point, then two handles, then a knife, etc. Thus the plow, which fortunately did not get stereotyped early, has passed through a number of stages still to be seen, and is now quite complete in form. In the case of the hoe and ax, wood has supplanted metal because more easily and correctly fashioned. The rake, shovel, pick, harrow, dray, pitchfork, snow shovel, ladder, stone boat, beetle, wedge, and gravel sieve, all show stages of improvement, and sometimes involve some skill in shaping or adapting wire, tin, etc. These tools are all very small, and not for the most part adapted to much real use, and quite disproportionately large as compared with the size of houses and men. Milk cans, pulleys, wheelbarrows, carts, wagons, and harnesses are made with still more skill. Harnesses have real collars, hames, bit, bridle, and string lines. Wagons have wheels (made of a section of a large curtain stick or of checkerboard men), brakes, end boards, kingbolts, neaps and shafts, stakes for hay, a high seat for the driver, etc. They can be made to tip up, and include many varieties, as a milk cart with money box, a long timber truck, market wagon, and others. Could the stages of evolution through which a few of these implements of farm work have passed be pinned on cards in their order of development and photographed, they would quite likely reflect in some respects the progress of mankind in their production. It is in connection with these products mainly that a patent office has been proposed, but up to the close of last season not established.

Carpentry has thus proved the most successful industry, and has of late slowly come to be largely the monopoly of Harry, who probably has most skill and the best tools. One boy made a croquet set of very miniature proportions. Another established brickworks, based on a careful study of those in Cambridge ; but the products of his yard, though admirably done, have not come into demand as building material. Another attempted molding and pottery, including baking, but with rather poor success. A tiny newspaper some three inches square, devoted entirely to the affairs of the " sand pile," was started, with seven subscribers, at a dollar per month in their peculiar currency, but the labor of duplicating soon caused its abandonment. At one time candles were manufactured in tiny molds. Two sailing vessels, the *Argonaut* and *Neptune*, were made and raced till boom and gaff were broken. Tiny pine trees were set out, and ash fertilizers prepared and used for crops. The farmers near by go to a distant meadow to cut marsh hay at low tide, and are gone overnight. This the boys parodied with a damp spot of mow land as a marsh, and the overnight part was represented by the interval of dinner. Cord wood of several lengths, with an inch representing a foot, and with both cleft and trash varieties, was cut down, piled, and sold. On one occasion the boys were observed creeping about one eighth of a mile and back, propelling their tiny horses held between their fingers, each span drawing a cart loaded with their wood. The functions of carpenter and doctor are fused in one, the office of the latter being chiefly to mend broken limbs, splints being used, but the regenerative force of nature being represented by the drying of glue.

Trade centered in the grocery store, of which Jack was one proprietor, the name of the puppet he represented being painted on the sign. A toy watch was hung in the gable to represent the clock over Faneuil Hall market, and a clay watchdog was on guard by night. Cans of pickles, partridge berries, and huckleberries were put up in small glass bottles; candy was sold by the barrel; tomatoes were represented by red barberries, and watermelons by butternuts. Grass put up in bags for cows and horses was sold by weight on a pair of small scales. Shelves and counters and a canvas-topped market wagon were the chief features of this establishment. Its goods were, however, for the most part, in a sense unreal, its business declined until at last its proprietors were obliged to declare themselves bankrupt, and a bill of sale and auction closed its career.

The need of a measure of value and a medium of exchange was felt early in the history of the "sand pile." A special kind of cardboard was procured, and later, as this material was found not to be proof against counterfeiting, a species of felt was used, out of which small ellipsoidal currency was cut with a gouge of peculiar curvature. These coins were of two sizes, representing dollars and half dollars, respectively. At the beginning of the first season ninety dollars and fifty half dollars were given to each boy, and the gouge and felt, representing mint and bullion, laid away, thus insuring a strictly limited circulation. This currency became so very real that actual silver dollars and half dollars were said, I know not how correctly, to have been vainly offered for their felt counterparts, the fluctuations in the silver value of which recorded the varying intensity of the play spirit of the "sand pile." When the grocer failed he became really a pauper on the community. He was, I think, the youngest boy, and his monetary ventures had gradually relieved him of his entire capital. He was aided in little ways, and meetings were held to discuss the best way of relieving him. One proposition was a general pro-rata subscription; another was a communistic redistribution of the money of the community. These schemes were successfully opposed, however, and it was at last agreed to inflate their first currency by issuing enough money to give each boy an additional sum of ten dollars. While this matter was under discussion, and redistribution was expected by some, prices were affected, and a few sales were made at prices so high as to cause embarrassment later.

Laws were enacted only to meet some pressing necessity. Town meetings were summoned by an elected crier, who shouted, " Ding dong, come to town meeting ! " These assemblages were at first held on and about the fence or near their hotel, each boy holding his little wooden dummy in his hand and turning up its arm when ayes or noes were called. Later a bell and hall were provided. The officers elected were president, flagman, whose duty it was to keep the flagpole in order and the flag flying, a pound-keeper to look after stray animals carelessly left lying about or lost by other boys, a surveyor of roads, whose duties were sometimes considerable after a shower, a janitor for the hall, and a sprinkler and waterer of crops, etc. A scheme of taxation was proposed, but as it was to be based mainly on land, and as the task of measuring the sometimes irregularly laid out farms was considerable, it was never carried out. A system of fines was also adopted, the enforcement of which led to quarrels and was stopped by parental interventions. A jail and a grogshop shared a similar fate. So great was the influence of proceedings in this community upon the general direction of interest and attention that it was feared that an undesirable degree of knowledge of criminality and intemperance would be fostered if these latter institutions were allowed to develop. It was at these meetings that the size of a cord of wood and an acre of land was settled. Judicial as well as legislative functions appertained to these meetings. After a firecracker had blown up a house a law was passed limiting the proximity to the village at which fireworks should be permissible. A big squirt gun served as a fire engine, and trouble was at once imminent as to who should control and use it, till it was enacted that it should be under the control of the boy whose buildings were burning. One boy was tried for beating his horses with a pitchfork, and another for taking down the pound wall and leading out his cattle without paying the fine. Railroads were repeatedly proposed, but never constructed, since the earliest days of the " sand pile," when they did exist for a short time, for the double reason that they would interfere with teaming, which was on the whole still more interesting, and because every boy would want to be conductor and president of the company.

"Why do you have no church ? " the boys were asked. " Because," they replied, " we are not allowed to play in the ' sand pile ' on Sunday, but have to go to church." " And why have you no school ? " " Why," said they, exultingly, " it is vacation, and we don't have to go to school."

The geography of the surrounding region is not well developed. The house in which the parents lived is called Cambridge, its piazza is Concord. A gully made by a water spout is Rowley. Another smaller sand pile once started near by is West B——. A neighbor's house, more recent, is Vermont. A place where worms are dug for fishing is called Snakeville, and another spot where some Oswego starch boxes once lay is Oswego. Boston is a neighboring settlement. The topographical imagination of these boys is far less developed than in the case of a group of school children the writer once knew, who played for years about a marsh half submerged in spots by high tide, and who had named continents, capes, bays, lakes, rivers, islands, promontories, to the number of perhaps several score, from real or fancied resemblance to great features of the world's surface on the map, and who had in a number of cases helped out resemblances by digging, and who carried on a brisk commerce between leading ports for entire summers, with many details and circumstances of real trade.

The conservatism of Harry and Jack and the boys that gathered about them was shown even in the name " sand pile," which the whole enterprise still bears. This designation is now entirely inappropriate, for all the sand originally dumped on the spot has been carefully removed and its place filled in with loam. Each spring, when the houses, barns, etc., are brought out and set up, the traditions of the preceding year are carefully observed in laying out the streets. Most boys hold that the monetary relations of the previous year should continue over to the new season, the rich at the close of the last year starting rich this year. This view generally prevails against the theory of an annual year of jubilee, and a release from last year's debts, that the poorer boys uphold. All the boys in town, even those who do not belong to the " sand pile," are not only greatly interested, but decidedly more proud than envious of it. It seems remarkable that during all the years of its existence no boy has been mean enough to injure or plunder it at night, or angry enough to demolish anything of importance. This latter is, of course, in part due to the gradual habit of settling matters of dispute that are wont to be brought to an issue with fists and feet or by meetings and speeches. The accumulation of values here as elsewhere begets not only conservatism but mutual forbearance and consideration. Most destructive in the " sand pile " are little girls, who quite fail to appreciate it, save in spots, as it were, and are therefore as far as possible excluded.

The institution is in general very real to the boys, though in different degrees to different boys, and some parts and some periods of it more so than others. Sometimes they are so in earnest that they rise early to play before breakfast. They pour out grain for the cattle, and tip them up on their noses that they may eat, and then must clean up after them. The cattle "promise" the younger boys not to eat the beans, and the wooden figures never talk about the boys behind their backs, for "they told us so," said one. Of all the names in use in the "sand pile," but one has been invented, all the rest having been copied from real persons about them. They are little troubled by incongruities of size. Some barns cover between one and two acres, and a horse could almost be ground up and put into a bushel measure, etc. Yet in a general way relative sizes are fairly preserved. It is a striking feature, to which I have observed no exception, that the more finished and like reality the objects became, the less interest the boys had in them. As the tools, houses, etc., acquired feature after feature of verisimilitude, the sphere of the imagination was restricted, as it is with too finished toys, and thus one of the chief charms of play was lost. Often the entire day was spent with almost no intermission in the business of the "sand pile," and all went very pleasantly when perfect harmony reigned. The boys most absorbed have devoted most of their playtime of nearly every day for several summers to its very diversified direct and indirect interests.

As boys reach the age of fourteen, more or less, the "sand-pile" gradually loses its charm, and seems childish and unreal. One member of the circle was, I think, fifteen, and had become quite alive to its fictitious nature. Unimaginative boys have proved mischievous and a source of constant annoyance to those who took everything in dead earnest. Thus it has been realized that to admit aliens indiscriminately, or especially boys who had begun to imagine themselves young gentlemen, was dangerous. Indeed, I fancy that the golden age of this ideal little republic has already passed, and that a period of over-refinement and enervating luxury is likely, if it has not done so with the close of the last summer, to end its career. It was known that I was to visit it in the fall again and perhaps write a brief sketch of it; it was decked out to be photographed; the young lady with her æsthetic paint brush had introduced new ideals, for paint decorates bad woodwork; the " sand pile," being near the roadside, attracted more and more notice. The carpenter took to making miniature saws, sawhorses, squares, screw-drivers, planes, vices, and other tools, copying his own tools for beauty more than for use ; and, in short, a gradual self-consciousness supervened, so that the boys came to have in mind the applause of adult spectators as well as their own pure interest. They have long been wont to call themselves, in some relations to their wooden figures, the *giants* — somewhat as their parents, in a sense, represent the blind fate that rules Jove himself, when they have occasion, as is most rare, to interfere. I thought that I observed that the giants were more high-handed, and prone to intervene in the natural working out of problems and events, as a miracle-working Providence is sometimes said to break in on the order of nature. There seemed to be a slowly decreasing autonomy, heralding the decline of full-blooded boyishness and the far-away dawn of a new and reconstructed adolescent consciousness.

Still, when the inevitable return to Cambridge and school comes at last, the boys, it is said, seem for some time to be left with less eager interest in events, and to be some time in getting up as strong a zest for anything else. It is not that they become indifferent or pessimistic in the least degree, yet possibly life seems a little cheap and servile. They tried to colonize the " sand pile " there, but Cambridge is too large to oversee and copy, and they were soon lost in trying to light their houses at night from within, and in constructing a system of drainage and sewerage, etc., and gave it up to spend playtime in the less-absorbing ways of following and imitating the college ball games, and making houses, horses, and new inventions for next summer's " sand pile."

On the whole, the "sand pile" has, in the opinion of the parents, been of about as much yearly educational value to the boys as the eight months of school. Very many problems that puzzle older brains have been met in simpler terms and solved wisely and well. The spirit and habit of active and even prying observation has been greatly quickened. Industrial processes, institutions, and methods of administration and organization have been appropriated and put into practice. The boys have grown more companionable and rational, learned many a lesson of self-control, and developed a spirit of self-help. The parents have been enabled to control indirectly the associations of their boys, and, in a very mixed boy community, to have them in a measure under observation without in the least restricting their freedom. The habit of loafing, and the evils that attend it, has been avoided, a strong practical and even industrial bent has been given to their development, and much social morality has been taught in the often complicated manner of living with others that has been evolved. Finally, this may perhaps be called one illustration of the education according to *nature* we so often hear and speak of. Each element in this vast variety of interests is an organic part of a comprehensive whole, compared with which the concentrative methodic unities of Ziller seem artificial, and, as Bacon said of scholastic methods, very inadequate to subtility of nature. All the power of motive arising from a large surface of interest is here turned on to the smallest part. Had the elements of all the subjects involved in the "sand pile" — industrial, administrative, moral, geographical, mathematical, etc. — been taught separately and as mere school exercises, the result would have been worry, waste, and chaos. Here is perfect mental sanity and unity, but with more variety than in the most heterogeneous and soul-disintegrating school curriculum. The unity of all the diverse interests and activities of the "sand pile" is, as it always is, ideal. There is nothing so practical in education as the ideal, nor so ideal as the practical. This means not less that brain work and hand work should go together than that the general and special must help each other in order to produce the best results. As boys are quickened by the imagination to realize their conceptions of adult life, so men are best stimulated to greatest efforts by striving to realize the highest human ideals, whether these are actualized in the lives of the best men, found in the best pages of history, or are the highest legitimate, though yet unrealized, ideals of tradition and the future.

G. STANLEY HALL

BIBLIOGRAPHY

Baldwin, James M. Social and Ethical Interpretations in Mental Development. Macmillan, New York and London, 1897. 574 pages.

Bradley, John E. "Relation of Play to Character," *Education*, Vol. XIX, pp. 406–413, 1898–1899.

Burnett, Frances Hodgson. The One I knew Best of All. Charles Scribner's Sons, New York, 1893. 325 pages.

Croswell, Thomas R. "Amusements of Worcester School Children," *Pedagogical Seminary*, Vol. VI, pp. 314–371, September, 1899.

Howells, William D. A Boy's Town. Harper & Brothers, New York, 1890. 247 pages.

Johnson, George E. "Education by Plays and Games," *Pedagogical Seminary*, Vol. III, pp. 97–133, October, 1894.

Johnson, John. Rudimentary Society among Boys, Johns Hopkins University Studies in Historical and Political Science, Vol. II, pp. 495–496, Baltimore, 1884.

Sheldon, Henry D. "The Institutional Activities of American Children," *American Journal of Psychology*, Vol. IX, pp. 425–448, July, 1898.

Stuart, Mrs. Ruth McEnery. Sonny: A Christmas Guest. The Century Co., New York, 1898. 135 pages.

A STUDY OF DOLLS[1]

Dolls have so long been one of the chief toys of children, and are now so nearly universal among both savage and civilized peoples, that it is singular that no serious attempt has ever been made to study them. The topic of this paper is not only relatively new, but the field it opens is one of vast complexity, many-sided interest, and of the greatest significance both for psychology and pedagogy. When a thoughtful mother asks what is the best form, size, material, amount of elaborateness or mechanical devices, dress, paraphernalia, degree of abandon in doll play, proper and improper imitations of human life, whether doll play is instinctive with and good for boys as well as girls, or for any generalizations concerning dolls' names, doll families, dolls' diseases, the age at which the doll instinct is strongest, when it legitimately declines, whether paper dolls precede, follow, or coexist with dolls of three dimensions, doll anatomy, doll psychology, the real source of the many instincts that are expressed in doll play, its form among savage races, whether it is related to idolatry, and if so, how, — for answer to nearly all these problems one would search the meager and fragmentary doll literature in vain. Indeed, this paper, imperfect as it is, is the first to call attention to the importance of a strangely neglected, new, but exceedingly rich psychogenetic field.

It was considerations like these that led one of us (G. S. H.), after a careful preliminary survey based on informal examinations of many children of different ages, in which he was greatly aided by Miss Sara E. Wiltse, to print and circulate

[1] Reprinted in abridged form from *Pedagogical Seminary*, Vol. IV, pp. 129–175, December, 1896.

among about eight hundred teachers and parents a questionnaire which brought the following returns: Miss Lillie Williams, State Normal School, New Jersey, 203 papers; St. George's High School, Edinburgh, Scotland, 67; Miss Jennie B. Merrill, New York City, 53; N. Y., 105; Miss S. E. Wiltse, 26; Miss Mary White, 18; and 176 from miscellaneous sources, making in all 648. These returns were of very varied degrees of merit. Some were long letters of reminiscence by adults, some were observations by mothers, and others were of the doll history of individual children. There were also school compositions by pupils of high and normal schools; 94 boys were reported on, the rest were girls; 96 were reminiscences, and the majority were written by females between fourteen and twenty-four. Altogether this constituted a stack of thousands of pages of manuscript. After a considerable time spent by both of us in a preliminary survey of this material, it was decided that, intractable, and lacking in uniformity as it was, it merited as careful a statistical treatment as could be given it, and this laborious task was finally undertaken by one of us (A. C. E.), who also conducted quite a voluminous correspondence, gathered the literary references with careful epitomes thereof, selected and condensed typical cases from the returns, preserving every salient phrase and incident, and issued a supplementary syllabus to get better statistical results.

These latter returns were given to Dr. Hall, under whose supervision they were tabulated, and to whom Mr. Ellis's tables, correspondence, digests, conclusions, suggestions, and everything else were turned over, and who must therefore bear the responsibility of the attempt herewith made to present such account of all these varied data as he is able to do under limitations of both time and space, which are such as leave much to be desired. He has also freely added inferences, data, etc.

MATERIAL OF WHICH DOLLS ARE MADE, SUBSTITUTES, AND PROXIES

Of 845 children, with 989 preferences, between the ages of three and twelve, 191 preferred wax dolls; 163, paper dolls; 153, china dolls; 144, rag dolls; 116, bisque dolls; 83, china and cloth dolls; 69, rubber dolls; 12, china and kid dolls; 11, pasteboard dolls; 7, plaster of Paris dolls; 6, wood dolls; 3, knit dolls; while a few each preferred papier-maché, clay, glass, cotton, tin, celluloid, French, Japanese, brownie, Chinese, sailor, negro, Eskimo dolls, etc. Many children gave several as equally desirable, or their preferences changed and many preferred the substitute to the real doll.

We have grouped as substitutes objects used and treated by children as if they were dolls. Such treatment always involves ascribing more or less psychic qualities to the object, and treating it as if it were an animate or sentient thing. Nothing illustrates the strength of the doll instinct and the vigor of the animistic fancy like the following list of doll substitutes. In answers to the first syllabus, pillows were treated as dolls by 39 children, who often tied strings around the middle of the pillow, using a shawl for the skirt; sticks, sometimes dressed in flowers, leaves, and twisted grass were used by 29; bottles, filled with different-colored water and called different people, some with doll-head corks, by 24; cob or ear of corn (red ears favored, corn silk for the hair, a daisy perhaps serving for a hat) by 19; dogs by 18; cats and kittens by 15; shawls by 14; flowers by 12; clothespins (one a sailor, one a woman, sometimes both, used as servants) by 11; blocks by 9; children by 7; pieces of cloth by 7; daisies (taking off all but two petals, marking eyes, and making grass mothers) by 6; newspapers by 6; stuffed elephants (seemed like a real baby) by 6; clothes pegs by 5; peanuts by 5; sticks of wood by 5; apples by 4; clay pipes by 4; kindergarten material by 4; handkerchiefs by 4; mud and clay by 4; chairs and stools by 3; buttons by 3; potatoes (one end the head, with eyes, matches used for arms and legs) by 3; wishbones by 3; nine-pins by 3; squashes by 3; toothpicks by 3; vegetables by 3; yarn strings by 3. The following are each mentioned twice as having been used as dolls: acorns, aprons, bootjacks, feathers, doughnuts, cucumbers, spools, shells, pumpkins (dressed in own clothes), towels (knotted in the middle), rubber balls, brooms (dressed in bolster case), nails, bedposts, sticks of candy (dressed), button hooks, keys, and umbrellas.

The following are each mentioned once as doll substitutes: box, jug, coat, orange peel, cribbage peg, chicken, whisk broom, board with face painted on it, croquet ball, dish top, finger of a person dressed as doll, hand dressed as doll, with thumb and finger wrapped up for arms, water bottle, celery, one corner of a blanket (the other was mother), log, shoe, curtain tassel, roll of batting, bundle from the store, turkey wing named Dinah, washboard (two legs, so much like a man), wooden spoon, weed, piece of lath, salt bag stuffed, fish, piece of Porterhouse steak, sweet potato, stuffed stocking, stuffed cat, hitching post (so dressed up as to scare horses), stick of stove wood, tongs, toy monkey, radish, scissors in a spool, sheet, shoulder blanket, stone block, spoon, petunia (stem pushed through for head and neck), pin, pronged stick (looked like arms and legs), linen book rolled up and marked, knife, fork and spoon (called servants), knitting needles, lead pencil, half-burned matches (black for hair), marbles, oranges, penholder, beets, grapes (pulps for heads, splints for arms and legs, set sailing in cucumber boats), geraniums, green peaches (with pins for arms and legs), gateposts (by a party of children), gourds, hickory nuts, hollyhocks, horse-chestnuts (pin for arms and legs), cuffs rolled up, dress folded, fuchsia, feather, forks, glass, corn husks, beans, berries, cradle quilt, carrot, crochet hook, hairbrush, cane, cricket, clamp, carpenter's plane, axle of toy cart, a bench, books, balls, and bric-a-brac.

In reply to the supplementary questions, out of 579 children 57 had used a cat as a doll; 41, clothespins; 26, sticks; 21, vegetables; 20, a pillow. Only 26 of all these were boys. As an instance of flower dolls one correspondent writes:

> I often took pansies for dolls because of their human faces; the rose I revered too much to play with, it was like my best wax doll, dressed in her prettiest, but always sitting in state in a big chair in some secluded corner where little visitors would not spy her out. I loved these nature dolls far better than the prettiest store dolls and ascribed special psychic qualities to them. The hepaticas seemed delicate children to be tenderly cared for but which soon drooped and faded. Violets were sturdy little ones which enjoyed a frolic and could be played with. The pansy was a willing, quick, bright flower child, the rose her grown-up sister, pretty, always charmingly dressed, but a quiet and sedate spectator. Violets were shy, good-natured children, but their pansy cousins were often naughty and would not play. The hepaticas were invalids and cripples who watched their livelier brothers and sisters and were entertained by stiff maiden aunts, marigolds, with long curls. The dahlias were colored servants and mammies; yellow violets were mischievous, fun-loving boys; sweet peas were the nurses with cap and kerchief on; the morning-glories were governesses and teachers. I often made little boats to give my flower dolls rides on the river. We built harbors, but in rough weather so many lives were lost that our pleasure was marred.

A kindergarten teacher writes:

> Nothing interests the little girls so much as to take a sphere, cylinder, or cube, wrapping it in a handkerchief to have "a baby," putting it into the long box of the second gift for the cradle; the boys often share this play.

A girl of three lavished her affection on a rude wooden footstool. It was set on end, its legs were arms and feet, and it was dressed, named "Stooly," nursed when sick, taken to bed and table, taught to read and write, fed, and various parts of the body imagined. A scratch on the joint was a sore. A child of two did the same with an old red slipper; another with a bottle with cork head, eyes, necklace; another with a bit of Parian marble; another with a covered brick, till her mother fancied living things grew uninteresting. My own boy had a long-continued craze for a big stuffed elephant and for a stove hook.[1]

Mud dolls are sometimes sick at first, but when dry are well. A shawl doll had no heart, so a ball was put in its folds so it could live and love.

Colored dolls sometimes need no clothing, "because they are so black nobody can see." A colored doll may be specially liked because others hate it, but fair hair and blue eyes are the favorites. When detected in " dollifying" very intractable objects children often show signs of self-consciousness and even shame. Besides the good and bad looks, dress, etc., of dolls, there are other influences that mediate likes and dislikes that we are not yet able to explain. A bottle resembled its giver and so took his name. Complimentary or uncomplimentary remarks of others often have much to do, but dispraise seems almost as apt to increase love as to diminish it. Real or fancied resemblance to people liked or disliked is a factor, and so is the feeling for the person who gave the doll, but why some dolls get all the whippings and others all the favors it is often very hard to ascertain.

The rudest doll has the great advantage of stimulating the imagination by giving it more to do than does the elaborately finished doll. It can also enter more fully into the child's life, because it can be played with more freely without danger of being soiled or injured. With rude dolls, too, the danger of both hypertrophy and of too great prolongation of the doll instinct is diminished. As between large and small dolls it would appear that dolls of from four to twelve inches are more common, and that interest in very large and very small dolls is later and less normal. It is opposed to large, elegant French dolls which teach love of dress and suggest luxury and dolls

[1] " Notes on the Study of Infants," *Pedagogical Seminary*, Vol. I, pp. 135–136, June, 1891.

with too many mechanical devices, as for winking, walking, speaking, and singing, against which the Russian Toy Congress has so strongly protested. Rather small and durable dolls, soft enough not to hurt, flexible, with two or three colors and not more than two or three plain garments, along with plenty of hints regarding clothespins, flowers, and other varied material, — something like this seems to be the suggestion for a first doll, with increasing variation in size, material, elaborateness, and number till the doll passion vanishes in two dimensions, with innumerable paper dolls, towards adolescence.

Dolls are often said to grow, more commonly large, but often when the owner is growing fast the doll grows small. A doll that squeaks is said to talk ; a coat of paint is a dress ; pictures of dolls sometimes take the place of dolls themselves ; new babies are sometimes treated as, and even thought to be, dolls ; children who have no proxies are few, and those who never played with dolls exceedingly rare. For dolls' hair, hemp ravelings, wool, split grass, corn silk, bits of fur, shavings, one's own hair, feathers, hair painted on, are used, and combing and dressing dolls' hair is a favorite occupation. Toilet accessories for this purpose are infrequent. Eyes are often made of buttons, seeds, pins ; rings are painted or inked on ; the brow is less cared for, but eyes that open and shut are greatly desired. Although the first feature to appear, young children care far less for eyes than for the softness and flexibility that appeals to touch. Open eyes are sometimes covered with bits of paper when the doll sleeps, or " to make it dark." The oldest child often cares less for dolls, or is interested in them later than the younger children. Dolls may lose the head, limbs, or body, and if they are replaced, generally, though not always, retain their identity. The first doll is sometimes remembered with peculiar interest. The function of joints suggests several interesting psychological problems regarding movement, will, expression, etc. A doll that can be taken everywhere as well as treated every way is a sure favorite. Cut-out pictures of the most varied things play an important rôle. Interest in school and books has an important influence on the doll passion, often eliminating it. Almost every conceivable whim and freak is illustrated here. Dolls that can be washed all over are often favorites.

Children are often under a long-continued delusion concerning the material of which dolls are made. Even long after it is *known* that they are wood, wax, etc., it is *felt* that they are of skin, flesh, etc. To find a doll's head hollow or that it is sawdust, while it suggests to very young children the same as contents of their own body, is with older children a frequent source of disenchantment and sometimes marks the sudden end of the doll period. In some cases allowances for the doll's moral or physical disabilities are made on account of the material of which they are found to consist. Wooden dolls will not bend; so are obstinate. Babies are differentiated as "meat dolls," but the differences of temperature are noted with strange rarity. It is singular how slow and late children learn what the "hard things" under their own skin (bones) are, and how easily, after a trifling injury, they think the body a bag of blood, or somehow get the impression that they are blown up and grow by inflation, or are themselves full of sawdust or of stomach, which fills even arms and legs. Discussions with skeptical brothers, who assert that the doll is nothing but wood, rubber, wax, etc., are often met with a resentment as keen as that vented upon missionaries who declare that idols are but stocks and stones, or, to come near home, upon those who assert cerebral, automatic, or necessitarian theories of the soul.

In our returns curly hair is preferred to straight; red cheeks are a special point of beauty, as are red knees in fewer cases. Boy dolls are only about one twelfth of all, and it is remarkable how few dolls are babies rather than little adults. Children are very prone to focus their interest upon peculiar slippers, shoes, the upward or downward look of the eyes, some peculiar turn and carriage of the head, some cute expression, "like a clown," "funny as if it was going to cry or shout," "stuck up," "smiling," "sweet," "tanned," etc. Some particular dress, name, complexion, or even defect is often focused on. Aversions follow the same rule.

Of 579 answers to questions 13, 14, and 15 of the supplementary paper, 463 reported for the age below five as follows: 266 preferred babies; 126, children; 71, adults. From five to ten, 314 reported, of whom 105 preferred babies; 159, children; 50, adult dolls. From ten to fifteen years of age, 45 reported a preference for babies; 64, for children; 32, for adults. On the whole, babies were thus preferred 416 times and children and adults 502 times. Children lead babies after the age of five, the ratio of adult dolls increasing with age. Boys' dolls are least often infants. Among 45 feeble-minded girls the ratio of dolls as babies is highest.

Out of 579 answers to the second questionnaire, 88 mentioned preference for blue eyes; 27, for brown eyes; and 8, for black eyes. As to hair preferences 118 mention light hair; 62, curly hair; 27, dark hair; 8, real hair; and 5, red hair; while 15 mention love for red cheeks; 7, nice teeth; 8, pretty hands or feet; 3, red lips.

Some children have a strong preference for old dolls, however ugly, and are indifferent to new ones, however fine; some love and some hate heirloom dolls. Some have sudden changes of affection; an old doll that has been long loved is perhaps suddenly repelled, thrown or given away, or even burned, and a new favorite chosen. Some never like lady or Japanese dolls, but their affection has a very limited range. Children with many dolls often have one for Sunday or one is queen, mother, or teacher; some profess to be absolutely impartial, loving all their dolls exactly alike. Often a sudden craze for doll dressmaking, hair combing, fantastic buttons, very small or very large dolls, shoes, hats, movable eyes, is reported, suggesting something akin to Kraft-Ebing's fetichism on the one hand, and the strange focusing on single features of face or dress seen in children's drawings on the other, and indicating how psychic growth tends to focalize, now in this, now in that direction. This we consider a point of great importance and suggestiveness for school work when fully wrought out. Mind may have its nascent periods like the body. Now interest centers on hair, which must be in long braids or otherwise done up, or be worn short, parted sideways, banged. Now it is a fat, round, baby face, plump red cheeks, teeth, pretty neck, joints, that are doted on. So it is with articles of dress, etc.

Psychic Qualities

The following psychic qualities are ascribed to dolls in the order of frequency of their recurrence, the figures indicating the number of cases: good 97, cold 54, jealous 46, bad 45, angry 38, naughty 36, loving 35 (bad and naughty together, equaling 81, should thus really be second in order), tired 33, pain 27, crying 18, feels 16, clean 15, feels warm 12, sleepy 12, tidy 12, cross 10, hungry 8, quiet 6, proud 6, sorrowing 6, mischievous 6, feeling hurt 6, stupid 6, modest 4, lonesome 4, kind 4, desiring something 4, dirty 4, patient 4, taste 4, seeing 3, talkative 3, obedient 3, smell 2, truthful 2, thoughtful 2, sly 2, stubborn 2, "sassy" 2. The following psychic qualities, as indicated by the following expressions, were fully brought out in individual cases: comfortable, contented, cleanly, blushing, honest, gentle, frightened, ill at ease, ladylike, makes faces, sings, scolds, sneers, is full of life, troublesome, too thoughtful, pure, proper, moral, lying, well educated, religious, prone to run away, democrat, Presbyterian, rich, Baptist, idiotic.

Of the 579 answers to the supplementary syllabus, question 26 foots up as follows : 230 children thought their dolls good ; 202 thought they felt cold ; 185, that they could love ; 183, that they felt tired ; 161, that they could be hungry ; 135, that they were sometimes bad ; 77, that they were jealous ; 58, that they hated. The smallest proportion of girls ascribing these qualities to dolls were over thirteen, and next least come the feeble-minded children.

Although these sixty-five terms can hardly be designated as so many qualities, they, too, open a rich field for psychology. Interesting essays are waiting to be written on such topics as modesty for dolls, what constitutes their goodness and badness, its relation to good and bad looks, being good and bad all the time and alternating, doll penalties, their sense of fatigue, their power to sit still, their stupidity and obstinacy, their propensity to sleep or be wakeful, their affection, etc. Out of 45 children specially cross-questioned, aged six to eight, 8 boys and 22 girls thought dolls felt cold, 1 boy and 13 girls thought not. Out of 34 children of the same age 4 boys and 18 girls thought dolls felt tired, 2 boys and 10 girls thought not. Out of 48 children of the same age, specially questioned, 3 boys and 8 girls thought dolls got angry, 6 boys and 25 girls said no, and 6 were in doubt. Of 45 children asked whether their dolls loved them, 10 boys and 29 girls thought yes, none no, 6 did not know. Of 45 children questioned 1 boy and 2 girls said dolls hated some one, 8 boys and 24 girls thought not, 2 boys and 8 girls were in doubt. Psychic qualities are often suggested by looks, dress, or fancied resemblance to some one thought to have good or bad qualities, while colored dolls, brownies, German, Chinese, and other dolls are often fancied, especially by boys, because they are " funny " or exceptional.

Almost all doll play involves the assumption of psychic qualities, but a few illustrations are added:

F., 18. I went to dolls with all my childish trials and felt relieved when I had poured out my heart to them.

F., 16. I supposed they were real children and would talk to them and laugh.

F., 15. Her name is a real person's name, and she is just as real to me as a real baby.

F., 16. I thought my dolls had the same feelings as persons.

F., 17. How would you like to be thrown down like that?

F., 7. Dolly was very angry when I would n't let her go to see the other children. I knew that my dolls had vitality and mind. My baby doll gives me no rest day or night; she is better if I take her out.

F., 11. When I found dolly laying out on the ground I thought I could see tears in her eyes, she was so hungry and cold.

F., 14. Two of my dolls had their heads broken off, but this made no difference in my treatment, for they seemed endowed with life and feeling. One day we were invited to a party, and I would not let Rose (dolly) go, because she had been naughty, but she cried so, and said she would be good, that I let her go.

F., 12. Dolly had been naughty, and instead of taking her out to ride I made her sit in a chair all day.

F., 11. [A fifth-grade girl would kiss and "poor" her doll after spanking her, but once, after a specially severe punishment, was filled with remorse for days.] I talked to my doll as if it could hear, and thought it could.

F., 12. Cut off her Japanese doll's hair, so she could never go back to Japan.

F., 6. Cut her doll's hair, thinking it would grow again.

F., 12. Said to her dolly, "There, I have fixed baby's hair and she did n't cry. Can't you be as good?"

M., 7. Screamed, saying, "Mother, mend the doll's leg," thinking such surgery painful.

F., 13. Would put molasses on doll's mouth, and then punish her for stealing it.

F., 13. Knocked Chinese doll against a window for crying and broke it.

F., 9. Sings dolly to sleep with her favorite songs.

F., 12. I thought all my other dolls jealous of the finest one.

F., 4. Dolls are good or bad as she is. If corrected for bad language, her dolls use it.

F., 11. Said, "Dolly was never on the cars to enjoy it before, but always went in the trunk.

F., 3. Her dolly often wants to go to the water closet, and is tenderly put on the stool by her little mother.

F., 6. Has great fears her dolls will feel lonesome.

F., 4. Now, dolly, I would like to give you a bath, but I must go up and see that other baby bathed, — the real one, you know.

F., 4. Will my dolly ever grow up to be a lady doll?

DOLL'S FOOD AND FEEDING

In our returns 90 children fed their dolls with both liquid and solid food; 75 sat at the doll's table; 68 touched food to the doll's lips and then ate it themselves (some speak of chewing it for the doll), or put it in doll's hand to make believe she ate it; 45 give it milk (16 of whom imagined water to be milk, and then played nurse the doll in natural way); 36 distinctly imagined the food; 33 set the dolls at table with themselves; 31 imagined or pretended growth, 8 of whom were positive the doll grew, thinking dresses grew short, or pulled doll's legs and found her to measure more; 29 say they never fed dolls or that they couldn't eat; 23 touched food to doll's lips, then threw it away, or put it in doll's mouth and took it out again; 19 distinctly imagined hunger; 19 declared that dolls preferred certain kinds of food to others; 15 were strenuous in urging real hunger; 2 said the dolls looked hungry; 9 thought them hungry when they were so themselves; 13 poked food inside the dolls' heads, where sometimes it accumulated and spoiled; 1 broke doll's tooth trying to get food in; 1 broke a hole to do so; 12 really put liquid into the doll; 1 had a rubber ball in the back of the doll's head to squirt it out; 13 reported spells of great regularity in feeding; 11, constant regularity; 9 used only liquid food; 7, only solid; 6 imagined they ate without any agency of the child; 7 used empty plates and imagined the food; 6 thought some foods especially disagreed with dolls; 11 seemed to think dolls really starved if not fed; 6 gave foods according to the age; 3 put the food down the neck of the doll's dress; 4 poured liquid food on the front of the dress; 8 always gave the dolls the same food as they had; 1 saw a healthy look in her doll from having slept and eaten well.

The following foods are also mentioned mostly by children between the ages of five and eleven: milk 88 times, bread 75 times, cake 62 times, water 45, candy 33, crackers 27, potatoes 19, tea 18, meat 15, sugar 13, pie 13, fruit 13, apples 12, butter 9, ice cream 8, cookies 7, all kinds of food 7, mud pies 6, coffee 5, sweetened water 5, dirt 3, gingerbread 3, grapes 3, nuts 3, strawberries 3, biscuit 3, apple juice 2, puddings 4, oranges 4, salt 4. The following were mentioned by two children: apple sauce, chicken, chalk and water, flour and water, gravy, cheese, chocolate, eggs, flowers, fish, mustard, lemonade, leaves, jelly, sand (for food, for flour, for sugar), soup, sweets. The following were mentioned once each: canned corn, blacking, beefsteak, buttons, brown paper, brick dust and water, boards in thin slices, beans, acorns, cocoanut, custard, cocoa, cinnamon water, crumbs, cream, flour, grass, green fruit, grasshopper (used as roast turkey), jumbles, lime, mush, mucilage and water, orange juice for soup, pears, pickles, pancakes, peaches, pictures of food (for paper dolls), rice, roast beef, starch and water for milk, also sticks, stones, sawdust, seed (in bottles for canned corn), soft food, soapsuds, vegetables.

Some children put food on the floor near the doll, others think it tries to eat or move the hand toward the food, forgets to eat, prefers cup, bottle, spoon, plate, glass, or to eat with fingers. Some are fed only when children play house, or Sunday mornings, or on coming home from school, or Saturdays, or going to bed, or between meals, or once a day. Out of 49, 19 say positively that dolls are never hungry, 14 are positive they are, 16 are in doubt, some think they are hungry all the time, others not often, or sometimes, or may be, or guess so. Out of other 49, 18 think dolls will not starve if not fed, 17 think they will starve if not fed, the others are divided.

F., 50. My dolls always went with me to the country, because they could not get out of the doll house to buy food.

F., 26. I fed one doll regularly until I found she would not grow, then only when I happened to think.

F., 6. Gives dolls flowers to smell for dessert.

F., 10. Once dolly got hungry and asked me for food. I fed liquids on a bib, thinking babies soaked it up that way.

F., 49. I put food on doll's mouth till it was dry, and thought the doll sucked out the juice.

F., 6. Uses doll biscuits, offering them first to the doll, then eating them herself.

F., 4. When her doll's head was knocked off, cried till uncle said he would fill it with meal before fastening it on; then thought she would get enough to eat and be well.

F., 14. Squeezed everything she could into a small mouth opening, fixed so it came out at the back.

F., 21. I used to worry lest I should not feed my doll and it would starve.

F., 4. Punished her doll by making it eat dirt, stones, coal, etc.

Dolls are weighed, and a few days later shot and stones are sewed in their clothes so they will weigh more. Children say of foods they especially like or dislike, that it is good or bad for their dolls. They often have recipes, as "flour, salt, sugar, milk, baked till brown." Sometimes the table ceremonies are elaborate, including grace, comments on food, courses, etc. At Thanksgiving dinners blocks are (play) boiled for turkey, round things for pies, and cakes and the rest pictures. When the food is not wholly imaginary, crackers may serve for every solid, and water for all drinks. Toy cook stoves are a great boon to children during the brewing and cooking age. If children eat too much or prefer the wrong kinds of food, dolls are accused of doing the same thing. They are counseled not to eat too fast, nor to be greedy, nor to slobber. If dolls are sick they must be fed accordingly. With some children the fire, stove, wood, dishes, and food are entirely imaginary; but more commonly something is imagined to be something else which it more or less resembles. Leaves and chips are plates, sticks are for spoons, bits of broken crockery are whole dishes, pieces of paper, petals of flowers, even figures on the carpet are dishes, so are shells and flat stones, acorns are cups and saucers, clothespins are sugar tongs, and napkins and every kind of table furniture is parodied. Soapsuds is ice cream, mud is chocolate cake, brick dust and water is tea, salt is imagined to be sugar, and sugar salt. Many kinds of seeds, buds, etc., are used. A barnyard weed has a tiny pod called cheese. Flag root and pods, birch bark, nuts, the honeyed ends of clover, honeysuckle, and other blossoms, green fruit, peppergrass, and many other things are used as dolls' food, and sometimes children are injured by eating what only their imagination makes wholesome.

SLEEP

329 papers speak of dolls' sleep. Most of these children are between six and eleven. 90 mentioned keeping others quiet while the dolls slept, 76 rocked the doll in their arms and sang to put it to sleep, and 76 put it in bed and did so, 55 rocked it to sleep without song, 37 used cradle and song, 33 took doll to bed with them, 12 expressly insisted that the doll really slept, 7 never put dolls to sleep, 3 shut the eyes of mechanical dolls only and called that sleep, 5 said that it made no difference to dolls whether there was quiet or not, 10 had dolls

say prayers, 2 said only dolls which closed eyes could go to sleep, 1 covered the eyes with paper, 4 rolled the doll in baby wagon, 7 jumped or trotted it, several told a story, others rocked it in a hammock, had it in the dark, shut it in a trunk, or thought it slept mostly when they were not present. 52 lullabys are named, "Rock-a-bye, Baby," leading all the rest, being mentioned 29 times. Others more often mentioned are the following: "Hush, my dear, lie still and slumber," "Bye, Baby Bunting," quite original lullabys, "La, la, la," "By-lo," Mother Goose rhymes, "Sweet and Low." Others mention "The Bowery," sacred songs, kindergarten songs, "Hush-a-bye, Baby," "Wee Willie Winkie," "Shut your eye, do not cry," Moody and Sankey songs, with exceptional things like "Rocked in the Cradle of the Deep," German songs, slumber songs, selections from *Pinafore* and other popular operas, "Comrades," and many others.

F., 10. I rock dolly and sing, and if this does not succeed, I walk the floor with her.

F., 10. Undressing and putting dolly to bed was the best play of all.

F., 15. Nights I undressed my dolls, put on their night clothes, had them say their prayers, and when all were in bed would sing to them.

M., 8. Hangs his doll on a chair papoose-wise to sleep nights.

SICKNESS

Dolls have many diseases. In our returns there were 63 cases of measles, 47 of scarlet fever, 34 of colds, 33 of whooping cough, 31 of diphtheria, 27 of members injured, 26 of headache, 23 of mumps, 22 of fever, 18 of chicken pox, 17 of smallpox, 16 of sore throat, 15 of colic, 11 of croup, 11 of surgical operations, 9 of stomach ache, 9 of toothache, 9 of leg broken, 8 of grip, 7 of consumption, 4 of typhoid fever, 4 of leprosy, and 5 were beheaded. The following occurred from one to three times: bronchitis, biliousness, cramp, catarrh, chills, teething, sore eyes, earache, dysentery, jaundice, heart trouble, chafed limbs, pneumonia, rheumatism, dyspepsia, brain fever, spells of vomiting.

The most common remedies are tapioca pills, water, sugar pills, poultices, plasters, quinine, paper pills, colored water, vinegar, menthol pencils, water and dirt, tea sirup, seltzer aperient, sweet oil, salt and water, sugar for powders, soap, peppermint, paregoric, potato and salt, castor oil, vaseline, cement, currant juice and water, camphor, candy, ice cream, bread pills, dirt powders, chalk and water, dissolved candy, hot bottles, mustard plaster, squills, laudanum, Hive sirup, castoria, drops, etc.

To treat these diseases the doctor in 48 cases is a boy, in 30, a playmate, sex not mentioned. In 25 cases the owner of the doll is the doctor, in 24 cases the doctor is imaginary, in 20 cases he is another doll. Sometimes father, mother, or even the real doctor, if he happens to be present, is consulted.

The remedy often aims to fit the disease. Fever may be put on with red paint and treated with Seidlitz powder or a drop of bismuth every half hour. A doll who lost her wig and had brain fever was bandaged and put to bed. Repairs are surgical operations and the repair shop is a hospital. In one case of toothache the face was broken in trying to pull the tooth. For dyspepsia burned rice was ground in a mortar. For sore eyes a veil was used. For sore throat flannel and salt gargle, pork rinds, red pepper, and ten minutes in bed. For stomach ache, after careful examination of the pulse, flannel, salt and water, tapioca pills, and darkness was the treatment. In smallpox, caused by spotting the waxed face of a doll, sugar and water cured. For measles, the head was bathed and tied up with imaginary brandy ; bread pills, a sweat, and hot water were given, which latter brought out the eruptions until the wax face was disfigured. For mumps the face is grotesquely muffled and tied up. Leprosy was suggested in the Sunday school and by the paint flecking off. In the case of a broken leg an ambulance, ether, etc., were extemporized. Eye water is squeezed into the socket of a knocked-out eye. Ink and catnip tea are good for sleeplessness. Orange marmalade, licorice, etc., is for teething. For colic, dolls must be laid on their stomachs and given warm drinks and tucked up with extra wraps. The best thing, says a boy of thirteen, is a good dose of bad medicine.

F., 10. My doll Liz had a headache, so I put on her "mikado" and read her some of Longfellow's *Hiawatha*, as she wanted me to.

F., 10. My baby doll is always sick, and I have Dr. Sam, a very old doll, come and treat her.

F., 8. Vaccinated all her dolls, putting in soap.

F., 12. My baby doll has colic every night, croup, pain, and all sorts of diseases, but the large dolls are very healthy.

F., 13. The paint came off my doll's face and she grew pale and sick.

M., 7. Takes his doll to the seaside for her health.

F., 12. Had 92 dolls; many were often sick; disease not always designated.

F., 10. Puts her colicky dolls across her knee and they soon recover.

F., 13. Rubbed red chalk on her doll's face to make a high fever seem more real.

M., 6. Has dolls that sometimes have three or four diseases at once; they must be rubbed, dosed, the room kept dark and quiet.

F., 12. Used to give tooth powder for medicine, but stopped when told it would not digest.

F., 13. I was once extremely anxious lest my doll baby should die, it was so sick.

DEATH, FUNERAL, AND BURIAL OF DOLLS

Sometimes these are quite isolated from each other and from sickness, and sometimes all follow in due course. Of all the returns available under this rubric 90 children mentioned burial, their average age being nine; 80 mentioned funerals, 73 imagined their dolls dead, 30 dug up dolls after burial to see if they had gone to heaven, or simply to get them back. Of these 11 dug them up the same day. Only 9 speak of them as dying naturally of definite diseases; 15 put them under sofa, in drawers, attics, or gave them away, calling this death; 30 express positive belief in future life of dolls; 8 mentioned future life for them without revealing their own convictions; 3 buried dolls with pets and left them; 3 said bad or dirty dolls went to the bad place; 14, that they went to heaven; 17 children were especially fond of funerals. 12 dolls came to accidental death by bumps or fractures, 1 burst, 1 died of a melted face, 2 were drowned (1 a paper doll), 1 died because her crying apparatus was broken, 1 doll murdered another, was tried, and hanged. Dolls of which children tire often die. 30 children never imagined dolls dead. This parents often forbid. 1 boy killed his sister's doll with a toy cannon, 3 resurrected dolls and gave them new names; 5 out of 7 preachers at dolls' funerals were boys, 1 was the doctor; 3 doll undertakers are described. 22 cases report grief that seems to be very real and deep; in 23 cases this seemed feigned. The mourning is sometimes real black and sometimes pretended. 19 put flowers on dolls' graves, 1 "all that week"; 28 expressly say that dolls have no souls, are not alive, and have no future life. In 21 cases there was death but no burial; in 10, funerals but no burials; in 8, funerals but no deaths.

F., 14. My dolls never die nor marry; they are babies.

F., 14. My dolls never die unless they get broken. I never allow them to, it is too painful.

F., 23. I never thought dolls dead till arms, legs, head were gone and often not then.

F., 13. Doll smashed, not dead, just thrown away.

F., 9. Doll broken, funeral just for fun.

F., 8. One particular doll for funeral purposes.

M., 10. Buries dolls' limbs, heads, etc., apart if they come loose.

F., 9. Very rarely had my children die, but had them come to life right away as a different person.

F., 6. Was given a doll so lifelike that she feared it, believing it a dead baby.

A teacher writes: " The true value of a good doll in molding a girl's character has not begun to be appreciated. I disapprove doll balls, theaters, marriages, and especially deaths and funerals."

F., 9. Whittled dolls rudely from sticks, buried them, covered the grave with flowers, and in a few days dug them up as mummies.

F., 16. It broke my heart when my doll broke her head, but I never thought of a funeral or future life.

M., 6. Hates dolls, " for they are all girls; they just keep their mouth shut and make believe children ; they never die because they don't keep their eyes always closed forever."

F., 11. Never played that dolls died lest she should die herself.

DOLLS' NAMES

Of dolls' names, 199 were given by a friend, 87, because they were pretty, favorite, or fancy names; 54, because of real or fancied likeness; 35, for a name in a story or some one heard of ; 33 were named from the giver ; 24 had no name save Dolly; 21 gave new names often ; 20 were named from some peculiar look or quality in person ; 9 took the owner's name ; 6 were named from the time or place of receiving the doll ; 5, from a feigned likeness ; 4 had purely imaginary names ; 2 had very unusual names. In some cases ugly names are given to dolls disliked, and in two cases the material of which the doll is made is the name. 10 very formal christenings are spoken of. Sometimes every doll in a family receives the same name. Dolls with names frequently changed rarely develop distinct personalities.

Some cases are the following: named Rose because of rosy cheeks. Some children cannot remember the names of their dolls, they have so many. A very short name sometimes goes with a very small doll. One boy three years old named his doll Family. The earliest dolls are rarely named. Sometimes qualifying terms are used, like " Birthday Mary," " Chicago Jane." A dent on the cheek suggested Dotty Dimple. A Christmas doll was named " Merry Christmas."

One doll was named Silk because always dressed in silk. Another named Jap because dressed like a Mikado. An invented name is Skidel, another Calambo. Some children hunt catalogues for new names. Some are named Lord, Lady, from vocations ; some from pet animals.

F., Had all dolls' names end in *ie.*

M., 11 (Bohemian). Named his doll My Friend.

F., 12. Now thinks it silly to name dolls, although she still plays with them.

F., 4. Gave a new name with every new dress. One doll was named Gingerbread, from the color of its stuffed-out head.

DISCIPLINE

In our returns are 41 distinct cases of punishment by being sent to bed, 34 spanked, 32 whipped, 25 scolded, 20 put in closet, 13 kept in, 12 shut up, 17 made to sit down, 11 shaken, 7 slapped, 7 severely talked to, 5 deprived of food, 2 tied to a post, 1 made to stand up and sing, 1 sent home from school, 1 had Cayenne pepper put on its tongue, 1 was punched, 1 had its legs pulled, 1 had its face covered, 1 was fed on bread and water, 1 was thrown downstairs, 1 made to sit on the door knob, 1 had to go to bed in the dark, 1 was hanged with due ceremony. Rewards are in the following order of frequency : taking out to walk, visiting, sitting up late, going riding, being kissed, going without nap, going shopping, being told a story, taken to party, given candy, cake, clothes, ribbons. Rewards are often promised or punishments are often threatened, but not given. There seems little disposition to make the punishment fit the crime. The qualities rewarded are the following in order of frequency: goodness, truthfulness, obedience, neatness, kindness, good nature, quietness, sweet temper, patience. Traits or acts punished are being naughty, not sitting still, quarreling, talking, answering back, not learning lessons, falling from chair, being " sassy," running away from baby doll, slapping baby doll, crying, being jealous, "won't stand," "won't sit proper," lying, being vain, angry, hitting or falling on small doll, being cross, upsetting things, stealing, flirting, saying " I won't," etc. 15 say they never discipline dolls, either because they are good, or too little, or they never thought of it.

In the supplementary answers 108 children whip, 108 never punish, 80 put to bed, 75 spank, 39 slap, 35 stand in the corner, 34 scold, 21 shake, 20 put in dark closet, 5 throw on floor. 4 broke their dolls, and several hanged them, pulled their ears and hair, stood them on their heads, shut them in a box, threw them up and let them drop, left them out in the cold. The age when punishments are most frequent and severest is below eight; thence onward they gradually decline in frequency.

F., 10. Punishes paper dolls by tearing their legs off.

F., 14. Punishes by keeping the dolls from the theater and rewards by letting them buy what they would.

F., 6. Beats and almost breaks her doll because she "wets herself most every day."

F., 11. Thought vanity and anger the worst faults.

F., 7. Whipped dolls for no reason but the pleasure of it.

F., 8. Flogs severely for the slightest error.

F., 5. When 4, whipped dolls, but at 8 loved them too much and reasoned with them when they were bad.

F., 8. Always scolds before whipping.

F., 6. Whips doll if not found where she thinks it was left.

F., 8. Gave prizes for neatness, her favorite doll getting all. She adds: " I did realize it was my fault if they were untidy."

HYGIENE. TOILET

Hygiene and toilet treatment is mentioned as follows: dressing, 18 times; washing face, 12; taking out of doors to get the air, 11; general bath, 10; dressed regularly, 7 times; hands washed, 7 times; bathed every morning, 5 times; hair combed, 6 times; braided twice, brushed twice, went in bathing twice, teeth brushed twice, nails manicured twice. Occasional mention is made of gargling throat, cutting hair, pure air in sleeping, water closet, massage, keeping home from parties to avoid late hours, not letting them go with boys, heavy clothing in cold and light in warm weather, putting salve in dolls' ears as wax to be cleaned out, and dirtying nails to clean out, wearing wrappers in the morning, plain dresses in the afternoon, and silk in the evening.

Dolls' Families, Schools, Parties, Weddings, etc.

153 returns mention families; 44 describe parties, teas, receptions, etc.; 33, schools of various kinds; 18, theaters, concerts, tableaux; 26, weddings; 25, excursions or rides; in 21 cases the child is the mother of her dolls; in 14 cases other dolls are the mothers; 14 played shopping; 14, visiting; 12, war; 10 played families only with paper dolls; 10, hanging or execution. Churches are described 7 times; Sunday schools, 6 times; ceremonial baptisms, 5 times. There were 4 dolls' swimming parties, in 4 cases all the dolls were cousins, in 2 cases the child was the grandmother and in 2 aunt of the dolls, 2 clubs, 2 plays of park with grand stand. Other social plays described fully once and often hinted at more times are fire company, slave selling, post office, country fair, sailing, prayer meeting, stepmother, imaginary mother. Till four, one boy was mother of his dolls and then father.

F., 10. Called a big doll her child, a small doll her grandchild. One boy was mother, and the father was at sea.

M., 7. I am the papa and the stuffed cat the mamma.

F., 5. Crucified boy doll with tacks on a cigar box.

F., 8. Kept doll boarding school.

M., 7. Executed criminal doll with popgun.

F., 11. Has wedding with doll bridesmaids, ushers, father, mother, invitations, and many dolls to look on, and rice.

F., 14. Thought giving presents between dolls was a great game.

F., 12. Thought married dolls had children; she tucked them up under the clothes and pretended they were born the regular way. When they grew up one was Longfellow and the other Louisa Alcott.

M., 2. Heard of crucifixion and tried to nail dolly to a board.

F., 8. Used to set her dolls in the parlor and play exquisite music; they applauded loudly and she bowed, although she did not know one note from another.

F., 4. Plays school, with dolls in a row and standing over them with stick, saying, "Be good."

ACCESSORIES

Counting the doll accessories, we find that 179 children mention clothes in general; 85 mention beds; 66, sets of dishes; 59, tables; 58, chairs; 57, trunks; 40, cradles; 32, houses; 30, bureaus; 23, toys; 23, furniture; 23, carriages; 22, brushes; 22, combs; 21, folding beds; 20, hats; 12, stoves; 10, shoes; 10, stockings; 10, bonnets; 9, quilts; 9, dolls' dolls; 9, underclothes; 9, toilet sets; 8, pianos; 12, washstands; 12, handkerchiefs; 6, cloaks; 6, chamber sets; 6, cupboards; 6, forks; 6, jewelry; 6, knives; 6, lounges; 6, mirrors; 6, mittens; 6, nightgowns; 6, picture books; 6, rattles; 6, sofas; 6, waterproofs; 5, capes; 5, aprons; 5, swings; 5, spoons; 5, towels; 5, veils; 4, caps; 4, hairpins; 4, newspapers; 4, pictures; 4, soap; 4, wash rags; 4, books; 4, carpets. The following are mentioned 3 times: bags, balls, bookcases, blankets, earrings, fans, flatirons, jackets, kitchen sets, muffs, mats, overshoes, parasols, parlor sets, pencils, pewter dishes, money purses, rings, shawls, slippers, sheets. The following are mentioned twice: bath tubs, blocks, bracelets, coats for boys, cribs, chests of drawers, candlesticks, comforters, Christmas trees, back combs, desks, furs, foot-stools, hoods, horses, high chairs, jardinières, kettles, nursing bottles, napkins, puff boxes, pillows, pincushions, sacks, sponges, sponge bags, tablecloths, tin kitchens, toothbrushes, toy dogs, toy cats, toy cows.

In issuing his supplementary syllabus it was Mr. Ellis's intention to have 100 boys and 100 girls from each grade to answer with a word each of his 29 questions. This would have given a more definite indication of the extent of doll plays, the doll age, effect of sex, etc. He also sought returns from idiots, blind children, children of foreign birth, etc., for comparative purposes. The returns, however, have been only 579 in all, and many of these fail to answer one or more questions. They have all been counted, and most of the results incorporated in the preceding table; and the rest, which could not be presented by this method, are inserted under their respective entries.

From tabulated results it appears that of average city school children below 6 years, 82 per cent. of boys and 98 per cent. of girls have played dolls; between 6 and 12 years, 76 per cent. of boys, 99 per cent. of girls ; of high-school girls, 100 per cent.

Those confessing that they have ever specially enjoyed doll play are : below 6 years, 77 per cent. of boys, 95 per cent. of girls ; between 6 and 12 years, 78 per cent. of boys, 97 per cent. of girls ; of high-school girls, 82 per cent.

Those ever having used substitutes are : below 6 years, 15 per cent. of boys, 48 per cent. of girls ; between 6 and 12 years, 35 per cent. of boys, 68 per cent. of girls; of high-school girls, 58 per cent. Thus girls appear to lead the boys in every grade. Nearly 50 per cent. of the girls and a little less of the boys, answering in all grades, said they loved the substitutes as much as real dolls.

Paper dolls had been used by 73 per cent. of those below 6 years, by 80 per cent. between 6 and 12 years and by 92 per cent. of high-school girls. Interest in other dolls was thought dulled by paper dolls by 34 per cent. of boys and 26 per cent. of girls below 6 years, 35 per cent. of boys and 15 per cent. of girls between 6 and 12 years, 44 per cent. of high-school girls.

Of all kinds of children, — blind, deaf, foreign, etc., — only 17 per cent. speak of lack of child companionship and 72 per cent. prefer playing dolls in company ; 38 per cent. say that love of dolls grew out of love of a real baby and 13 per cent. transferred their doll love to babies ; 79 per cent. had tried to feed dolls ; 66 per cent. have thought dolls hungry; 68 per cent. have ascribed to dolls some of the psychic qualities mentioned ; 67 per cent. have thought them sick.

MISCELLANEOUS

Relative frequency of some forms of doll play. In the supplementary reports to question 27, 266 children mention a
fondness for dressing dolls; 218 like to wash them; 189 have
a love of doll parties; 183, a love of sewing for them; 176, a
love of playing school; 169, love of putting to sleep; 137,
love of weddings; 93, of nursing; 82 mention treating them
as companions, telling secrets, etc.; 79 love to feed them; 49,
to punish them; 36, to play funerals.

The relations of doll and baby. If the wig comes off dolls,
they are often treated as babies; sometimes they are made
bald-headed to be babies. For some little children dolls with
hair have no charm, and as children grow older they dislike
baby dolls. Transference of affection from dolls to a new baby
is often noted. Some are afraid of dolls till acquainted with
babies and then become very fond of them. Some children
think babies, like dolls, are filled with sawdust. Some experiment on babies, putting fingers in their eyes, etc., and treat
them generally as they have been used to treating dolls.

Paper dolls. Some children never care for paper dolls;
some think them best to play or act fairy stories. Of 27 boys,
aged seven, 5 played with and preferred paper dolls. Some children prefer them to all others and play with them longer. As
they grow older paper dolls have a peculiar fascination. One
girl of seventeen ended doll play by putting her paper dolls in
a scrapbook as a house. School, collective games, and families
are more often played with paper dolls.

Maimed dolls. If dolls lose their heads, eyes, or get otherwise deformed, little children are often afraid of them. Some
are horrified if the wig comes off; some little children fear
everything in human shape, perhaps, till they make the acquaintance of a new baby and then love dolls. Some suddenly
conceive lifelike wax dolls as real dead persons and have

sudden aversions for them. Some like to maim dolls, pulling off their limbs, perhaps killing them, in order to have a funeral. Sometimes it is thought rather disgraceful to both doll and owner to have new heads, limbs, etc. Accidents to dolls sometimes cause sensitive children to faint.

Influence of age. Very rare are those who begin doll play in the cradle and keep it up through life. The doll passion seems to be strongest between seven and ten, and to reach its climax between eight and nine.

In the supplementary papers 55 stopped playing dolls because they liked other things better; 50 ceased to care for them without being able to give a reason; 46 stopped because they were too old; 44, because too large; 22, because too busy and had no time; 15, because ashamed; 11, because they loved a real baby. Others gave their dolls away, preferred new playmates, were made to stop, dolls were worn out, etc.

Persius tells us how the young Roman girl, when ripe for marriage, hung up her childhood's dolls as a votive offering to Venus.

Froude, in his life of Carlyle, tells how Mrs. Carlyle at the age of nine made an end of doll play. It had been intimated to her, by one whose wish was law, that a young lady reading Virgil must make an end of doll play. She decided that dolly should die like Dido, so with her many sumptuous dresses, her four-post bed, a faggot or two of cedar allumettes, a few sticks of cinnamon, a few cloves, and a nutmeg, her funeral pyre was built, and " the new Dido having placed himself in the bed, with help, spoke through my lips the last sad words of Dido the first, which I then had all by heart as pat as A, B, C. The doll having thus spoken, kindled the pile, and stabbed herself with a penknife by way of a Tyrian sword. Then, however, in the moment of seeing my poor doll blaze up (for being stuffed with bran she took fire and it was all over in no time), in that supreme moment my affection for her blazed up also, and I shrieked and would have saved her and could not, and went on shrieking, and everybody within hearing flew to me and bore me off in a flood of tears."

Girls often play with dolls regularly until thirteen or fourteen, when, with the dawn of adolescence, the doll passion generally abates. It is then realized more distinctly than before that dolls have absolutely no inner life or feeling. Some girls play with dolls with great pleasure, but secretly, till well on in the teens and often in the twenties, and occasionally married women, generally those without children, or single women, play with dolls all their lives. Several of our returns report infants as interested in dolls very early in life, — one fully reported case at thirty days, another at thirteen weeks, and several cases before one year old. For the second year of life our reports contain about twenty cases of developed love of dolls. Near the end of the second year one child was observant enough to take the rectal temperature of her doll.

Some children prefer naked dolls, and persist in playing with them in this condition, imagining that thus they can love them more. Some children have special aversions, now to dolls with brown eyes, now to light- or dark-haired dolls, those with long or short hair, etc.; some children compose stories and even poems for or about their dolls; a six-year-old boy, e.g., says: "I have a little dolly, she sits in a chair. Her name is Polly, and I comb her hair." "One doll would not stand and I was angry, knocked out its eyes and gave it away." "To tell my dolly she looks ugly makes her good." "I imagined my dolly cruelly treated for what it never did, but loved to tease it and pretended she said bad words." "My dolls all kept individual characteristics, often suggested by the faces." "I could never understand why dolls needed to be whipped, and thought them so good that I was greatly hurt when they were accused of faults." "I thought dolls greatly pleased with new clothes, toys, etc."

Influence of dolls on children. All opinions received are rudely classified as follows: 44 adults simply report the influence of dolls on children as good; 41 think dolls help parenthood; 39 think rude dolls best to cultivate the imagination; 38 think dolls fit for domestic life; 38 think they develop moral qualities; 35, that they cultivate taste in dress; 35, that they teach to sew; 29, that they teach tidiness; 25 like rude dolls best; 25 think that they develop the social nature; 24, that they teach to make clothes; 24, that they teach thoroughness; 24 report that there was no regularity in the care of dolls; 23 thought the religious nature strengthened; 21, that they teach neatness; 21 say dolls are better cared for if lifelike; 13, that they are better loved when lifelike; 12, that they teach carefulness; 7, that the care of dolls helps in care of children; 6 think the doll passion makes no difference with children; 6 report great regularity in care of dolls; 6 say that it develops love of children; 6, that doll play is better for children in every way; 5, that imitation is stimulated; 4 each specify that playing with dolls' clothes helps children to combine colors, makes them more obedient, keeps them quiet, keeps them out of mischief, keeps them from bad company, makes them more tender, more thoughtful of others, and that expensive dolls are best. Three each specify improvement in dress, knowledge of color, say that children are more affectionate, more orderly, more sympathetic, that they never learn anything from doll play, that they have spells of regularity in caring for dolls, and that lifelike dolls are best. Two each think that dolls teach children to appreciate parents' care, make them more cheerful, help power of conversation, help design, teach knitting, to make patterns, make the child more observing, more persevering, more stylish, more gentle, more refined, exercise a softening influence, and that dolls should be in kindergarten. One each thinks that dolls help to care for baby, housekeeping, industry, kindness, that the finer senses and emotions are developed by them, and that they make children more courteous, that they teach embroidery, inspire desire for motherhood, philanthropy, love of beauty, memory, mending, originality, patience, power, womanliness, truthfulness, show mother the child's traits, make pure in thought, respectful, that there is danger of too many accessories, that the child's attitude toward dolls is harmed by too light treatment and remarks by parents, and that care for the doll's body helps children to know and care for their own.

Some individual opinions of parents and teachers are quite fully expressed: "they keep children from growing old"; "best of all is the reflex influence on the child of trying to teach her doll and of trying to set a good example "; "nice dolls make children more careful of them and they ascribe human qualities to them, while rude dolls that can be banged about and made to take any part stimulate a more elementary type of imagination "; " to imagine the rug an ocean and have a stick doll with a frock that can be washed, gives the fancy something to do "; "she learned to read in order to read her doll a story "; " I had a strong wish to be as good as I thought my dolls were "; "children who care least for dolls love their own babies most later "; "dolls hurt my health by making me sit indoors and care too little for the company of other children, but they help me put myself in my parents' place "; " too fine dolls check fancy, beget restlessness and desire for everything, so there is a limit beyond which dolls should not go "; " when mothers fail to impress certain virtues they need but to say, ' How would you like to have your doll do it ? ' to score their point "; "dolls might aid in teaching geography, language, history, and drawing, by playing journeys to different countries, the use of foreign money, dress, food, or being engineers, sailors, etc. "; " dolls might be brought to school and by teaching them children could learn their own lessons better "; "doll play reveals character and ideals "; "excess of the doll passion makes excitement, nervousness, worry, and some girls are teased into nervousness by their brothers for playing dolls."

The number and vast variety of objects more or less dollified well illustrate the remark of Victor Hugo — that as birds may take almost every material for a nest, so nothing resists the childish instinct to find or make dolls out of everything, and stones, books, balls, buttons, stove hooks, nails, bricks, washboards, flowers, pins, articles of food, objects with no trace of anything that can be called face, limbs, or head, are made dolls. Hugo's Cossette dressed, hugged, and put to sleep a naked sword. Occasionally immovable things like posts, stumps, and even trees are more or less dollified. The quick imagination of childhood makes an eye out of a speck or dot, and perhaps imagines the other features. This instinct cannot be entirely explained as nascent parenthood, but must include some elements of the widespread animism, if not fetichism, of children and savages. The valuable study of Dr. Fewkes, the Roman

games, the Doll Feast of Japan, and some of the etymologies
point this way, as do, perhaps, the rare cases of children who
make God dolls, whipping them for watching, etc. The fear
of the spirits of burned dolls, of black dolls, of evil eye, and
some forms of special aversion point the same way. As the
optic nerve, whether heated, chilled, touched with chemicals
or electricity, can only respond by giving the sensation of
light, so primitive humanity sees personality in everything.
This again is abundantly proved in returns to another syllabus
already worked up, illustrating children's feeling for inanimate
as well as animate nature. However disconnected the words
doll and *idol,* some psychic connection cannot be doubted.
Not only are dolls personified as the visible form of a non-
existent person, as of Queen Victoria, the Court, and theatrical personages ; in Japan, of the Mikado and his wife ; and of
other orientals, of ancestors, but they may represent mythological beings or demigods, and evil or beneficent deities. Greek
statues of the Olympians have been called stone dolls, and the
iconoclastic rage which destroyed many of them expressed the
instinct of the first commandment. As object lessons setting
forth invisible beings in concrete form, idolatry is perhaps as
much more persistent than dolls, as memory of abstract is more
persistent than that of concrete words in progressive aphasia,
and for analogous reasons. Idols may, perhaps, be valuable
object lessons in religion for children at the low pagan stage
and may yet have a rôle to play in elementary religious training, but their danger is analogous in kind to that sometimes
feared for excessive and too prolonged doll cult, viz., that it
may arrest the higher development of parental instincts, check
interest in free play with children, and place puppets and
dummies where real personalities ought to be. If deities were
certain to appear later in concrete form and break the charm of
idols, so that the danger of forever putting an unworthy symbol in place of that which it symbolizes could be as effectually

obviated as interest in "meat babies" and live children is sure to supplant dolls, idolatry would lose its dangers. Both the psychological significance and the educational value of the image worship of the Catholic church and of religious pictures, figures, and of spiritual beings are topics upon which carefully made home experiments and observations, which would be of great value, are needed and could be made.

The relatively small proportion of dolls which represents infants, and the large proportion representing adults, shows again that the parental instinct is far less prominent in doll play than is commonly supposed. Nearly all the 132 dolls of Queen Victoria were adults and represented prominent personages. On every hand we see that a large part of the charm of doll play is the small scale of the doll world, which brings it not only into the limited range of the child's senses and knowledge, but focuses and intensifies affection and all other feelings. A large part of the world's terms of endearment are diminutives, and to its reduced scale the doll world owes much of its charm. The cases of fear of dolls are almost always of large dolls, the charm of which comes out only well on in the doll period and as exceptions to the rule. Even feared and hated objects excite pleasure when mimicked on a small scale. Moreover, relations are better seen in a world of small things. A small eye or mind cannot readily take in a fully dressed lady. Yet again the child can work its feeble will on objects with a completeness which is inversely as their size. Smallness of size indulges children's love of feeling their superiority, their desire to boss something and to gain their desire along lines of least resistance or to vent their reaction to the parental tyranny of anger. Maggie Tulliver drove nails through her doll's head to vent her anger at her aunt, but when the reaction came drew them out and poulticed the wounds. There may often be danger in a scale too small, as that of Queen Victoria's dolls ranging from three to nine inches long, for thirty-two of which she made dresses, working handkerchiefs half an inch square ; yet to make small will always be of itself alone a most effective pedagogic method, and will always exert a potent fascination. In Japan, it is a fashion to make everything severely small for children. Our returns do not show any law of relationship between the size of the doll and the size or age of the child, save that the extremes of large and small develop their chief charm well on in the doll period. Things large, like things far off, fail of exciting interest and of being comprehended by children, and are almost as effectively out of their range as things microscopic are for adult eyes. As the microscope and telescope bring minute and distant objects within our purview, so a doll microcosm opens up a world of relationship so large, and simplifies things so complex, as to be otherwise closed to the infant mind. If we take a large view of the doll problem, it thus comprises most of the most important questions of education.

That boys are naturally fond of and should play with dolls as well as girls, there is abundant indication. One boy in a family of girls, or boys who are only children, often play with dolls up to seven or eight years of age. It is unfortunate that this is considered so predominantly a girl's play. Most boys abandon it early or never play, partly because it is thought girlish by adults as well as by children. Of course boy life is naturally rougher and demands a wider range of activities. The danger, too, of making boy milliners is of course obvious, but we are convinced that, on the whole, more play with girl dolls by boys would tend to make them more sympathetic with girls as children, if not more tender with their wives and with women later. Again, boys as well as girls might be encouraged to play with boy dolls more than at present, with great advantage to both. Boys, too, seem to prefer exceptional dolls, — clowns, brownies, colored, Eskimo, Japanese, etc. Boys, too, seem fonder than girls of monkey and animal dolls, and are often very tender of these, when they maltreat dolls in human shape. Again, dolls representing heroes of every kind and non-existent beings, dragons, and hobgoblins find their chief admirers among boys. A boy of six I know was fascinated with a rude Jack-o'-lantern, would lie on the floor and talk to it by the hour, ask it questions and get what he deemed real answers, and was charmed by its horrid features. Boys are little prone to doll luxury or elaborate paraphernalia and are content with ruder dolls than girls, and the doll function is naturally far less developed than with girls.

In discussing the degree and kind of reality of the doll world, we approach one of the most difficult of psychological problems. Children seem to delight in giving way to illusions, and even delusions here, which it is extremely difficult for the adult mind to understand. Often in the midst of the most absorbing play, the slightest criticism, a word of appeal to reason, the most trivial fact of real life, annihilates in an instant the entire doll cosmos. The wedding, school, or funeral is left unfinished, the half-dressed doll dropped in the most painful attitude and left in the cold for perhaps an indefinite period. Sometimes we see traces of a struggle almost painful between faith and doubt, either of which may triumph. The doll may have a definite personality, be a real member of the family and not a toy, or a "hybrid between a baby and a fetich," be a real part of the child's self, be fanned, its bruises rubbed and wept over; or, again, as in one case, may be the hero of a vividly fancied romance, lose money, work its way out West, become rich, travel east, be shipwrecked on a desert island, etc; real personalities may lose interest in comparison with it, and all this may be kept up with some consistency for years, — one normal woman of twenty-seven and another of forty still play with dolls, — absorption in the play blotting out the grossest incongruities, the doll being a real companion and crony sharing every secret and confidence in solitude *a deux*, on journeys, and elsewhere, so that the child's psychic life seems entirely bound up with it. The subjective and objective, will, feeling, and knowledge are strangely mixed. One child had tried all her life to keep her doll from knowing she was not alive. Dolls are buried without dying, fed without eating, bathed without water, are now good, now bad, now happy, now tearful, without the slightest change, the child furnishing the motive power and all its moods being mirrored in another self. It seems to be at about the age of six, three years before the culmination of the doll passion, that the conflict between fancy and reality becomes clearly manifest. Abandonment to the doll illusion and the length of the doll period seems less in the western than in the eastern children, and decreases as dolls and their accessories become elaborate. With every increase of knowledge of anatomy or of the difference between living tissue and dead matter, between life and mechanism, this element of doll play must wane.

Perhaps nothing so fully opens up the juvenile soul to the student of childhood as well-developed doll play. Here we see fully revealed things which the childish instinct often tends to keep secret. It shows out the real nature which Plato thought so important that he advised drunkenness as a revealer of character. The doll often fears ghosts or lightning, and becomes conscious of sex as the child does. Flogging the doll for not being in the right place, being untidy, etc., often marks the rise of the child's consciousness of order and cleanliness. Whispered confidences with the doll are often more intimate and sacred than with any human being. The doll is taught those things learned best or in which the child has most interest. The little mother's real ideas of morality are best seen in her punishments and rewards of her doll. Her favorite foods are those of her doll. The features of funerals, weddings, schools, and parties which are reënacted with the doll are those which have most deeply impressed the child. The child's moods,

ideals of life, dress, etc., come to utterance in free and spontaneous doll play. Deaf girls teach their dolls the finger
alphabet, blind ones sometimes want bandages or glasses for
their dolls. I know a mother of a sickly child who says she
can anticipate the symptoms of all the illnesses of her daughter
because they are first projected upon the doll before the child
has become fully conscious of them in herself. Children often
express their own desire for goodies euphemistically by saying,
" Dolly wants it." Thus the individuality of children sometimes is more clearly revealed in the characters they give their
dolls than in their own traits. Long-kept dolls thus often grow
up, as it were, with the child, their infantile qualities expanding
into those of childhood and then youth. Paper dolls, often with
picture food, which seem more ideal and more often associated
with fairy stories, betray the evanescent stages of the doll psychosis as it fades into adult life.

Is doll play an early cropping out of mother love as Schneider
and Victor Hugo and others think ? And are dolls represent-
atives of future children ? This appears to be true only in
a limited and partial sense, and we must readjust our views
upon this point. Some mothers, very fond of their children
now, never cared much for dolls, while many of our returns
show that unmarried women and childless wives have been most
enthusiastic devotees of dolls, and in such cases the doll cult
seems often to be most prolonged. It also seems natural for
small boys. Certainly other functions are more pronounced.
There seems to be a premonition of the parental instinct in
early childhood, which fades as the dawn of adolescence ap-
proaches, as the fetal hair falls off to make place for a ranker
growth much later. The saying that the first child is the last
doll is, I believe, not true of normal women. The treatment of
and feeling toward a doll and a child are more unlike than the
teeth of first and second dentition. That the first may hypertrophy and dwarf the second is undoubted. Indeed it is just

possible that the ideal mother never plays dolls with great abandon. Despite the increased extent of doll play, its intensity seems a little on the wane among the best people, and too many accessories lessen the educational value of this play in teaching children to put themselves in the parent's place, in deepening love of children, and of motherhood.

The educational value of dolls is enormous, and the protest of this paper is against longer neglect of it. It educates the heart and will, even more than the intellect, and to learn how to control and apply doll play will be to discover a new instrument in education of the very highest potency. Every parent and every teacher who can deal with individuals at all should study the doll habits of each child, now discouraging and repressing, now stimulating by hint or suggestion. There should be somewhere (1) a doll museum, (2) a doll expert to keep the possibilities of this great educative instinct steadily in view, and (3) careful observations upon children of kindergarten, primary, and grammar grades should be instituted, as at an experiment station, in order to determine just what is practicable. Children with French dolls incline to practice their little French upon them ; can this tendency be utilized in teaching a foreign language to young children ? Some children read stories in order to tell them to their doll, and one learned to read by the strength of this motive. With what proportion of children can this be helpful ? Many children learn to sew, knit, and do millinery work, observe and design costumes, acquire taste in color, and even prepare food for the benefit of the doll. Children who are indifferent to reading for themselves sometimes read to their doll and learn things they would not otherwise do in order to teach it, or are clean, to be like it. They are good in order to set it a good example, compose poetry, and write compositions for it, their naughtiness is reduced by asking them how they would like their dolls to do so ; and to be as good as they think their dolls are is sometimes a high ideal. Goethe reproduced dramas with puppets in a doll theater as several of our correspondents have done. To make them represent heroes in history or fiction, to have collections illustrating costumes of different countries, the Eskimo hut, the Indian teepee, the cowboy's log cabin, to take them on imaginary journeys with foreign money, is not merely to keep children young, cheerful, out of bad company, but it is to teach geography, history and morals, nature, etc., in the most objective possible way. Plenty of toy animals, figures representing different vocations and trades, poor and rich, etc., would be not only taking the dolls to kindergarten and school, but would also bring rudimentary sociology, ethics, and science in their most-needed and effective form. Dolls are a good school for children to practice all they know. Children are at a certain period interested to know what is inside things, especially dolls ; could not manikin dolls be made that were dissectible enough to teach some anatomy ? Would not dolls and their furnishings be among the best things to make in manual training schools ; and why are dolls, which represent the most original, free, and spontaneous expression of the play instinct so commonly excluded from the kindergarten, where they could aid in teaching almost everything ?

ANTHROPOLOGICAL NOTES

Doctor Gustav Schlegel writes : " Dolls are of recent origin in Europe. In the beginning of the fifteenth century, during the reign of mad Charles VI of France, an Italian, named Pusello, came from Padua to France with thirty mules packed with boxes and hung with jingling bells. He had in these boxes wooden images of ninety-six empresses and other celebrated women of the old Roman Empire, carved after statues and coins. He showed them everywhere, gaining a considerable fortune by their exposition. At last the counselors of the king called him to court in order to amuse His Majesty.

When he came to the explanation of the statuette of *Poppœa*, who, it is pretended, was killed by Nero by a kick in her belly, the king listened with the greatest attention, and at last bought the statuette of Poppæa for fifty Parisians sols, about three hundred francs of present currency. The king's example was soon followed, and every nobleman bought such a little statue ; and ever it appears that such pouppées, or dolls, came at that time in vogue as playthings for girls.

"Children in Amoy play with solid puppets made of baked clay, called *Hai dzi-a*, or 'babies' ; and Douglas even quotes the saying *Kah na hai dzi-a*, equivalent to our saying, 'As fair as a doll,' said of a pretty child.

"Puppets for theatrical performances were long known in China, but from these to the doll as a plaything for little girls is a long distance, and Chinese girls never played with them.

"Probably the doll, as an article to play with for little girls, has been equally imported into Japan by the Dutch."

Dr. J. Walter Fewkes writes : " The Tusayan custom of giving the symbolism of a god to the doll, to which you refer, may be limited to that interesting people, but I suspect that it has a deep significance, and may show a universal relationship between child concepts and primitive social cult development. The Tusayan name for a doll is *tihu*, personification, not far from εἴδωλον in meaning. A dramatic dance in which gods are personified by men (masked) is spoken of as *tihuni*, —we personate (gods). I find, in studying the Tusayan calendar, as a whole, that dolls resembling Katcinas [1] are made in *Powamu*, the February ceremony, as well as at *Niman*, in July, and presented to the little girls in the same way ; never given to boys.

[1] Masked figures, or images of them, who take part in the religious ceremonies of the Tusayan or Hopi Indians. Their exact significance is somewhat doubtful.

"Just before I left Cambridge last November I installed my collection of Tusayan dolls in the upper story of the Peabody Museum, and if you happen that way, you may find it interesting to see them. A few more were collected last summer, but all duplicates. I noticed last August that one Tusayan child had a China doll hanging to the rafters of her mother's home with her *Katcina* dolls, and she supposed it represented a *Pahano* (American) *Katcina*."

W. E. Griffis, in his "Games and Sports of Japanese Children,"[1] says: "On the third day of the third month is held the *Hina matsuri*. This is the day especially devoted to the girls, and to them it is the greatest day in the year. It has been called in some foreign works on Japan, the 'Feast of Dolls.' Several days before the *matsuri* the shops are gay with the images bought for this occasion and which are on sale only at this time of year. Every respectable family has a number of these splendidly dressed images, which are from four inches to a foot in height, and which accumulate from generation to generation. When a daughter is born in the house during the previous year, a pair of *hina*, or images, are purchased for the little girl, which she plays with till grown up. When she is married her *hina* are taken with her to her husband's house, and she gives them to her children, adding to the stock as her family increases. The images are made of wood or enameled clay. They represent the Mikado and his wife; the *kuge*, or old Kiôto nobles, their wives and daughters, the court minstrels, and various personages in Japanese mythology and history. A great many other toys, representing all the articles in use in a Japanese lady's chamber, the service of the eating table, the utensils of the kitchen, traveling apparatus, etc., some of them very elaborate and costly, are also exhibited and played with on this day. The

[1] *Translation of the Asiatic Society of Japan*, Vol. II, pp. 132–133, London, 1882.

girls make offerings of *sake* and dried rice, etc., to the effigies of the emperor and empress, and then spend the day with toys, mimicking the whole round of Japanese female life, as that of child, maiden, wife, mother, and grandmother. In some old Japanese families in which I have visited the display of dolls and images was very large and extremely beautiful.

" On this day the entire female sex appears in holiday attire. The whole household store of dolls, among which are many old family treasures, is brought out for the girls and set up in a special room. The living dolls entertain the dead ones with food and drink, the latter consisting, in the absence of milk, of *shiro-sake* (white sweet cake). In Kio-bashidori, at Tokyo, where the shops are large and splendid and some of the dolls expensive, there is great activity on this day. Formerly the ' Feast of Dolls' fell, as a rule, in April, when the favorite sakura trees are in blossom, and as it resembles our peach tree, Europeans have named it the ' Festival of the Peach Flowers.'

"On this occasion mothers adorn the chamber with blossoming peach boughs and arrange therein an exhibition of all the dolls which their daughters have received; these represent the Mikado and Court personages, for whom a banquet is prepared, which is consumed by the guests of the evening.

" The greatest day in the year for the boys is on the fifth day of the fifth month. On this day is celebrated what is known as the ' Feast of Flags.' Previous to the coming of the day the shops display for sale the toys and tokens proper to the occasion. These are all of a kind, suited to young Japanese masculinity. They consist of effigies of heroes and warriors, generals and commanders, soldiers on foot and horse, the genii of strength and valor, wrestlers, etc. The toys represent the equipments and regalia of a daimiô's procession, all kinds of things used in war, the contents of an arsenal, flags, streamers, banners, etc. A set of these toys is bought for every son born in the family. Hence in old Japanese families the display of the fifth day of the fifth month is extensive and brilliant."

In Korea, at the children's festival, which falls on the eighth day of the fourth month, toys are universally sold, the most popular being the Ot-tok-i, or erect standing one. This is an image made of paper, with a rounded bottom filled with clay, so that it always stands upright; it is feminine, and has many counterparts throughout the world, and is a possible survival of the image of a deity anciently worshiped in Korea at this season, the above date being the birthday of Buddha, and this toy perhaps having once been his image. Still more anciently this was the date of the celebration of the vernal equinox.

In Japan the sitting toy is made to represent the Indian saint Daruma, and its name, Oki agari koboshi, means the little priest that rises up. They must be weighted to rise quickly. Tsuchi-ningyo means clay images of men and horses once buried with the dead to take the place of living sacrifices. Its French name, Le Poussah, is Buddha. This toy, therefore, is a common plaything, carved by an idol maker, and once an object of worship.

M. Ollivier Beauregard [1] says that there are two chief theatricals of dolls in Java, — the Topeng (mute mask), and Wayang (spectacle in shadow). In the latter a sort of bard rhapsodist operates the dolls and tells them their rôles of love and war to musical accompaniment. The dolls represent historical and mythological personages, and this is thought the best means of teaching history and enforcing its morals early. The spectators are often so interested that they watch the play all night. These Javanese marionettes are of three kinds : (1) very

[1] *Bulletins de la Société d'Anthropologie de Paris*, December, 1894, p. 689.

ancient gods and heroes; (2) celebrants of special festivals; (3) common dramatic figures. This is the most important of the native amusements coming at the time of the New Year's feast, which, in 1890, was from April 21 to May 21. W. Basil Worsfold, in his *A Visit to Java,* says : "This is very simple business ; beneath a Punch and Judy show in point of art, but the audience watch the puerile display for five or six hours without intermission. The theater consists of panto-mimic representations with which is mingled a ballet, the basis of which is ancient tradition."

James Mooney, of the Bureau of Ethnology, writes: "Among the Mokis and Pueblo tribes, generally, dolls are commonly representations of mythologic characters, and consequently have some religious significance. I doubt if this be the case among any other tribes, unless, possibly, among the totem-pole tribes of the northwest coast. Among others, probably, and with the prairie tribes certainly, dolls are simply girls' toys, as with us, and have no other purpose and are not used by boys. In other words, as you say, their use is from 'a common human instinct.' The Kiowas, with whom I am most closely asso-ciated, have a religious dread of making tangible representa-tion of mythologic beings. Little girls frequently carry and dress up puppies as dolls. Boys never play with dolls. Girls 'play house' with their dolls, as with us."

He adds : "With Kiowas and other prairie tribes dolls are simply girls' toys. The dolls represent both sexes, but, so far as my observation goes, are used only by girls. Indians lay great stress upon manly distinctions, and boys and girls rarely use the same toys or games."

R. J. Dodge says: "The little Indian girls are very fond of dolls, which their mothers make and dress with considerable skill and taste. Their baby houses are miniature tepees, and they spend as much time and take as much pleasure in such play as white girls."

Speaking of Eskimo toys, sledges, and dolls, Dr. Boas[1] says : "The last are made in the same way by all the tribes, a wooden body being clothed with scraps of deerskin cut in the same way as the clothing of men."

Clay MacCauley, in the same report, says : " The Seminole has a doll, i.e., a bundle of rags, a stick with a bit of cloth wrapped about it, or something that serves just as well as this. The children build little houses for their dolls and name them 'camps.' "

We see thus that among the Pueblo Indians, the Koreans and Chinese dolls are exact imitations in miniature of old tribal fetiches or idols no longer worshiped, made or sold on a special feast day or given only to girls with formal ceremony. Among the Pueblos this day was the primitive corn feast. Among the Koreans and Chinese it was the day once celebrated as the birthday of Buddha. In both these languages the word for *doll* is from the same root as the word for *fetich* or *idol*. In Japan, at a yearly feast, all the dolls of many generations are present, and the living dolls entertain the dead ones. Again it is possible that the ancient custom of Roman maidens of hanging up their dolls to Venus when they loosed their girdles was primitively a religious rite of consecrating play children to the goddess of fecundity. Still, in most languages the word for *fetich* and for *doll* have at best only a secondary connection, and that doll play is degraded fetich worship is certainly unproved. The exact origin and meaning of the Lares and Penates is too uncertain to base argument upon.

Dolls are found buried along with the children in the sarcophagi of the ancient Egyptians. A little girl figure was found in one of the buried cities with a doll clasped to her breast.

[1] *Annual Report of the Bureau of American Ethnology, 1884–1885*, p. 571. Washington, 1888.

Baring Gould says: "A white marble sarcophagus occupies the center of one of the rooms in the basement of the Capitoline Museum in Rome. The sarcophagus contains the bones and dust of a little girl, and by the side is the child's wooden doll, precisely like the dolls made and sold to-day. In the catacombs of St. Agnes one end of a passage is given up to the objects found in the tombs of the early Christians, and among these are some very similar dolls taken out of the graves of the Christian children."

W. H. Holmes [1] thinks that dolls found with other relics in graves in the province of Chiriqui were possibly toys, but more probably tutelary images.

Miss Alice Fletcher writes: "Among the Indian tribes with which I am familiar there is no special treatment of dolls. All depends upon the particular child's imagination and imitative powers.

" As far as my observation goes, and I can learn, the religious ceremonies of the tribe are not mimicked, although some of the practices of the same are. The religious rites of the white race are reproduced by the children. As far as I can yet discover, there is no relation between dolls and a fetich or any emblem."

During the two years that have intervened since the first syllabus was issued this subject has steadily grown in both interest and importance to the editors' minds, until this paper seems but the faintest and feeblest beginning of the many more special investigations that ought to be made in its field. Where could the philologist, for example, find a richer field for the study of the principle of analogy, the law of diminutives and of conferring names generally, and I know not what else, than in a far more extended and systematic investigation of dolls' names? The whole subject of idolatry, the use and

[1] *Annual Report of the Bureau of American Ethnology, 1884–1885*, p. 152. Washington, 1888.

psychology of images and pictures of God, Christ, angels, saints, etc., suggests, but only begins to reveal its richness here. When we reflect on the rôle that tutelary and ancestral images, puppets, heroic and mythological dolls have played in the past, the question must force itself upon our minds whether some well-devised form not only of image worship but even of fetichism might not be made as helpful in early religions as object lessons have been in secular education since Comenius. We do use pictures and statuettes of classical mythology to great advantage. Are we now advanced and strong enough to utilize the powerful instinct of idolatry still further, so as to get its stimulus and avoid its great and obvious dangers ? Children's ideas of life, death, soul, virtue and vice, disease, sickness, all the minor morals of dress, toilet, eating, etc., of family, state, church, theology, etc., are all as open as day, here, to the observer, and, although unconscious to themselves, almost anything within these large topics can be explored by the observing, tactful adult, without danger of injuring that naïveté of childhood which is both its best trait and its chief charm. What topic yet proposed for child study is not, at least in part, illustrated here ?

Imperfect as this study is, however, alas for the tact and intuitive power of the parent and kindergartner that does not find in the children's and mothers' records a wealth of helpful and immediately practical suggestions for their daily task of unfolding childhood from within. We have carefully refrained from psychologic or pedagogic generalizations, which have been often very tempting, because the time has not yet come for conclusions or specific rules of application. Prematureness and rashness here would involve danger of great harm ; but, as further researches are needed on the scientific side, special studies on the practical side are no less desiderated.

A. Caswell Ellis
G. Stanley Hall

204 CHILD LIFE AND EDUCATION

BIBLIOGRAPHY

Baring-Gould, S. Strange Survivals. Methuen & Co., London, 1902. 287 pages.

Chamberlain, Alexander F. Child and Childhood in Folk Thought. Macmillan, New York, 1896. 464 pages.

Compayre, G. L'Évolution intellectuelle et morale de l'enfant (chapter on Les Jeux, pp. 270–278). Hachette & Co., Paris, 1893. 371 pages.

Dodge, Richard Irving. Our Wild Indians. A. G. Nettleton & Co., Chicago, 1882.

Fewkes, J. Walter. "Dolls of the Tusayan Indians," *International Archiv für Ethnographie*, Vol. VII, pp. 45–73, 1894.

Griffis, W. E. "Games and Sports of Japanese Children," *Trans. of the Asiatic Soc. of Japan*, Vol. II, pp. 132–133, London, 1882.

Keller, Helen. The Story of My Life, pp. 22–24. Doubleday, Page & Co., New York, 1903. 441 pages.

Lazarus, M. Ueber die Reize des Spiels. Dümmler, Berlin, 1883.

Lombroso, Paola. Saggi di Psicologia del Bambino. Fratelli Bocca, Torino e Roma, 1894. 126 pages.

Low, Frances H. "Queen Victoria's Dolls." George Newnes, London, 1894.

Lubbock, Sir John. Origin of Civilization, Appendix, p. 545. D. Appleton & Co., New York, 1902. 577 pages.

Rein, J. J. Japan: Travels and Researches (translated from the German). Hodder & Stoughton, London, 1889. 534 pages.

Sidney, Margaret. Five Little Peppers Grown Up. Lothrop Publishing Company, Boston, 1892.

Stewart, Culin. Korean Games (with notes on the corresponding games of China and Japan). University of Pennsylvania, Philadelphia, 1895. xxxvi + 177 pages.

Sully, James. Studies of Childhood. D. Appleton & Co., New York, 1896. 527 pages. See index for many references, especially George Sand's doll experiences.

THE COLLECTING INSTINCT[1]

The "treasures" of children are cherished by them with feelings of sacredness, pride, and importance which can hardly be appreciated by the adult, unless he be blessed with a bit of foolish sentiment himself or possessed of a vivid memory penetrating back into the recesses of his own childish heart. Even more than in the single object of affection, — the pet chicken, the especial pride of a top, the beloved scrap of colored ribbon, the little shining stone fostered almost as a fetich, — the "treasure" feeling in children seems to expand and thrive especially when bestowed upon a collection of objects, objects which are not only a possession, like the single cherished fetich, but a seemingly great possession, commanding the admiration which repetition and numbers always invoke, and a possession, too, that may be compared proudly, or at least stimulatingly, with similar possessions of childish compeers and rivals. The single fetich treasure twines about the heart in a more or less indefinable, unreasoning sort of way. It strikes a cord of fancy or sentiment, perhaps through some association, or perhaps merely as a fragment seemingly unrelated to any other feeling and not based on any reason. But the collection treasure arouses, besides and along with the feeling of kinship and close relationship between "me" and "my possession," a more objective interest based on more definable even if more varied motives.

A study of the collecting instinct, craze, fad, or interest, however one may choose to designate this widespread phenomenon, is the object of this paper. Mrs. Annie Howes

[1] Reprinted in abridged form from *Pedagogical Seminary*, Vol. VII, pp. 179–207, July, 1900.

Barus has given an interesting biography, recorded from observation, of her own little boy's passion for bottles, beginning in his first year as a fear and mystery fetich-feeling for a particular huge green bottle, and developing into an affection for bottles in general and love of many bottles. Professor Earl Barnes contributes a reminiscent study based on the recollections of ninety-two adults, and Sara E. Wiltse and Dr. G. Stanley Hall have also made a study from a large amount of data.

The data which I wish to present here have been gotten from the reports of children themselves. A certain fifth grade in the schools of Santa Barbara, California, exhibited in connection with their nature study and history work a very lively interest in collections, and all the children were anxious to tell of their birds' eggs, their Chinese coins, their Indian arrows, and to bring specimens to the schoolroom. This collection interest had developed in the children spontaneously, and its extent and intensity were a surprise. In order to gain more definite information in regard to the nature of this interest, the children were asked to make out a list of all the things they had ever collected, tell when they began and when they stopped any collection, give the number of objects in each, and tell also various things about them, as will be discussed later. The results proved so fertile that a set of questions was made out and given to most of the teachers in the city, to be filled out by the children, and a similar set was gathered from school children of Santa Rosa. Several days were allowed in order that they might have time carefully to think up, look up, and count up their collections, and jog the memory of their mammas, also, as to their past collections. In some cases, as when an enterprising youth of ten years recorded sixty-six collections, fifty-five of them still continuing, the teacher herself consulted the mother and made sure that all were verified.

Records were obtained from 510 Santa Barbara children and 704 Santa Rosa children, in all 607 boys and 607 girls, or 1214 children.

The universality of the collecting interest was strikingly brought out. Only ten per cent. of the boys and nine per cent. of the girls were not actively making collections at the time, while but three per cent. of the boys and one per cent. of the girls said they had never made any collections, slightly fewer girls than boys being exempt.

The intensity of the collecting interest is shown in the number of collections made, as given in the following tables (I and II):

TABLE I

Present and Past Collections

Boys	. .	2874 Collections	Average to the boy . 4.7 Collections
Girls	. .	3261 Collections	Average to the girl . 5.4 Collections
Children	.	6135 Collections	Average to the child 5.1 Collections

TABLE II

Present or Active Collections

Boys	. .	1937 Collections	Average to the boy . 3.2 Collections
Girls	. .	2115 Collections	Average to the girl . 3.5 Collections
Children	.	4052 Collections	Average to the child 3.3 Collections

It will be seen that the girls slightly exceed the boys in the average number of collections made, as well as in the number making collections.

That the children on the average were in process of making from three to four actual collections bespeaks a considerable amount of energy being drained off through the channels of this instinct. But the generalities of the average cover up the "spots" where the instinct breaks out with remarkable intensity. There were six boys and ten girls making 9 collections each; seven boys and four girls making 10 collections each; three boys and five girls making 11 collections each; one boy and two girls making 12 collections each; one boy making 13 collections; one girl making 14 collections; one, 16; one, 18; one, 32; and one boy making 55.

The age development in regard to the number of collections made is worthy of notice. The following table (III) shows the variation of the average number of actively continuing collections for ages from six to seventeen years.

TABLE III

Average Number of Active Collections for Different Ages

Age in Years		Average per Boy	Average per Girl	Average per Child
6	. . . .	1.2	1.9	1.4
7	. . . .	2.1	2.6	2.3
8	. . . .	3.5	4.5	4.
9	. . . .	3.9	4.1	4.
10	. . . .	4.4	4.4	4.4
11	. . . .	3.4	3.3	3.3
12	. . . .	3.	3.	3.
13	. . . .	3.5	3.4	3.4
14	. . . .	3.	3.	3.
15	. . . .	2.7	3.2	3.
16	. . . .	2.1	3.3	2.8
17	. . . .	2.	3.	2.5

The impulse to collect, as shown by the reports on past collections, manifests itself at an early age, at least by three years. It develops rapidly from six years on and reaches its greatest intensity from eight to ten or eleven years, being strongest at ten years; then it continues with moderate force into adolescence. From fourteen years on the boys show declining interest, while the interest of girls continues more steadily. The high-tide mark is shown by the average number of collections at ten years, being then 4.4 collections for both boys and girls.

The question as to what children collect is best answered by asking what they do not collect. The consciously applied genius of man could hardly concoct a more numerous and diversified set of objects, — objects ranging from the utterly absurd, the useless, the grotesque to the really valuable; ranging from the commonest, meanest things to the rarest; objects appealing to all sorts of interests and allied with a variety of motives.

The following alphabetical list of nearly three hundred varieties of collections serves well to impress the vagaries of the collecting instinct, — to show how, in its intensity, it squeezes into any little channel that circumstance may open up. The classification is of course somewhat arbitrary. I have given as far as possible the specific collections as reported by the children. For instance, doll buggies, doll dresses, doll dishes, doll hats, and doll quilts might be summed up under doll belongings, but the children gave them separately. While, on the other hand, the term *pictures* might be divided into numerous classes, as funny pictures, pictures of noted men, of actresses, of poets, of singers, of babies, of animals, of flowers, war pictures, war-ship pictures, fashion pictures, mythological pictures, all of which were mentioned by the children. But as the majority who collected pictures simply gave the general term, I have combined under it all these special terms.

The boys and girls show about an equal variety in kinds of collections, the former making 215 different kinds and the latter 214.

In the following table the alphabetical order has been followed as the form most convenient for reference. The classification under subject-headings to show distribution of interests among the various groups of objects included in the collections, and the relative popularity of each group among boys and girls, is given in Table VI.

TABLE IV

List of Collections with Number of Boys and Girls making Each Kind

	Boys	Girls		Boys	Girls
Acorns	4	7	Breastpins		1
Advice (bits of) . . .	1		Bullets	2	
Animals	1		Butterflies	29	20
Antlers (deer) . . .	2	1	Buttons	84	154
Arrowheads	19	2	Buttons (cuff) . . .	1	1
Autographs	4	19	Buttons (picture) . .	39	32
Autograph sentiments .		3			
			Calendars	7	15
Badges	23	15	Candies		7
Bald-headed men counted		1	Cans	1	
Balls	1		Cards (calling) . . .		3
Beads	5	39	Cards (cigarette) . .	38	16
Beans	2	4	Cards (election) . . .	36	9
Bees	1	1	Cards (merit)		1
Beetles	1	1	Cards (picture) . . .	57	204
Belts		1	Cards (report) . . .		1
Bills		1	Cards (tally)		1
Birds	16	5	Cartridges	13	2
Birds' beaks and claws	1		Caterpillars	1	2
Birds' eggs	289	81	Cats	7	3
Birds' nests	17	7	Certificates		1
Birds' wings	2		Chalk	4	2
Blocks	4		Charm-strings	1	3
Bones	5	5	Chickens	7	3
Booklets		1	Chillicotes	8	5
Books	40	70	China (painted) . . .		1
Books (advertisement)		1	Chips	1	
Books (school) . . .		1	Christmas berries . .		1
Books (scrap) . . .	6	15	Chrysanthemums . .		1
Books (song)		2	Cigar-box papers . .	3	
Bottles	9	13	Cigar holders		1
Bottles (perfume) . .		1	Cigar ribbons	6	11
Boxes	12	16	Cigar tags	389	149
Bracelets		2	Cigar tins	1	
Brass	1		Cigar stamps	4	

	Boys	Girls		Boys	Girls
Clay		1	Ferns	7	29
Clocks	1		Fish	7	6
Clothespins	1	1	Fishhooks	1	
Clothes stamps . . .		1	Flags	8	12
Clover (four-leaf) . .		2	Flint	18	4
Cocoons		2	Flowers (paper) . . .		4
Coins	41	28	Flowers (pressed) . .	16	58
Compositions		1	Fossils		2
Cookies		1	Frogs	3	1
Coupons	14	9	Furs	1	1
Cows	1				
Crabs	2		Games	1	3
Crystals	4		Glass (pieces of) . .	17	35
Cups and saucers . .	3	14	Glasses		4
Curios (Alaskan, Indian,			Goats	1	
etc.)	29	17	Gopher skins		1
			Grass	1	3
Dishes	2	15	Guns	1	
Dishes (broken) . . .		11			
Dolls	1	95	Hair (locks of) . . .	5	17
Dolls (paper) . . .	4	106	Handkerchiefs . . .	1	1
Doll buggies		1	Hats	2	1
Doll clothes		17	Hat tips counted . . .		4
Doll dishes		1	History scraps . . .	1	
Doll hats		1	Horses	1	
Doll quilts		1	Horsehair chains . .	12	6
Dogs	6	2	Horseshoe nails . . .	4	
Dogs (rubber) . . .	1		Horseshoes	16	7
Dragonflies		1	Horses counted (white)	6	41
Drawings	2	6			
Dresses		2	Insects	9	4
Ducks	1		Invitations		1
			Iron	3	
Earrings		2			
Easter eggs	1	3	Jackstones		1
Envelope rings . . .	1	2	Jewelry		8
Envelopes	1		Jugs		1
Fans		4	Keys	1	
Feathers	6	8	Kites	2	

	Boys	Girls		Boys	Girls
Knives	7		Nuts (Chinese)	1	
Knots in ropes	1		Nutshells	1	
Labels	7		Oak balls	1	
Lace		4	Oil cans	2	
Lead	4		Opals		1
Leaves	40	68			
Leaves (decayed)		1	Padlocks	1	
Letters	4	10	Paints	1	
Lizards	1		Pans	1	
			Pant guards	1	
Magazines	4	9	Paper articles		1
Maps	3	1	Paper (colored)	1	10
Marbles	221	136	Paper (tissue)	2	4
Marbles (agates)	25	3	Papers (French)		1
Match-box tops	1		Papers (perfect)	1	
Matches	1	1	Papers (school work)	1	5
Medals	2	1	Papers (Sunday school)	1	7
Mice	1		Peas (wild)	2	
Minerals	22	10	Pebbles	15	41
Money	10	10	Pencils	2	6
Monkeys	1		Pennies	1	5
Monograms		5	Pens		3
Moss (sea)	19	58	Periwinkles	1	
Moss (wood)	3	7	Pets		3
Music	1	2	Photographs	8	25
			Pictures	58	132
Nails	3	1	Pictures (kodak)	4	13
Names (authors')		1	Pieces for quilts		14
Names (of books read)	1		Pieces of calico, cloth, silk,		
Names (Christian)		1	velvet	6	110
Names (of legal holidays)	1		Pigeons	25	8
Napkins	2	24	Pinks	1	
Neckties	2		Pins	10	31
Needles	1	1	Pins (hat)	2	3
Newspaper covers	1		Pins (scarf)	1	
Newspaper scraps	1	9	Pins (stick)		6
Newspapers	5	4	Plants	7	19
Nickels	1		Poems	2	23

	Boys	Girls
Polliwogs		2
Postal cards	1	
Posters		2
Postmarks	2	8
Programmes (theater, dance, etc.)	4	5
Puzzles	2	4
Quartz	2	
Rabbit ears	1	
Rabbits	27	12
Rags	2	16
Rats (white)	6	1
Red-headed girls counted		1
Ribbons	8	58
Ribbons (men-of-war) .	1	
Riddles		3
Rings		3
Rocks	67	53
Rose petals		4
Rubber (sheet) . . .		1
Rubbers	1	
Sachet bags		1
Sacks	5	1
Sayings (of all descriptions)		6
Sayings (witty) . . .	2	7
Seals		3
Seeds	6	8
Shark eggs	1	
Shells	113	223
Shoes (old)		1
Shot		1
Silkworms	2	2
Skeletons	1	
Skins	3	
Skins (rattlesnake) . .	1	

	Boys	Girls
Sloyd models	11	
Sloyd sewing		4
Snake eggs	1	1
Soils		1
Songs	1	16
Souvenirs	3	14
Spiders		1
Spools	18	22
Spoons	1	15
Stamps	365	240
Starfish		2
Sticks	1	
Stingaree stings . . .	1	
Stones	43	26
Stories	2	5
Strings	6	23
Tags (shipping) . . .	1	
Tags (tin)	2	
Tags (tobacco) . . .	32	10
Teeth (cats')	1	
Thread		1
Tickets	2	1
Tiles	1	
Time-tables	1	
Tin	1	
Tintypes		2
Toads	1	
Tobacco sacks . . .	1	
Tools	4	
Tops	38	3
Toys	4	1
Trade-marks (soap, etc.)	2	2
Trees	3	
Turtles	10	1
Valentines	1	3
Vases		3
Vegetables	3	

	Boys	Girls		Boys	Girls
Wagon wheels . . .	1	1	Weapons	1	1
Walnuts	1		Woods	15	3
Wampum	3		Woods (petrified) . .	3	2
War (pieces about) .	1		Wrappers (fruit, yeast,		
War relics	1		etc.)	1	3
Water (colored) . . .		1			
Water colors		2	Zoölogical specimens .	1	1

PROMINENT COLLECTIONS

Certain collections stand out much more prominently than others, especially cigar tags, stamps, birds' eggs, marbles, and shells. These are prominent among both boys and girls, though all but shells much more so among the boys. Certain collections rank high, but more particularly among the girls, as picture cards, pictures, buttons, pieces of cloth, silk, etc., dolls, paper dolls. Then follow some, as books, rocks, leaves, flowers, ribbons, and others, which have a fair following. The remaining classes of collections were made by only a few children, and ninety-seven kinds were made by only one child each. Table V gives a list of the more prominent collections, with the percentage of boys and girls who were making or who had made them.

It will be seen that the boys concentrate more on a few things which run as crazes through very many groups. About three fifths of the boys had collected cigar tags and stamps, and nearly half of them had collected birds' eggs. Nothing attains such widespread interest among the girls, although between thirty and forty per cent. of them had collected stamps, shells, and picture cards, but a greater number of things have considerable runs with them. The table shows that only seven things were collected by ten or more per cent. of the boys, — cigar tags, stamps, eggs, marbles, shells, buttons, and rocks; while sixteen things were collected by ten or more per cent. of the girls, — including the same things as in the case of the boys, except rocks, — all in the following order : stamps, shells, picture cards, cigar tags, buttons, pictures, marbles, pieces of cloth, etc., paper dolls, dolls, eggs, books, leaves, sea mosses, pressed flowers, and ribbons.

TABLE V

Prominent Collections and Proportion of Children making Them

	Boys Per Cent.	Girls Per Cent.		Boys Per Cent.	Girls Per Cent.
Cigar tags. . . .	64	24	Flowers	2	10
Stamps.	60	39	Ribbons	1	10
Birds' eggs . . .	47	13	Stones	7	6
Marbles	36	22	Pebbles	2	7
Shells	18	36	White horses counted	1	7
Picture cards. . .	9	33	Picture buttons . .	6	5
Pictures	9	22	Coins	6	4
Buttons.	14	23	Pieces of glass . .	3	6
Pieces of cloth, etc.	1	20	Butterflies. . . .	5	3
Paper dolls . . .	1	17	Election cards . .	6	1
Dolls		16	Beads	1	6
Books	7	12	Spools	3	4
Rocks	11	9	Badges.	4	2
Leaves	7	11	Strings	1	4
Sea mosses . . .	3	10			

COLLECTIONS MADE BY BOYS OR GIRLS EXCLUSIVELY

Certain kinds of collections, eighty in all, are found only among the boys, and certain kinds, seventy-nine in all, only among the girls, one hundred and thirty-five kinds being common to both. Only boys report such collections as birds' beaks, claws, and wings, crabs, dogs, ducks, goats, lizards, mice, monkeys, rabbit ears, shark eggs, skeletons, rattlesnake skins, cats' teeth, toads, in the way of animals ; brass, bullets, cigar tins, clocks, crystals, horseshoe nails, iron, keys, lead, nickels, oil cans, padlocks, paints, pans, quartz, tin, tiles, in the way of mineral and mechanical miscellanies; blocks, balls, fishhooks, guns, kites, knives, tools, in the line of toys; war relics, pieces about the war, history scraps, names of legal holidays, in the historical line; neckties and scarf pins, in the way of toilet articles. Only girls mention autograph sentiments, calling cards, report cards, tally cards, invitations, monographs, tintypes, in the line of things savoring of the souvenir sentiment; belts, perfume bottles, bracelets, breastpins, dresses, earrings, fans, jewelry, lace, sachet bags, stick pins, in the line of toilet articles; painted china, posters, paper flowers, jugs, vases, in the decorative line; baldheaded men counted, red-headed girls and hat tips counted, and four-leaf clover, in the way of luck collections; and doll belongings, in the way of toys.

INDIVIDUALITY VERSUS IMITATION AND FADS

Without doubt the collecting instinct, if such we may call it, is largely dependent on imitation as its tinder. There are large blazes that spread rapidly and widely, and small blazes that still affect their many. The elements of imitation and its specialized form, faddism, are unmistakable. Five sixths of the six thousand collections reported were, each, one of from ten to three hundred or so similar collections in the same town. About one sixth, or a thousand collections, were in runs of less than ten in the same town, showing some considerable individual independence. Ninety-seven children, as already mentioned, — fifty-five boys and forty-two girls, — or eight per cent. of all the children, made collections reported by no other child, — collections that were the product of individual fancy. If we found the most widespread crazes among the boys, as in the case of cigar tags, so too we find, on the other extreme, slightly more marked individuality among them. Some of the collections to which only one child stood sponsor were bits of advice, chips, rubber dogs, envelopes, knots in ropes, match-box tops, names of books read, Chinese nuts, nutshells, oak balls, pant guards, perfect papers, rubbers, stingaree stings, time-tables, bills, advertisement books, merit cards, dragon flies, gopher skins, jack-stones, decayed leaves, Christian names, old shoes, soils, shot, spiders.

DISTRIBUTION OF INTERESTS

While a study of the collections of specific objects may show, perhaps, the influence of imitation and circumstance and environment, a combination of the heterogeneous varieties of collections under a few general headings may show real trends of interest and inclinations of mind. For instance, we find that the Santa Barbara children, living in daily contact with the sea-beach, collected more shells and sea moss than the Santa Rosa children, who, living in an interior, agricultural valley, depend solely on summer vacations for their acquaintance with the ocean and its treasures. This is the result of environment. But we should hardly conclude anything as to general nature interest from these two collections alone. The Santa Rosa children may show their nature interest in channels more in accordance with their own immediate environment; as, for example, we find bird-egg collections in excess there. But a combination of all the nature collections in both places will in some measure indicate the comparative place the nature interest occupies among other interests. This combination I have made, and also a separate grouping of the animal, plant, and mineral collections. Under animal collections we have birds, birds' eggs, nests, wings, insects, rabbits, pigeons, and other animals, silkworms, skins, furs, etc.; under plant collections, ferns, flowers, leaves, woods, moss, seeds, grass, etc.; under mineral collections, minerals, shells, rocks, stones, pebbles, flint, quartz, petrified wood, etc. Besides the nature collections I have combined the other collections under eleven further headings, as shown in Table VI, which gives the proportion of collections found under each. The percentages are made on the whole number of collections. A few of the headings need illustrative explanation. "Playthings" include dolls, marbles, tops, tools, guns, kites, etc. Under "literary" are placed books, magazines, poems, sayings, stories, etc.; under "historical" there are curios (Alaskan, Chinese, Indian), arrowheads, historical scraps, pieces about the war, etc. "Personal adornment" embraces ribbons, hats, stick and breast pins, lace, fans, feathers, neckties, dresses, etc.; "sentimental" includes locks of hair, autograph sentiments, valentines, souvenirs, etc.; "useful" includes quilt pieces, handkerchiefs, spoons, cups and saucers, etc. The "miscellaneous trivial" collections are those chiefly of the younger children, of things such as bottles, sticks, strings, boxes, pieces of cloth, etc., which seem to be more or less purposeless, and which are easy to obtain. The second heading is a specific one, — "cigar tags, stamps, etc." No general term seems to cover these collections. Badges, picture buttons, and others are included, and all seem in a way related. These things, like the miscellaneous trivial things, are easy to obtain, but at the same time there is a sort of official importance about them that perhaps appeals; they have the fascination, too, of connection with the outside world, and their quantities and currency quality facilitate the interesting transaction of trading.

Taking the boys and girls together it is interesting to notice that the nature interest ranks highest. With the boys by themselves the cigar-tag, stamp, etc., interest leads the list, but this is practically equaled by the nature interest. In the nature line (see Table VII), interest in the animal world far exceeds that in the plant and mineral worlds, with the boys.

Minerals rank next, then plants, while with the girls the order is mineral, plant, animal. The next greatest number of collections with the boys is in the line of playthings; then come miscellaneous trivial things and pictures; literary and historical interests follow with modest steps. With the girls the nature interest ranks higher than that in cigar tags, stamps, etc. Miscellaneous trivial things come next, then pictures and playthings, followed by the other classes in much less degree. Boys exceed girls greatly in the cigar-tag, stamp, etc., collections, considerably in the nature collections, and very slightly in the historical collections, while girls exceed boys in the other classes except in playthings, where both have an equal interest. The greater interest of girls is most marked in picture, literary, and personal adornment collections. In the subdivisions of nature collections boys exceed girls only in the animal collections.

TABLE VI

Distribution of Interests shown by the Relative Proportion of Various Groups of Collections

COLLECTIONS	OF ALL CHILDREN Per Cent.	OF BOYS Per Cent.	OF GIRLS Per Cent.
Nature	29.	32.4	26.
Cigar tags, stamps, etc.	24.	33.8	16.
Miscellaneous trivial	12.	8.	15.
Playthings	12.	11.	12.
Pictures	10.	6.	13.
Literary	3.	2.	5.
Historical	2.	3.	2.
Personal adornment	3.	1.	5.
Sentimental	1.3	.7	2.
Useful	1.3	.6	2.
Luck	1.	.8	1.5
Unclassified	1.4	1.7	1.5

TABLE VII

Distribution of Nature Interest

COLLECTIONS	BOYS Per Cent.		GIRLS Per Cent.	
Animal	17.6	⎫	6	⎫
Plant	4.9	⎬ 32.4	9	⎬ 26
Mineral	9.9	⎭	11	⎭

AGE DISTRIBUTION OF INTERESTS

Some of the collections are found at all ages, beginning in childhood and lasting on into adolescence. Others show an especial prominence at certain ages. We may notice the age distribution of a few of the more prominent collections.

The marble collection begins at least by six years, with a small number of followers, and reaches its height from seven to ten years, but especially at eight and nine years. After this age it declines, and from thirteen years on plays a small part. Stamps hold their own from seven to fifteen years, declining thereafter. The prominent ages are from nine to fourteen years. Collections of cigar tags are rather full-fledged at as early an age as six years. The craze increases, reaching its greatest intensity at twelve years, and then diminishes, dying out practically at sixteen years. This collection is prominent through a greater number of years than any other collection. The bird-egg fever begins mildly at seven years and increases, reaching its height from twelve to fourteen years.

The greatest intensities of these four collections seem to follow one another like the crests of succeeding waves. The marble crest, at eight and nine years, is followed by the stamp crest from nine to eleven years ; then comes the cigar crest at eleven and twelve years, and then the bird-egg crest from twelve to fourteen years. The cigar-tag craze remains highest, the stamp craze next highest, through all ages. The marble line of interest and that of birds' eggs cross between eleven and twelve years and supplement each other.

With the girls the interests in stamps, cigar tags, and birds' eggs follow about the same lines as with the boys, reaching their heights a little earlier if anything, while the greatest interest in marbles comes a year or so later.

Noticing now other nature collections besides birds' eggs, we find that rocks are about the first to appear upon the scene. The little child of four seizes upon crude, irregular bits, lumps, and masses. Beauty, form, and color seem to play little part at first. The collecting of rocks continues until about ten years, and in the latter part of this period is largely superseded by the collecting of smoother stones, often " colored stones " and "pretty stones." In contrast with crude rock lumps, the collection of pebbles begins also at three or four years and lasts about the same length of time. Leaves have their dominant period before ten years, while flowers, sea mosses, and shells come especially between eight and eleven years, chiefly with the girls, and butterflies at this age with the boys. Spontaneous nature interest, as far as collecting goes, seems to be especially from eight to eleven years. Birds' eggs are about the only nature collection that continues to show any prominence in adolescence.

The collection of miscellaneous trivial things — buttons, spools, strings, glass, beads, pins, broken dishes, etc. — begins at about three or four years of age and lasts to about seven or eight years. The collection of picture buttons is an adolescent affair, together with badges. Doll collections, beginning at three or four years, reach their height at nine or ten years, while those of paper dolls are strongest a year or so later. The collection of pieces of cloth follows the trail of the doll interest, and is superseded in early adolescence by that of ribbons. Picture cards rage from four to eleven years of age. Pictures have two periods, — the childhood period of scrapbook pictures up to nine or ten years, and the adolescent period of better pictures from twelve years on. The interest in books begins at about eight years and continues through adolescence. The "luck" interest is from eight to twelve years. The "historical" interest comes from eight to thirteen years, continuing into adolescence.

STAGES OF DEVELOPMENT IN THE CHILD

Looking now at the age progress from the standpoint of the child rather than from that of the various collections, we may combine the prominent interests of each age and note certain well-marked stages of development in the collecting mania. Up to eight years of age the collecting impulse is crude, groping, undirected. Collecting at this period seems to be an instinct rather than an interest. Things are collected which are absurd, valueless, trivial, mechanical, scrappy, simple, and easy to lay hands upon. There are bottles, boxes, pins, clothes-pins, strings, sticks, matches, buttons. The crudest nature collections come at this age, — acorns, rocks, pebbles. Things which are purposeful at this age are really possessions rather than collections, as toys, dolls, doll belongings, scrapbooks, etc.

Following the childhood period is what we may call the pre-adolescent period, from eight to eleven or twelve years. Here collections reach their height in quantity and genuineness. The crude instinct seems to develop into a more conscious interest. There is more interest in the things themselves, as well as in the collecting of them. The interest is more directed, more purposeful, answers the call of inner needs more strongly. On the other hand, we find the imitative element very strong at this period. On the side of "inner need" we notice that the play interest reaches its height here, as shown in the marble, doll, etc., collections; and also the nature interest is more prominent at this age than at any other, shown in the collections of flowers, stones, mosses, butterflies, shells, eggs, etc. On the side of "imitation" we find the cigar-tag and stamp crazes more widespread at this age than earlier or later. At this age, too, the "possession" idea of childhood seems to develop into love of quantities. The largest collections come now.

Then follows the adolescent period from about twelve years on, a period not so much of interest in the things collected, not so much of large crazes and widespread imitation and love of quantities, as a period of social associations, a period of fad and fashion on smaller scales. The pre-adolescent child is a spontaneous naturalist: he gathers in his quantities. The adolescent, entering into his heritage of logic and reason and understanding of relationships and of cause and effect, passes out of the "naturalist" stage; but at the same time he does not seem to develop spontaneously into the later scientific stage of digestion and classification and explanation in connection with his collections. Scientific development at this age, when the individual is less the product of the race and more susceptible to the influence of environment, especially of human environment, needs direction and encouragement, if it would continue in its normal path. We should naturally expect collecting, which before adolescence has been more or less of an end in itself, now, if carried on, to be used as a means, as a handle, to higher scientific interests. But such does not prove the case. For want of direction the collecting impulse in reality continues into adolescence as a vestige, as it were, a remnant, of the real instinct. It dribbles off into sentimental lines, as in the collection of party souvenirs, theater programmes, etc.; and into social fads, as in the collection of spoons, hatpins, etc. The spontaneous nature interest largely dies out, except in the case of birds' eggs, where other instincts, as the roaming and hunting, continue to supply incentive. The stamp and cigar-tag interests, which continue, are now closely associated with the passion for trading.

But while, in general, collecting in adolescence lingers as a degenerate form, as it were, or as a cat's-paw for other passions, as the sentimental and social, the hunting and the trading, we still find that it does continue as a real and genuine interest in two lines, the literary and the æsthetic. The collecting interest is a beginning interest in any subject. Logical and analytical interest comes later. Now, in the child as in the race, the nature interest develops earlier than the literary and æsthetic, and hence it is natural that the collecting period in the former line should normally precede that in the latter lines. The literary and æsthetic interests, beginning largely in adolescence, are initiated by a collecting stage. So, here, collections of books, pictures, etc., come normally, and true appreciation of them follows later. As a pedagogical conclusion we may here suggest that while nature collecting should be followed in adolescence by more analytical work, literary and æsthetic work, on the contrary, may begin in early adolescence with the encouragement of this very collecting instinct.

Methods of obtaining Collections

The children were asked to tell how they obtained their various collections. The data given here are from the Santa Rosa children only. The methods of getting collections simmer down to a few. The things were found or hunted for by the children themselves, that is, obtained by their own exertions, were given to them, were traded for, were bought or won. Table VIII and Chart I show the relative proportion of the methods given.

Table VIII

Methods of obtaining Collections

	Boys' Methods Per Cent.	Girls' Methods Per Cent.
Finding	39	36
Given	26	48
Trading	16	6
Buying	13	9
Winning	4	

CHART I

Methods of obtaining Collections

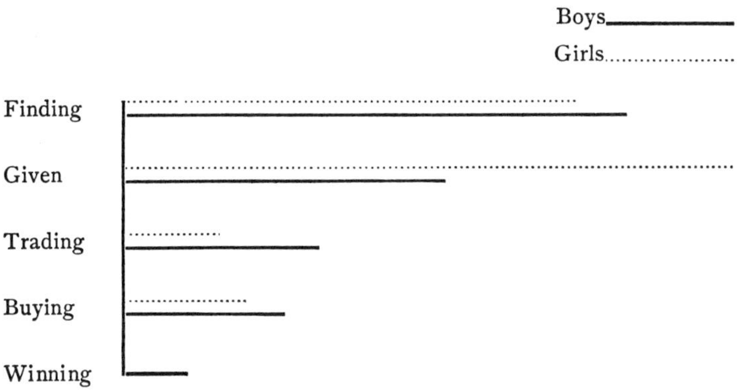

Boys_____
Girls...................

Finding

Given

Trading

Buying

Winning

With the boys the chief method of getting their collections is by their own exertions, finding them, or hunting for them. Then follow "given," "trading for," and "buying." "Winning" is insignificant and applies practically only to marbles. Nearly half of the methods mentioned by the girls came under the head of "given." Then follow "finding," "buying," and "trading," the latter two being comparatively unimportant. The boys exceed the girls somewhat in finding and hunting, and considerably in trading and buying. The girls exceed the boys very greatly as passive recipients of outside assistance, in having their things given to them by brothers, sisters, parents, uncles, aunts, and friends. But this excess of passivity on their part is not balanced by any special decrease in the method of finding, but it rather balances the excess of trading, buying, and winning among the boys.

These different methods vary somewhat with the different ages of the children. For boys we find that the prominent ages for being given their objects are seven, eight, and nine years, after which there is a general decrease in this method.

The prominent age for finding and hunting immediately follows the more passive period and comes at nine and ten years. The "given" and "finding" are equal just before nine years, the latter waxing greater at that time and continuing so throughout. From eleven years on, the "finding" continues rather evenly, but is less than before on account of the rise of the buying and trading tendencies. The prominent ages for buying and trading follow next after those for finding, and are from eleven on through adolescence. The winning tendency maintains a humble but even course.

The greatest activity among the children in obtaining their collections by their own exertions comes in the pre-adolescent period, which has already been noticed as the age of greatest intensity and genuineness of interest in collections, and also as the age of greatest interest in nature collections. With adolescence the commercial spirit comes in to mar the naturalist spirit.

I give some of the responses of the children to the question, How did you obtain your collections? The first one is very typical of the younger children.

F., 9. My cousin gave me my paper dolls. My aunt gave me my box of shells. My papa and mamma gave me my picture cards and scrapbooks. And my grandma sent me my rocks. And whenever I find a pretty rock I take it home.

M., 10. In collecting cigar rings it is very hard to find many good ones, because most every boy is collecting them, but in San Francisco you can find a great many, but still the boys collect them.

M., 10. I got my marbles in playing for them and bought a few.

M., 10. I started to count white horses when I was eight years old and ended when I was nine. It brought me good luck. I got to go to a show.

F., 12. I obtained my stamps in several different ways, hunting for them myself, buying them, getting friends to collect for me, and trading with other people. I have about 600 varieties and 1000 stamps.

F., 13. I asked my friends to get me all the cards they could, and if I happened to get two of a kind I traded with some one.

F., 13. Buttons are very foolish and easy things to collect, but I had the craze as most girls do. I had my grown friends give me all the odd ones they had in their button baskets.

The replies in regard to the nature collections are the fullest and most enthusiastic, especially in the case of birds' eggs, and often give additional information about the objects collected.

F., 11. I hunted for sea mosses along the seashore, and then I wet it and put it in the sun to dry. The sea moss grows on rocks out in the ocean. When there is a storm it breaks the sea moss off the rocks, and it floats in to the shore.

F., 11. I hunted for shells on the seashore. There are many different kinds of shells, and some are very pretty. There are two kinds called rice shells and coffee beans. You find these in little alcoves where the water is always washing up on the sand.

M., Grade VI. Butterflies are quite hard to get. Sometimes when standing in the yard I would see a butterfly, then I would take my hat off and throw it at the butterfly, and that would scare it. Then I would chase it around the house a few times, then the butterfly would start off in a different direction and probably go over a swamp, and then I would wade through and get my feet wet rather than let the butterfly go. Sometimes I would run after them three or four hours.

M., 15. I used to live on a ranch in Colusa County. I had about 15 quails' eggs. These the men who worked for my father would bring in in haying season. The quails would build their nests in the shocks where the men would find them. I had some doves' eggs; these I would find on the ground after the hay was cut. I had some small owls' eggs and linnets'. The swallows made their nests in the cottonwood trees that grew around the house.

Only two or three children suggest qualms of conscience in collecting birds' eggs.

M., 13. I think I like to collect birds' eggs better than anything else. But I think it is not right to take our songsters' eggs.

F., 13. I started to collect birds' eggs, but when I saw how badly the birds wanted them I would just climb down that tree and up the next, where the same performance was apt to occur, and so I failed.

MOTIVES FOR COLLECTING

The children give a variety of reasons as to why they made their collections, as shown in Table IX. They collected because others were collecting, because an older brother or sister, or Johnny Jones, or the "other boys," were collecting, that is, as a matter of imitation or fad.

M., 9. I began to collect cigar tags because I saw the other boys collecting.

M., 11. As all the other boys were collecting stamps I thought that I would get a collection of them, just for the fun of collecting.

M., 10. I got birds' eggs because my relatives got them.

F., 13. The reason why I collected the dolls was because it was a fashion to play with them and have as many different kinds as possible, and I had to follow the fashion, and because I considered it great fun to play with them.

F., 13. I suppose my weakness or craze (in regard to buttons) was because I am a girl and all girls are afflicted with it sometime during their life.

The influence of others is sometimes in the way of rivalry rather than mere imitation.

M., 9. I started to collect cigar wrappers because my chum started and I wanted to beat him.

M., 12. I began collecting cigar wrappers because I saw another boy collecting, and so I thought I would see if I could get as many as he had.

F., 13. Cigar rings, I am ashamed to say, I commenced collecting because a girl I knew and did not like had 500 or more different kinds and I wished to get ahead of her, and I did.

The interest in quantity, in numbers, is very great. To get as many as possible possesses a great attraction. Interest in quantity far outweighs interest in kind.

M., 11. I thought I would collect election cards to see how many I could get.

F. I wanted to see how many cigar wrappers I could get in three weeks.

There is some interest, however, manifested in kinds, in varieties, as well as in mere numbers.

M., 11. I thought I would collect buttons and birds' eggs to see how many different kinds I could get.

F., 16. I commenced my collection with the purpose of seeing how many different kinds I could obtain, and because I am interested in them.

Many vague reasons are given by the children, showing a more or less purposeless and nebulous state of mind. They "just wanted to"; they collected "just for fun"; they had a "good start" or an accidental start; they thought it was "nice"; some one suggested the idea; the things were "easy to get"; or they accumulated in some way or other. Some of the children give no reason; others say they "don't know why." All these replies I have classed in the table under the head of "Indefinite."

M., 9. I just collected shells for fun. I just collected stones for fun.

M., 10. I found two nests with eggs, and I thought if I was started I might as well collect, so I did.

M., 10. A boy said to me why did n't I get some pigeons. So I asked my father, and he said Yes, and I made a house and collected pigeons.

F., 13. I do not know why I commenced collecting dolls, probably because I am a girl.

Some collect with the idea of enjoying their collections in some way, of using them, of playing with them, or for the pleasure of looking at them.

M., 8. Marbles I began to collect because it would be fun playing with them.

M., 12. History scraps, puzzles, games, I got to play with on rainy days.

M., 12. Pictures of ships and famous men I got just to keep and look at.

Besides the enjoyment of the objects collected there is pleasure in the mere collecting, in the activity as a pastime.

M., 12. I got birds' eggs just to pass away the time.

Differing from the use or enjoyment of the collections is the more intellectual interest in them and desire to study them. The curiosity interest may be included under this head.

M., 11. I collected my minerals because I liked to take an interest in them.

F., 10. I liked to collect polliwogs because I tried to find out all about them and see them turn into frogs.

The interest in the objects collected is sometimes an æsthetic one. The beauty of the object attracts.

M., 10. I got pebbles because they were pretty.
M., 10. I got picture cards in stores because they were pretty.

The commercial motive appears consciously to some extent.

M., 10. I collected eggs because I can sell them. In collecting rings I most always sell them. I collect stamps because when you get a set of them you can sell them for a great deal of money. You can sell flint if you chip an arrowhead out of it.

M., 14. I collect stamps because the stamps that I have collected for years are worth very much money. I keep on collecting them now because I was offered for my collections twenty dollars, but they are worth more.

M., 13. Collected minerals of attractive form and color to sell as souvenirs to summer visitors.

Objects are also collected as souvenirs, and a few other miscellaneous reasons are given, such as for luck, for trading purposes, to give to others, to exhibit, to have or keep, for school work.

Table IX and Chart II show the relative proportion of these various motives, and differences for boys and girls.

TABLE IX

Motives for Collecting

	Boys' Motives Per Cent.	Girls' Motives Per Cent.
Imitation (because others did)	29	25
Rivalry (to get as many or more than others)	2	4
Quantity interest (to see how many) . . .	20	15
Interest in kind (to see how many kinds) .	3	6
Indefinite	8	6
Enjoyment, use, of objects	7	10
Pastime (pleasure in collecting)	4	3
Interest in objects collected	7	9
Æsthetic attraction of objects	3	8
Commercial motive	7	2
Souvenir interest	2	5
Miscellaneous	8	7

Motives for Collecting

CHART II

Imitation	
Rivalry	
Quantity interest . . . . , .	
Interest in kind	
Indefinite	
Enjoyment, use, of objects . .	
Pastime	
Interest in objects collected .	
Æsthetic attraction of objects .	
Commercial motive	
Souvenir interest	
Miscellaneous	

Boys ——
Girls ············

Imitation looms up as the strongest influence in setting the collecting instinct in action. Then follows the interest in quantity, in numbers, in large possession. In contrast with imitation, or doing as others do, rivalry, or doing more than others do, seems to hold a comparatively small place; and in contrast with interest in quantity, interest in variety, in kind, is insignificant. The interest in kind and the genuine interest in the objects themselves approach most nearly to the conscious scientific attitude. The considerable percentage of indefinite reasons given seems to suggest the instinctive side of the collecting interest. Some start, some suggestion, some idea perhaps not remembered or known, supplies the incentive to an instinct that seemingly requires very little inducement to call it forth.

Some sex differences may be noticed. Boys yield slightly more to the imitative influence than girls. This has been already shown in the record of their collections by the fact that they exhibit more widespread crazes. As imitation takes on the character of faddism in adolescence, the girls give this motive oftener than the boys. Boys, too, exceed slightly in the love of quantity and large possessions. This is shown also by the fact that their collections are carried to a far greater extent than those of the girls. They often collect thousands of objects, while girls are content with hundreds. Girls show somewhat more maturity in their greater interest in kinds and in the objects collected. Without doubt the interest in kind is larger for both boys and girls than is here represented. It is less of a conscious interest, and at the same time it is an interest in quantities of kinds, which is not very different from interest in quantities of objects. In the commercial motive boys outrun the girls, while the girls balance their lack in this line by a disinterested pleasure in the æsthetic and sentimental attractions of their collections.

Certain motives are more dominant at some ages than at others. Imitation is given as a motive by boys chiefly before adolescence, and by girls chiefly during adolescence where it takes on the character of faddism. Interest in quantity comes chiefly from ten to twelve years, before adolescence. Rivalry is scattered along, but does not appear before nine years of age, and is, perhaps, a trifle the strongest just before adolescence. The motive of enjoyment and use appears largely in the ten-to-twelve period. The scientific, the æsthetic, and the commercial interests come principally in adolescence. The indefinite motives appear to a great extent before eight years of age.

Summarizing, we find childhood the period of blind yielding to instinct; the preadolescent years, from nine or ten to twelve, the age when imitation, competition, interest in quantity, and enjoyment of the objects collected act as motives. In adolescence come faddism and also the commercial, æsthetic, sentimental, and scientific interests.

ARRANGEMENT OF COLLECTIONS

A study of the arrangement or classification children make of the contents of their collections shows that they are in the stage of the naturalist rather than of the scientist. There is comparatively little classification of objects according to any scientific basis, that is, according to variety and kind. The large majority of the collections are simply "kept together" with more or less care. They may be in "no order," just "mixed together," "arranged any way," kept "in a pile," or, as may be stated more definitely, they may be kept in the barn or the shed, in a drawer, a box, bag, envelope, book, trunk, pocket, basket, bottle, or can, on a shelf, or fastened on cloth, paper, ribbons, or on a string.

There are many evidences of care if not of arrangement.

M., 10. I had my birds' eggs in a cigar box. It is filled with sawdust. Sawdust is very soft and will not break the eggs. The eggs are very tender. I think that the humming birds' eggs are tenderest.

The first appearance of classification is on the basis of size or color, or both. Butterflies may be arranged according to color, eggs according to size or color.

M., 9. I put the birds' eggs in a glass box, large eggs in the bottom and small ones on top.

M., 9. The cards I put in my scrapbook, small ones on one page and large ones on another.

There is some classification of objects according to kinds, but this does not imply much knowledge of varieties.

M., 13. When I got birds' eggs I went to work and got a pasteboard box about three inches deep, one foot wide, two feet long, to put them in. Then I got some long strips of pasteboard and fenced off one kind of eggs from another kind; then I put in these places cotton so the eggs would n't break.

Then there are miscellaneous methods of arrangement, for example, according to age (as magazines or theater programmes), according to beauty, difficulty of getting, value, rarity, shape, alphabetical arrangement, or some arbitrary arrangement, as in rows.

F., 13. My minerals I arrange in a cabinet in whatever way they look the best.

M., 9. I put my cigar wrappers in an old composition book, and instead of putting them in rows I would make a star.

M., 12. History scraps I put in books according to the way they fit in.

F., 12. Arranges shells and pebbles in a cabinet to show them to the best advantage.

In some cases the objects collected are used for decorative purposes, perhaps hung on the wall or from the ceiling, as pictures, picture cards, badges, feathers, nests, antlers, strings of eggs, buttons, etc.

Table X and Chart III show the relative proportion of the various methods of arrangement.

TABLE X

Arrangement of Collections

	BOYS' METHODS Per Cent.	GIRLS' METHODS Per Cent.
Things kept together (no special order) . .	80	80
Classification according to color, size, or both (size predominating)	9	6
Classification according to kind	8	5
Miscellaneous arrangements	1	4
Decoration	2	5

CHART III

Arrangement of Collections

No special order .
Accord'g to color, size
According to kind .
Miscellaneous . .
Decoration . . .

Boys_____
Girls..........

There is very little spontaneous classification. This is natural, as quantity is evidently more interesting than kind. Throughout all ages the care of collections, the simply keeping them together, far outweighs any classification or arrangement of them. This is the only method up to nine years of age, when there is a small proportion of miscellaneous arrangements and of classifications according to color and size, with some few instances of classification according to kind. But these arrangements and classifications appear chiefly after eleven years of age. Decoration comes in chiefly from fourteen years on. Boys show more sense of classification than girls, and girls exceed in decorative and miscellaneous arrangements. Boys and girls show the same large proportion of "no special order."

To summarize the facts which this study seems to indicate, we find :

1.. The collecting impulse is practically universal among children.

2. It is an impulse of great strength, leading the child generally to make collections along several lines. It has its rise in early childhood, develops rapidly after six years of age, and is strongest from eight to eleven years of age, just before adolescence, the greatest number of collections per child occurring at this time, after which it declines in intensity.

3. A remarkable variety is shown in the kinds of things children collect. What they collect seems to be largely the result of circumstance, environment, suggestion, or imitation, but *to collect something* seems to be the part of instinct.

4. Certain collections are very prominent and have a widespread following, showing the part imitation plays as incentive to the collecting instinct. The imitative influence is strongest in the preadolescent years, while in adolescence a specialized form of imitation appears in the way of faddism.

5. Certain inherent interests, however, are shown by groupings of the various collections. Of these the nature interest appears to be strongest. The next greatest number of collections is in the line of stamps, cigar tags, etc. ; then come the trivial childish collections of sticks, glass, buttons, etc., and the collections ministering to the play interest ; and then those pertaining to the æsthetic interest. Collections along literary, historical, sentimental, commercial, useful, and "luck" lines are comparatively few.

6. The collecting impulse shows a certain trend of development in its character. In childhood there appears the crude instinct to collect anything, however trivial, — anything simple and easy to obtain. In the preadolescent years the collecting interest reaches its height in genuineness. Interest in the things collected is here strongest. At this age nature and

play collections are more prominent than at any other age. There is also greater susceptibility to the imitative influence at this age. In adolescence the instinct declines, and degenerates into a matter largely of fad and fashion, along sentimental and social lines.

7. In obtaining their collections the young children are given their things largely; the children in the preadolescent period are most active in obtaining their specimens by their own exertions; in adolescence the commercial spirit, as shown in buying and trading, appears as an additional factor.

8. As to motives for collecting, the influence of others, shown in imitation and rivalry, appears strongest. Then comes the interest in quantity, in large numbers, and great possession. The interest in kind and in the things themselves as specimens is small. Other motives also appear, such as the enjoyment and use of the objects collected, the pleasure in collecting as a pastime, the æsthetic and commercial attractions of the objects. A considerable proportion of vague reasons for collecting is given by the children.

9. In arrangement of their collections children show very little sense of classification. The large majority of children keep their objects in no order, simply keeping them together. There are some attempts at arrangement, as, for example, according to beauty, value, shape, and in arbitrary forms. The first classifications appearing after nine or ten years of age are on the sense basis of color or size, classification according to kind, what there is of it, coming a little later.

We have made no attempt to go into the psychology of the collecting instinct. In the mere calling of collecting an instinct, however, we have assumed considerable psychology, perhaps more than is warrantable. But certainly this phenomenon is no accidental affair, no merely acquired trait.

When we consider its universality, its widespread affection; when we consider its intensity, the number of collections children make and the interest they take in them; when we consider the variety of the things collected, showing that the mania seizes upon any and practically every outlet imaginable, and showing, too, that to collect is more important than what is collected; when we consider, moreover, that the phenomenon has a definite progress, — a rise, a growth and a decline, an age development, — we are inclined not to hesitate in calling it an instinct.

But, at any rate, whatever the psychological interpretation, the fact remains that the collecting instinct, passion, or interest is wonderfully universal and wonderfully intense among children, and that consequently it may be used to practical pedagogical advantage.

Again the question may be raised, Admitting that collecting is a genuine interest, is it an interest in the scientific sense? The scientific collection is made not for the purpose of obtaining quantity but for obtaining varieties in completeness, and for the purpose of classifying those varieties. But children care more for quantity than kind, they desire to possess things rather than to illustrate principles, and they show very little sense of classification. However, in scientific development there seems to be room for a purely naturalistic stage preceding the analytical stage, a stage of going out and gathering in before sitting down to staid induction, a stage, too, of mere gathering before the stage of searching along the line of any hypothesis. Children seem to be in this more primitive naturalistic stage, and as in such we must deal with them.

The age at which the collecting interest is of greatest pedagogical importance is largely in the preadolescent period, before which collecting is more or less a blind, groping, purposeless instinct, and after which it largely loses its purity by being bound up with other associations, but during which period it reaches its greatest intensity and genuineness. Here we find the greatest reveling in quantity, here the time when the instinct acts most easily through the incentive of wide imitation, here rivalry comes in to add zest, here the true naturalist's spirit of finding and hunting, as opposed to receiving or buying, is most prominent, here the beginnings of a sense of classification develop. In fact, at this period the instinct seems to be at its height. Its tractability, too, through the incentive of imitation, makes it most practical now for use in education. So much for the period when the collecting instinct is most important as an educative channel. What content interest of most value appears at this preadolescent time? Here we find the nature interest at its crest, and this is the time for sending children forth to gather in nature's stores, to let them roam and wander, to encourage their naturalist clubs where they may proudly exhibit their collections, where they may compare their treasures with those of the other children, where they may be stimulated to relate how and where they found their specimens and to tell all they know about them, not in any methodical way but in their own way, where what they have imbibed naturally or with unsuspected stimulus may overflow in the telling.

As we have suggested before, the naturalistic interest is a beginning interest, and the collection passion may be used normally as a beginning help in literary, historical, and artistic studies in adolescence, in the same way that it may be used in nature lines in the preadolescent period.

CAROLINE FREAR BURK

BIBLIOGRAPHY

Barnes, Earle. "Children's Collections," *Studies in Education* (edited by Earle Barnes), Vol. I, No. 4, pp. 144–146. G. E. Stechert & Co., New York, 1896–1902.

Barus, Mrs. Annie Howes. "History of a Child's Passion," *Woman's Anthropological Society, Bulletin No. 4*, Washington, D.C.

Darwin, Francis. The Life and Letters of Charles Darwin, pp. 28, 31, 37, 38, 43. D. Appleton & Co., New York, 1901.

Hall, G. Stanley, and Wiltse, Sara E. "Children's Collections," *Pedagogical Seminary*, Vol. I, pp. 234–237, June, 1891.

Loti, Pierre. Story of a Child (translated by C. F. Smith). C. C. Birchard & Co., Boston, 1901. 304 pages.

Sisson, Genevieve. "Children's Plays," *Studies in Education* (edited by Earle Barnes), Vol. I, pp. 171–174. G. E. Stechert & Co., New York.

Smith, Fred. The Boyhood of a Naturalist. Blackie & Son, Ltd., London, 1900. 227 pages.

Stuart, Mrs. Ruth McEnery. Sonny: A Christmas Guest. The Century Co., New York, 1898. 135 pages.

THE PSYCHOLOGY OF OWNERSHIP[1]

The present study is an attempt to investigate the origin and nature of the instincts and motives that operate in the accumulation of property, and to describe more thoroughly than heretofore attempted those mental states arising from the consciousness of things owned ; also to indicate the rôle played by property as a mind-developing agent. For these purposes the sciences of biology, anthropology, social economics, child study, and history furnish analogies and illustrations.

BIOLOGICAL

Property, defined biologically, is anything that the individual may acquire which sustains and prolongs life, favors survival, and gives an advantage over opposing forces.

What are the conditions and circumstances attending the acquisition of property among the forms of animal life ? Some of the most fundamental of these are hunger, thirst, cold, and the multiplication and distribution of species, any detailed consideration of which would lead us far into biological fields. A complete history of distribution alone would involve a consideration of the majority of biological problems. For our purposes it will suffice to call attention to a few of the most obvious results.

1. Distribution has subjected innumerable forms to the wide fluctuations of cosmic forces. This is notably true of the life in temperate zones. Nearly all forms of life in these zones (save domestic animals) either migrate, hibernate, or lay in a store of food at the approach of winter, — a fact of value for

[1] Reprinted in abridged form from *Pedagogical Seminary*, Vol. VI, pp. 421–470, December, 1899.

the present investigation. The ant, bee, rat, squirrel, polecat, hamster, mole, not only burrow spacious underground dwellings, but also fill them with a store of winter food. Observations of these activities are so frequent, and the literature so accessible, that to give examples is unnecessary. Many birds also possess the hoarding activity, and all are more or less able architects. The owl buries its surplus provisions like the dog. The shrike, or butcher bird, having appeased his appetite with grasshoppers, mice, and small birds, still continues to slay and kill. His victims he hangs or rather impales on the thorns of bushes or on twigs. A California woodpecker bores holes in trees wherein to place his booty. In autumn he may be seen pecking away at pines and oaks, and slipping acorns into the cavities thus made.

2. Distribution has caused highly complicated relations and interdependencies among all forms of animals, even plants. All this has created new instincts and habits, and in some cases has modified structure and intensified, if not necessitated, the accumulation of property.

An illustration of multiplication and distribution modifying structure and necessitating the accumulation of a special kind of material is seen among different species of ants.

"Amongst the Amazon ants (*Formica rufescens*), who not only do not debase themselves by working, but even have the food put into their mouths by their slaves, the jaws have become elongated, narrow, and powerful, and project in sharp points, very suitable for piercing an adversary's head, but unfit to lay hold of food. When one of these Amazons is hungry she taps with her antennæ upon the head of a slave, who injects food from her own mouth into that of her mistress."

The yellow ant has domesticated the plant lice (aphides) for the milk that they furnish. "As soon as one of those new herds is found by an ant, she returns to the nest and informs her companions. One or two ants then accompany her to the treasure, which in the future remains, night and day, under their watchful care. As the herd increases in numbers additional herdsmen are called into service." The constant guarding of the aphides is due to the fact that they are eagerly sought for by ants from other colonies, and especially by the swift-flying ichneumon, which uses the body of the aphides as a depository for its eggs. It is observed that when one of these flies is seen hovering over the herd, the ants at once endeavor to chase her away whenever she alights. In addition to slaves and cattle, the products of agriculture as well as the grains of uncultured plants constitute a species of property prized by the ants of the southern portions of the north temperate zone. I need only call attention to the harvesting ant of Texas. Moggridge, one of the earlier scientific observers of the harvesting ants of the Old World, writes: "I then selected a nest where the coarse and hard rock lay much nearer to the surface, barring the downward course of the ants and compelling them to extend their nest in a horizontal direction. Here . . . I came upon large masses of seeds carefully stored in chambers prepared in the soil. Some of these lay in long subcylindrical galleries, and, owing to the presence in large quantities of the black, shining seeds of amaranth, looked like trains of gunpowder laid ready for blasting. . . . On carefully examining a quantity of the seeds and minute dry fruits he found more than twelve distinct species of plants belonging to at least seven separate families. The granaries lay from an inch and a half to six inches below the surface and were all horizontal. They were of various sizes and shapes, the average granary being about as large as a gentleman's gold watch."

3. Multiplication and distribution have thrown together in the same area or in adjacent areas different species and even members of the same species whose interests continually clash. Witness the extensive warfare among different colonies of ants

or the fight to the finish between the rabbit and the comical little puffin, when the latter attempts to take possession of the rabbit's burrow for breeding purposes, or the terrific battles between the male seals for the possession of a nuptial court.

"The lion lives alone, or at most in a temporary family; but he needs a vast hunting ground. This territory must be well furnished with game, and he chooses it himself. Having done so, he will allow no intruder to poach there. He has fixed its boundaries. . . . If another animal of his own species ventures to infringe upon this domain, . . . he protests, lays a complaint against the invader after his own fashion, and, if the latter does not attend to him, has recourse to the *ultima ratio* of kings and lions, — a battle."

"The wandering dogs of Egypt have similar customs; each pack chooses a habitat, and, says an eyewitness, 'Woe to the dog that strays into a neighbor's territory. Many times I have seen the other dogs fall upon the wretch and tear him to pieces.' The pariah dogs of India quarter themselves in the part of the town where they are born. Each of them has his district, 'police fashion,' which he clears of intruders, while for his own part he never crosses its boundaries."

Again, natural history abounds in observations of conflicts in bird families while defending their domain and hunting ground. More severe and even deadly are they if the contestants are flesh feeders or fishers. In these cases ownership in a given area as a hunting ground is absolutely necessary to the maintenance of life.

In October, 1889, the writer [Kline] saw an army of large black ants near the banks of the Colorado in Texas, carrying roundish pieces of leaves cut from the grapevine. The army was twelve feet long and eight inches wide. They were marching with "closed ranks," and at a distance looked not unlike a monster green serpent. I followed this military procession with the interest of a schoolboy. The march was brought to a close by the arrival of the ants at their nest. This consisted of a mound of earth about four inches high and three feet in circumference. Many carried their burdens in at once, others dropped them a few inches from the entrance and went in without them. I cut open a section of the nest and found the leaves in small pockets, though in some places they seemed to be scattered without care. Some of the leaves were dry and crisp, others damp and covered with fungi, which growth I am now persuaded was the object of this vast leaf gathering.

The storing up of honey and pollen by bees for young and self is a common observation by every one. Among the fishes the stickleback and hassar, sometimes called hardback, of tropical America are noted for the elaborate preparation in their nest building and for the care they maintain over the eggs and young until committed to the water. The nest and its contents constitute the only property acquired by these species.

For the purpose of obtaining data a topical syllabus was distributed to teachers, students, and others. On this point of the property instinct 325 answers were received, of which 145 were from males and 175 from females.

While the reminiscences and observations obtained from this syllabus offer nothing that is brand-new, they do continually remind one of his own experiences; they tap, as it were, the reservoir of the common mind and set flowing afresh the stream of life's experiences. And what do we read in them? First, that property getting in childhood is instinctive, an activity not to be suppressed or thwarted. What the child collects is a matter almost wholly of environment. The intrinsic value of the article plays no rôle, but collect it must and will; second, that this promiscuous but continuous gathering is modified somewhat and directed to the accumulation of articles that can be worked upon, articles on which the motor apparatus of the child may repeatedly operate and not unfrequently develop a rude mechanical skill (these mechanical and industrial activities appear more or less prominent in the years just preceding puberty); that at adolescence the desire for material inanimate things is transferred to those of the animate, social, and spiritual world. Now the friendship, the good opinion, the good will, the love, the confidence of and for others constitute the world of values. For these things individual life itself is not too dear a sacrifice. The adolescent must love and be loved, must have friends and associates. " I used to collect picture cards, now I collect photos." " I grew tired of monograms, and have instead a fan with my friends' names written on it." " I gave up dolls and the like and collected napkins and other souvenirs that would remind me of stated occasions."

Childhood wants objects satisfying the senses and the instinct to have; adolescence wants friends and society to whom it may offer sacrifice. It is the beginning of the operation of that universal principle which offers up the best that is in the individual as well as his most valued belongings to the welfare of the species. As the ferment of the adolescent simmers down and the possibilities of his future begin to take shape he sets himself to accumulating goods and valuables that shall meet the drafts upon him at the time when life's stream is broadest and deepest, — the period of fatherhood.

ANTHROPOLOGICAL

In order to see the general ideas of the savage in regard to property, it is necessary to find how much property the savage had, what his relation to this was, how held, etc. Some savage peoples, such as those found wandering in the woods of Borneo, Forest Veddahs of Ceylon, and others, possess almost nothing. In this respect they are inferior to some animals. Others have merely their rude weapons. Of necessity these can accumulate nothing; as Mr. Keary says: "In order that social customs should attain any development, the means of existence must be sufficiently abundant and easily procurable to permit some time to be devoted to the accumulation of superfluities or supplies not immediately required for use. The life of the primitive hunter and fisher is so precarious and arduous that he has scarcely either the opportunity or the will for any other employment than the supply of his immediate wants." It is the satisfaction of these wants that measures his desires. The little he has is mere physical possession.

When we do, however, find primitive man holding property, it is to a large extent property in common. "A large body of facts combines to show that property was a social before it was an individual sentiment, and distinction between owners was at first assigned to one tribe of gens rather than to another. The first notions of property seem to be communal." "The several forms of ownership tend to show that the oldest tenure by which land was held was by the tribe in common." Many other investigators have held this view to a greater or less degree. They find traces of the system in Europe, Asia, Africa, North and South America, Australia, and the Malay Archipelago. Everything leads us to believe collectivism was at its maximum and individualism at its minimum. The reasons for this are apparent. First the very weakness of man made coöperation, a combining of strength and effort, necessary. As Topinard says, "Man lives in society because he has to do so like many animals." Property thus was acquired in common. Furthermore it was necessary to the existence of the horde or tribe that it should be at peace with itself, — the closer solidarity the greater power. This would tend to a common ownership. As long as the savage has food to eat and shelter from the cold he was satisfied. We must remember that the savage is a being of very limited experience, that his ideas of the relation of things are very vague. He has the physique of the man with the mind of the child. His conceptions of himself and his own body are weak and unanalyzed. Individual ownership implies that the particular object is shut off, boxed up as it were, labeled *mine*. This is beyond the savage.

This primitive communism gives us a fair index of savage character and mind. It is the best of evidence of mental dullness, physical laziness, and primitive lethargy. It shows that the savage had not risen to the level of progression ; it demonstrates the lack of individuality, of that self-assertiveness and push so essential to development. Men living under a system of communism are, as Dr. Brinton says, "classified like so many bricks." It is primarily a system of monotony revolting to an independent, virile manhood, and to that active type of mind which glories in life as a struggle. This régime, however, had its use. Long continuance under a communal system developed those sentiments of respect for and toleration of another which are so essential. Human society is based on mutual toleration, on each man's giving up something for the good of all.

It was when man began to get clearer ideas of his own body, to distinguish between the self and non-self, that the idea of individual ownership became possible. The savage's lack of knowledge of the limits of his own self are surprising.

When man arrived at a clear notion of himself as an isolated individual, began to look in upon himself, he must have begun to get glimpses at the concept of individual ownership. For we find that the concept *mine* and self-consciousness are mutually dependent. Those states which come up into consciousness one can be aware of, but not unless they are tagged *mine* will there be self-consciousness. It is here where the term *mine*, the conscious idea of ownership, must have originated in giving expression to these internal psychic states. The concept *mine*, then, is the focal point in self-consciousness. In order that a person may recognize these parts of himself as parts of himself, they must be recognized as *his* own. Neither memory of nor cognition of experiences or psychic states can be recognized as being a part of the ego if this concept *mine* is not present in them ; if the individual does not recognize himself as the *owner*. So it must have been that the idea of individual ownership arose in recognizing internal psychic states, together with one's body and bodily feelings as being parts of self or belonging to self.

The earliest forms and usages of individual property show there was a sort of transition period ; that the savage could not entirely think of external objects as *mine* and *mine alone*, unless they had a subjective element or subjective relation. Letourneau says : " The first private property was in objects forming, so to speak, part of the person, such as weapons and ornaments made by the possessor himself, and generally put in the grave with him." "Australians possess for personal property the objects attached to their persons, such as arms or ornaments in the ear, lips, and noses ; or skins of beasts for clothing ; stones laid in baskets woven of bark fastened to body of the owner ; personally appropriated by them, so to say, incorporated with them. These objects are not taken away from them at death, but are burned or buried with the corpses. Names are among the primary individual property we meet with.". . . "Rude weapons, fabrics, utensils, apparel, implements of flint and stone, personal adornments, represent the chief items of property in savage life.". . . "In primitive society property extended to single personal belongings, to articles of adornment, to trophies of the chase or war, and to tools and weapons." Dr. Rink says that the Eskimo recognizes ownership only in weapons, fishing boats, and tools. Von Martius, speaking of certain Brazilian Indians, says : " Scarcely anything is considered strictly as the property of the individual except his arms, accoutrements, pipe, and hammock. Every man claims a right in what he can make." Haddon, in describing a stone ax found among the people inhabiting the islands about New Guinea, says: "The value of such an object seems to depend on the amount of work required to produce it; thus we arrive at certain primitive ideas. Work done gives ownership."

We see from this that early ideas of individual ownership in regard to external things rose out of the idea of work put on them. The savage only possessed those things he made with his own hands, as his weapons, tools, utensils, etc. These things first existed as ideas in his mind, — he thought of these in a subjective way as his own. And when these, through the molding and forming of material with his own hand and by his individual labor, took on external form, it was but natural that the idea of individual ownership should extend to them. The fact that nearly all objects of personal property are attached to body, and the custom of burning, breaking, or burying these articles with man at death, is evidence of the close relations of the internal concept of ownership and externality. Another suggestive fact is that the earliest forms of weapons were pushing weapons. This seems to point to the belief that the savage considered his weapons almost as a part of his body rather than as some external object he could wield.

This attaching and putting of articles owned on the body intensified the feelings of ownership, through the feeling of pleasure arising from continual contact, and because of the idea of permanence of ownership arising from the feeling that articles were safe from danger when on the person. This element of safety played a great part in the savage mind. Can we not account for the rise of ornaments in this way? Did not the attaching of things on the body for ornament take origin originally in this putting things owned on the body? Can we account in any better way for some of the absurd customs of loading one's body down with trophies, presents, weapons, etc.? That this custom of wearing property prevailed, resulted from the fact that the savage learned the value of individual property in individuating, in marking one man off from another. And so ornaments in general may have taken rise.

This whole development of the idea of individual ownership in the savage mind but indicates one of the great influences property has had in the evolution of mind. As has been shown previously, the savage was originally in a state of lethargy. The only incentive to activity was to satisfy bodily desires. But when man had the notion of acquiring, in order to individuate self, to increase self-importance, when he began to realize what individual property could do, life took on a different aspect for him. He broke away from his laziness, threw off his lethargy. His mind was stirred into activity. His desires became more numerous and extended to various things. And, above all, the desire for individual property is his first great incentive to labor. The effect of all this on developing mind can hardly be overestimated. Self-consciousness, together with all those feelings of pride, emulation, rivalry, and competition, arise out of this. Perhaps there is no one greater result arising from this than the development of attention; as Ribot says, voluntary attention is the product of civilization, and that it is easily shown that before civilization voluntary attention did not exist, and that work is the concrete, the most manifest form, of attention. But the ability to work has not come without a struggle. For, as Ward aptly puts it, " Labor is not the natural condition of man. It must have acquired a powerful motive to curb and steady the wild and adventurous desires of the human heart and compose them to the monotony of toil." This incentive was the desire for individual property and the love of power that property brings. The labor may have been the enforced labor of women and slaves, but property was its incentive ; and if attention has resulted from continued labor, we owe its development originally to individual ownership.

With the idea of individual ownership firmly rooted in the human mind, the tendency would be for the individual to claim all things he desired. The question now arises, not what are the motives for individual acquisition, but what are the motives which cause men to respect each other's possessions. If you presuppose that the proprietary right is an inherent characteristic of mankind, this question of toleration or respect for the property of one another is easily done away with. This is exactly the view the popular mind and superficial considerations would assume. Occupancy was possession. Each man recognized the natural right of the occupant. This is Blackstone's view, that of Roman law, and the view in general. Sir Henry Maine shows that this view of the property right being inherent in man is unscientific and irrational. Men had to learn to respect the rights of one another, and the proprietary right, as every other such abstract notion, was a growth in the mind of man.

If some right to possess individually did not exist, the idea of individual ownership could never have gained strength. For to own a thing implies a feeling of permanence in it ; that one will possess it for some length of time. As the bulk of property was common in savage communities, and as the individual property was slightly confused with one's body, the idea of respect for possession among one another did not have to be very strong. As is natural under these conditions, individual ownership only cropped out at first in those things which naturally fell to the share of individuals and those things which did not interfere with common ownership. Among these might be classed presents given to those performing brave deeds in time of war, trophies taken on the field of battle or in the chase, and rewards of bravery, all of which were great stimuli for protecting and looking after common interests. Another way private property gained admittance was through inheritance. Sir John Lubbock thinks that in cases of legal revenge and punishment we can trace the origin of private property. He says: " When any rules were laid down regulating the amount or mode of vengeance which might be taken in revenge for disturbance, or where the chief thought it worth while himself to settle disputes about possession, and thus, while increasing his own dignity, to check quarrels which might be injurious to the general interests of the tribe, the natural effect would be to develop the idea of mere possession into that of property."

The reason woman is held as property is due to her physical weakness and her peaceful character. As to why she was held as private property instead of common, there are several reasons. Women were more numerous than men. For while men were killed in war, women were held as captives. A man could generally have a sufficiency of wives without interfering with the interests of others. In addition to this Westermarck has clearly shown that among all savage peoples some definite marriage relation existed, which would naturally result in the ownership of woman being individual. It is readily seen what a valuable chattel woman must have been. For all the hard work, all the drudgery, she performed. She, too, had to use all her ingenuity to provide food for her husband when he returned unsuccessful from the chase. If not, she might become a victim to his appetite. " Among savages it is really the women who perform all the real labor of their societies."

The growth of agriculture, together with domestication of animals, caused a revolution in property and property ideas as well as in society. From it resulted the introduction of slavery among men, the domestication of animals, abolition of cannibalism, and the growth of agriculture, requiring more laborers. The domestication of animals and the growth of slavery gave rise to a value which could be accumulated and something that could be used as a commodity in exchange. Agriculture and the domestication of animals, by making means of subsistence procurable without coöperation, did away gradually with all ownership in common, the idea of proprietary right having gradually developed through an ever-increasing individual ownership. The domestication of animals must have had great effect on the primitive mind, for here, as Morgan says, was a "possession of greater value than all kinds of property known previously put together. They served for food, were exchangeable for other commodities, were useful for redeeming captives, for paying fines, and as a sacrifice for the observance of religious rights. Moreover, as they were capable of indefinite multiplication in numbers, their possession revealed to the human mind its first conception of wealth." This conception of wealth has played no mean rôle in the evolution of mind as well as civilization.

Dress is a class of property which also has had much influence on the development of mind. "Dress," says Professor Starr, "generally has been developed out of ornament. That it has, after being developed, often been turned into a modest covering and a protection, is unquestioned." "Ornaments are of two kinds, — those directly fixed into the body, and those attached by a cord or band. As soon as man hung an ornament on such a band dress evolution began." Dress had a great influence on mind because it is one great means of expressing one's individuality by external show, and also because of its power in marking off or individuating. The only individuality that some people have is that expressed in their dress. So it is that, as Professor Starr says, "in looking over the history of the race, we find many inventions have resulted, many discoveries been made, many arts been developed, in pursuit of new materials for attire, and general intelligence has been increased thereby."

In connection with property, especially property as power, are found some psychoses of not a little value : obedience to command and willingness almost amounting to a desire among a mass of people to be led ; the tendency of people to believe in and give way to a man who makes large assumptions ; the general feeling of contempt for a man who performs manual labor, in particular the agriculturist, arising from the time when no man who labored was a gentleman ; considering wealth instead of merit the mark of superiority ; feelings of servility and littleness in the presence of wealth. Pride is but a sense of superiority arising from the fact that one owes much of value and worth to society and friends. Vanity is the same feeling minus any such possessions.

And it was wealth which, by easing the hard struggle with cosmic forces for a few select ones, made possible and gave opportunity for the rise of that learning and culture which has had such a great effect on the development of mind as well as civilization.

The history of the evolution of culture has been the history of the leisure class. The leisure class had its birth with the beginning of wealth, and was alone made possible by the establishment of ownership.

In the light of the preceding we cannot but conclude that there has been no greater factor than property in broadening and developing mind and civilization.

OWNERSHIP IN CHILDREN

The study of the child mind in relation to ownership takes on an increased interest and value, if its property activities be regarded both as *recapitulatory* of the racial attitude to property and *anticipatory* of the adult's serious wrestling with property and fortune. Cataloguing the activities under these two categories is left largely to the reader. We indicate here, from answers to the questionnaire, the beginnings of the sense of ownership and property-getting activities in general as found in child life.

In answer to the request for cases in which a child for the first time evinced signs of ownership, 185 returns were received, — 93 males and 92 females (ages from 3 months to 72 months). These are divided into six groups, — 3 to 6 months, 7 to 12 months, 13 to 18 months, 19 to 24 months, 25 to 36 months, 37 to 72 months. The following examples are typical.

First group (3 to 6 months), 39 cases

F., 4 months. Cries whenever bottle is taken from her. Even if bottle was empty, would not let it leave her sight unless given another.

F., 4 months. Never showed sense of special ownership until another baby was brought to visit her. The second child was given F.'s rattle, whereupon F. began to cry and reach for it.

F., 6 months. In trying to amuse this child I took her rattle. She at once stretched out her hands, uttering little sounds as *um, um,* — first time she had laid claim to anything.

F., 4 months. Played with a rubber ring. I picked it up; she began to cry and hold out her hands. Put it down and she stopped crying. Repeated with same result.

Second group (7 to 12 months), 58 cases

M., 8 months. Was given a go-cart, and after riding in it at different times M., aged 7 months, sat in it. M., 8 months, cried, pulled his dress and hair until he got it.

F., 12 months. Was given a little white rocking-chair in which she sat most of the time; would not let any one touch it.

F., 12 months. Very fond of her cradle, always liked to be in it. If she saw any one sitting in it, she would endeavor to pull them away and would cry.

F., 11 months. Before she could walk or talk, seemed to think she owned her mother's lap, and cried when any one else attempted to occupy it.

Third group (13 to 18 months), 27 cases

M., 13 months. When Edward saw another child sitting in his little red chair, he at once wanted to sit in it. He would not sit in his sister's chair.

M., 18 months. Owned a cap. My brother put it on his head. The little boy ran to him and cried, " Take that off; that Harry's hat."

F., 18 months. Had a little blanket she would not go to sleep without. She always cried, " My blankie, my blankie," till she got it.

Fourth group (19 to 24 months), 23 cases

M., 20 months. Had been given a great many playthings, but the things he seemed really to care for and *to own* were a woolly lamb and some building blocks.

M., 24 months. Given a jumping-jack. He never seemed to make any claim to it until one day a stranger said it was his. Immediately he declared that it was his.

M., 24 months. Showed plainly he owned a toy express wagon by taking it away from a boy who came to see him, saying, " That's my waggie."

Fifth group (25 to 36 months), 24 cases

M., 36 months. Claimed one of his father's canes as his horse.

M., 27 months. Had a piece of clothesline which he was very fond of. He used to throw it over the back of a chair and play horse with it.

F., 36 months. When two years old saw a toy kitchen which she called a dustpan. From the day she saw it she was never quiet until her mother bought her one to play with.

Sixth group (37 to 72 months), 10 cases

F., 48 months. When she was four years old everything that was given her she kept in a box placed in one corner of a room. She was much displeased if any one should even raise the lid of the box.

F., 72 months. Owned a ball of which she was very fond. Kept it hid where no one could find it.

Having a place for and hiding articles possessed are the common features of this group.

Our interest in these returns lies in what they suggest as to the way in which the property *instinct* and *concept* became etched so deeply into the mind.

It appears that those things which give satisfaction to the sensory side of the human organism are the earliest to be drafted in as property. Gradually objects that may be acted upon, that exercise the motor side, are laid claim to. The human infant, like the young of all vertebrates, reacts the earliest and most vigorously at all those points that give information about want-satisfying objects. It goes without saying that objects which satisfy these " want points " are the ones first claimed. It is not chance, then, that the highest per cent. of objects claimed by infants 3 to 6 months of age should be those that satisfy hunger or are instrumental in doing so. In the second group — 7 to 12 months — objects appealing to sight are far in the lead. Objects satisfying the sense of touch rank next, followed by those appealing to taste and smell (hunger). The eye soon becomes the chief mind feeder. Its objects have a permanency essential to the growth of the property concept. Objects that administer to bodily comforts, as a "special chair," "mother's lap," "a carriage," etc., begin to be appropriated at this age. Preferring certain spots in exclusion to others apparently as comfortable is a widespread animal trait. This is true of nearly all domestic animals. The third group — 13 to 18 months — introduces for the first time articles of motion, for example, go-cart, buggy, toy engines, etc., and articles of dress. At this age the motor side begins its call for objects on which it may operate. In the fourth group — 19 to 24 months — articles of motion are predominant. Articles used in imitation plays come in. The fifth group — 25 to 36 months — shows that articles used in imitation plays are most frequently claimed and owned. The articles appropriated in the last group — 37 to 72 months — are of a miscellaneous character. The most interesting and significant fact presented is the effort of the child to hide whatever possessed.

The sense of ownership finds expression in children not able to talk in those "expressive" movements of body: of the hands, reaching and clasping; of the feet, kicking; of the face, anger, pleasure, satisfaction; by crying, laughing, and other characteristic sounds common to infants.

These are the objective facts noted by the observers. Here and there we get hints of the child's attitude — consciously and unconsciously — toward property. The following facts may be noted: (1) In every case, from the youngest to the oldest, it was necessary that the child have the article entirely to itself; communism was out of the question. Extreme selfishness seems to be the rule. (2) Generally the child does not lay claim to an object until it sees the object in the possession of another, or when some one else tries to take the article; in fact, at this point the sense of ownership first gives itself definite objective expression. (3) The extreme forms of isolation and exclusion, two fundamental elements in the sense of ownership, crop out in the child hiding its possessions. I have found no case of hiding articles under four years of age. (4) The child may have a fairly clear idea of possessing an article himself, while not conceiving the same feelings to be present in any other child.

Here the question may be raised, At what age does the child have a clear notion of the concept *mine*? It is believed that the child under three years has an inadequate knowledge of his own body and of self. Up to the second year it does not use *me* or *mine*, and very probably then does not understand their significance. To illustrate this, Dr. Ladd one day asked a little girl what the *I* was that loved papa. She seemed not to understand for a minute; then she said, "Oh, now I know; it is my arms, because I hug him with them, and my lips, because I kiss him with them." Sully says: "In this crude idea of self, before the meaning of the *I* becomes clear, we have to suppose that the child does not fully realize the opposition of self to not-self, but rather tends to regard himself as a kind of thing after the analogy of other objects." In the anthropological section of this paper it was maintained that it was impossible for the savage to have a clear conception of ownership until he had learned the boundaries of his ego, to distinguish self from not-self, and the same holds true of the child. No being can conceive of an article belonging to himself, if that self is not to some extent known. The conscious concept of property and of self thus seems to develop along parallel lines.

In answer to the question regarding children's collections, 188 answers were received — 88 describing females and 100 describing males, ages one year to fourteen years. The following articles were collected by 188 children: money, stones, blocks, cards, stamps, drawings of engines, marbles, bottles, handkerchiefs, spools, pipes, pieces of dress goods, nails, leaves, nuts, buttons, strings, insects, butterflies, beetles, pencils, frogs, carpenter's tools, garden utensils, flowers, dishes, broken china, shells, dolls, ribbon strings, pins, acorns, tin articles, paper dolls, old kid gloves, balls, fans, corks, saltcellars, ink bottles, hats, cigar pictures, colored glass, seeds, toy boats, knives, keys, boxes, colored rags, sleds, wagons.

The articles that the child collects, as previously shown, depend on the environment and home training. The child inherits only the activity to collect. To have something, to own something, is needed to fill up an empty gap in the child's life. The article may be utterly useless: a heap of stones, pieces of wood, leaves, old gloves, rotten strings, — things for which the child itself could not invent a reason for collecting. The treatment of the collection is probably the best evidence as to the motive for collecting. It appears that the majority of children from 2½ to 6 years old either neglect their collections as fast as made, or hide them, taking a peep at them from time to time, but never making any use of them. This period of collecting might be termed a purely instinctive one. It would be worth some one's time to gather a wide range of data upon this one point. Our own returns (188) are inadequate to warrant conclusions. From 6 to 14 years the disposition of the articles is indeed varied. They are hidden or forgotten ; traded for others ; kept to show playmates ; kept through imitation and emulation, in order to get more than some one or any one else ; sold for money ; kept to play with ; kept as ornaments, as beautiful shells, flowers, etc. ; and kept to work with. The motives prompting and controlling the collecting activities of the child appear then to be instinctive,[1] imitative, emulative, utilitarian, love of display, and love of the beautiful.

The most widespread and interesting phenomena connected with collecting is hiding the articles. The child takes a keen pleasure in having things that it may " use and abuse," hidden in some place which no one else knows about. Displaying them to friends occasionally is a pleasurable act, but the pleasure is much sweeter if the articles are produced from quarters known only to itself. The love of displaying possessions, thereby attracting attention and eliciting praise, is characteristic of very young children. Sully thinks love of approbation in the child is one way in which self-consciousness is developed. The following cases are typical of a number received on this point.

F., 7. Made a large collection of shells which she kept on a stand in the sitting room. She was very fond of showing them, but did not want any one else to touch them.

M., 5. Collects all the spools he can get, makes no use of them, but when his mother has company he brings them out to show.

---

[1] Kleptomania is an abnormal instance of this instinct. The subject cannot control his impulse to take any article he sees. He does not care for it afterward particularly. He must needs take it to satisfy his impulse.

The collecting of money among children is common. This perhaps is due as much to suggestion as from any primary realization on the part of the child of the value of money. Collecting money is common to all ages from one year to fourteen years. The per cent. of boys is larger than that of girls in 135 cases.

M., 3. Asked every one who came to the house for money. If they gave him a silver piece, his eyes would sparkle and he would say, " That is worth something "; but if given a penny, he would look at it and say, " Not worth much." Both, however, he would put away and not spend.

M., 2. My brother began to collect money when about two years old. Would ask his father for money and do things to earn money. Would not spend a cent, but continually tried to get more.

It appears that money is not collected with an idea of its purchasing power, but rather as something desirable to hoard, something not to use but to save. We do not, however, put much faith in money collecting and saving as an activity reflecting a "money sense," for getting money is a thing which parents are constantly suggesting and encouraging in their children.

Interesting in this connection are the money superstitions current among children.

I remember two superstitions about money. One was a pot of gold at the end of the rainbow, and the other, if a piece of down from milkweed came to you and you caught it and told it to bring you twenty-five cents, it would surely do so.

I had a superstition about money, and that was, I thought when there were bubbles on the coffee, if it was a large circle I was surely going to get fifty cents or a dollar, that is, if I could drink it without separating it; and if it was smaller, I was going to get a less amount of money.

If a number of names beginning with the letter *m* were placed under a mossy stone and left there a week, you would find money at the expiration of that time.

Very often I would make a hundred marks on a paper, each representing a white horse I had seen. I would then place it under a stone and expect to find money within a certain number of days.

One superstition I had was, if a person had white specks on the finger nails, one would be rich. Another, that if you had long hair on your wrist, you would be rich.

If the palm of the left hand is itchy, you will receive money.

If you dream of counting your money, it is a sign of acquiring wealth.

If you found any money and did not keep it, you would not have good luck.

I had great faith in "find a black tin, find a dollar."

I thought if I got money on New Year's Day, I would get money every day in the year.

One very common superstition was the saying " money " three times, every time we saw a star fall.

If we ever found a horseshoe with any nails in it, we were to obtain or receive a hundred dollars for each one. To find a pin with the head pointing toward you was thought to be a sign of increase in finances.

We would go around and ask each person to bow his head, and when we got a hundred crosses on a paper, each cross representing a bow, we would put it in the ground and would expect to find money in its place after three days.

One thing impressed upon me very much as a child was that my arm being so long was the sign of riches. I knew also that the finding of silver money was a warning of coming riches.

The only superstition I had about money was that some day I would be rich because my two front teeth were separated quite a little, and I was told that was a sign.

We asked for a description of a child who wants to own everything ; who steals, begs, and cheats to acquire property. 406 cases are described, — 262 males and 144 females, ages from one year to seventeen years.

Nearly every return gave an instance of a child who wished to own property far in excess of his wants or his ability to use the same aright. And over 80 per cent. of the 406 cases described a child who would beg, cheat, or steal to get the coveted article. Value did not seem to be taken into account.

They were not regarded by the observers as peculiar or exceptional children. They would seem to be anybody's children, — the average child. The following are typical cases :

M., 4. Wishes to own everything he lays his eyes on, — cards, stamps, bottles, pictures, etc.; he steals and begs and uses various schemes to get what he fancies. Makes no particular use of them, just wishes to keep them.

M., 5. Is fond of slate pencils; often steals pupils' slate pencils when they are not in their seats. When questioned by his teacher how the pencils got into his pockets, he answered, " They must fall in my pocket."

M., 5. Frequents our house when we are eating. He will say : " What is that ? I wish I had some. We never have that at our house, but it looks good."

M., 8. Is always getting things by begging, cheating, and stealing. Tells his mother that they were given to him. He begs things for the church and keeps them for himself. He tells the neighbors' servants that such a boy sent him for his football, and then runs home with it.

Pedagogical inferences and suggestions are in the main patent. In some schools pedagogy is already plying her tools to this never-failing ore supply. We venture the suggestion that collecting may advantageously be connected with nature study, geography, art, etc., making what might be a laborious task coincide with a fundamental desire. The child who makes collections of insects, birds' eggs, leaves, or flowers translates the beauties of nature into terms of self. They become thus a part of him, and nature is brought nearer. Emulation and rivalry in collecting would help to make the study more easy.[1] Another fact of not a little value is the habit of neatness, arranging by order, giving an idea of system and method, which collections bring out in the child. A large per cent. of children in the returns were most particular in regard to this. The power of observation is trained in the child's always having an eye out for certain things. Furthermore the child in

[1] In some schools this is carried out, and with advantage.

making collections puts his own labor in the gathering. Hence these collections represent his own self. This is why the child will consider collections of old stones, or other objects of little worth, of much more value often than his brightest and most attractive toys. His own labor has given them their value. In our anthropological section it was seen that the first idea of individual ownership arose in those things in which man had put his labor, his inventive genius in making. The stamp of his own personality was on them.

The writers believe that as in labor ownership was conceived, so in labor are its real sweets to be found ; and that ownership in general, which does not result from labor of some kind, has an artificiality about it : though it stands for the real thing, it is not. It is this artificial notion of ownership which has created the idea that manual labor is degrading, and which, in fact but a few years back, held that all labor was degrading, — beneath a gentleman.

Here lies the true value of manual training in our schools : that the child may learn how much more valuable is the article which he had made with his own hands by his own labor. It gives a knowledge from whence the sweetness of possession derives its source. The technique is of practical use, the learning how is valuable ; but much more valuable is it for the child to learn the divinity of labor. No one who has worked with hammer and saw, and learned how rich in pleasure is the possession of an article derived from hard labor, can consider work a degradation. It puts the child in sympathy with labor and the laborer. Looked at from this point of view, no one factor has greater possibilities of developing the child than that of manual training. It puts the child in sympathy with men. He rubs in large grains of the stuff we call humanity, and for this reason it is essential that the child should be allowed to make things he wants, and also that the things made should *belong* to him.

We have found that the desire to own is one of the strongest passions in child life; that selfishness is the rule; that children steal, cheat, or lie without scruple to acquire property; that they have no idea of a proprietary right. These generalizations will hold almost without exception for children under five years, for many children under ten, and in some cases even up to fifteen years of age. These things are natural in the child. Parents as a rule are continually struggling to keep them down; to teach principles of unselfishness; to teach not to lie, steal, cheat, and beg; to respect the rights of others. This method may meet with more or less success. The writers of this paper are inclined, from reading over the returns and from personal experience, to say less. The problem is, What is the right method? Shall we hold with Calvin that the child is naturally a depraved being, and that by hook or by crook we must take it out of him, or with Rousseau that by nature the child is good, and that nature wills the child to be a child before he is a man, and so "let children be children"?

Do we believe that the child recapitulates the history of the race? If so, we may not be surprised to find the passion for property getting a natural one, nor that the child lies, cheats, and steals to acquire it, nor that selfishness rules the child's actions. Selfishness is the cornerstone of the struggle for existence, deception is at its very foundation, while the acquiring of property has been the most dominant factor in the history of men and nations. These passions of the child are but the pent-up forces of the greed of thousands of years. They must find expression and exercise, if *not in childhood, later*. Who knows but that our misers are not those children grown up whom fond mothers and fathers forced into giving away their playthings, into the doing of unselfish acts, in acting out a generosity which was neither felt nor understood. Not to let these activities have their play in childhood is to run great risk. It does no good to make the child perform moral acts when it does not appreciate what right and wrong mean, and to punish a child for not performing acts which his very nature compels him to do is doing that child positive injury.

During the period of adolescence generosity and altruism spring up naturally. Then why try to force the budding plant into blossom? Instruct them by all means, teach them the right; but if this fails, do not punish, but let the child be selfish, let him lie and cheat, until these forces spend themselves. Do not these experiences of the child give to man in later life a moral virility? Is not a man the stronger man for having in childhood done some of these acts? Has he not a more robust personality after them? He knows what it is to have sinned. He knows what he has to meet or stand against. These rank, selfish deeds are giving the child an idea of self. The child must learn by them the idea of ownership before he can appreciate ownership in others.

The next topic discussed was, Describe a child who persists in amassing a special article; also a child with a passion to trade. Very little is brought out in answer to the first of these topics. Cases of girls collecting were much more numerous than those of boys. Trading is peculiarly a boy's trait, very few instances of girls being given. Every return described a boy who had a passion for trade. How strong this passion is among boys everyday experience teaches us.

M., 7. Had a knife he was very proud of, but when T. came to house with a drum H. wanted to trade the knife for the drum. When he obtained the drum he traded it for a bat, then the bat for a toy gun. He did the same way with all his possessions, even wished to trade his clothes. One day he traded his old straw hat for a marble, and was very proud of the deal.

M., 8. Has a great passion for trading. Everything he gets he tries to trade, not for the sake of gaining, for most of the time he loses, but just to satisfy his passion. He one time traded his hat; one warm day after school he traded his shoes. He even speaks of trading his father's house.

Any one who knows boys knows how strong is their passion to trade. It seems necessary for their development. The trading is not so much for gain or for any specific article as it is to satisfy the desire or passion. It but emphasizes again how much property and property getting makes up of life. In the history of the race, when men began to trade it marked the beginning of a great epoch. Dr. Chamberlain says that variations in the race commenced when men began to trade and fight. Trading is certainly a controlling element in the nature of developing the boy. It is an activity which could be used to much advantage in attracting boys to school. What interest it would rouse in the boy, bubbling over with the desire to trade and do business, if there were some system of banks or trading posts connected with the schools![1] It is these things that the nature of the child goes out to that education needs to discover.

Detailed descriptions of children's quarrels over the ownership of some article were asked for and 187 answers were received, — 74 cases being females, 67 males, 42 where quarrel was between male and female, 4 sex not given, ages of children from 3 to 14 years. The quarrels were decided in five ways: (1) by some older person stepping in (78 cases); (2) by strength or force, one child taking possession and holding it (27 cases); (3) by children coming to some agreement, as dividing, neither having article, or by one making some compensation to others (27 cases); (4) by destruction of article either during quarrel or after it, so that neither child becomes the final possessor of it (21 cases); (5) by one child giving in to another because of its persistent selfishness or strong will (17 cases).

[1] School savings banks have been established in France with great success, and to some extent in England and America. Some very interesting articles have been written on this subject, showing the advantages of school savings banks.

F., 2, and F., 3. K. and R. were given blocks to play with. One of them kept taking the other's blocks. Then they began to quarrel; neither one would give up her blocks. Finally they became so angry that K. up and danced around the floor in her temper, while R. sat on the floor and cried. The mother heard the noise and came to the rescue. She took the blocks away from them.

M., 7, and M., 8. Walking with me over a field one day these two boys simultaneously found a watermelon. Each, of course, wanted it; it was a very small one and not even ripe. They quarreled until one got it from the other, and taking it, threw it on the ground as much as to say, "There, you got it!" I know many similar cases. Boys quarrel, then one gets it, and instead of keeping it, as one might suppose, he throws it away or destroys it.

In nearly all cases it was found that if one child got the article it did not seem to care about the article itself; and if the other child was not around so that it could show its possession and thus tantalize the other child, it cared no more about it. The object in asking this question was, if possible, to get some light on the problem. What conception of right or privilege of possession in another has the child? How does the conception of proprietary right rise in the child? Is such a conception to be presupposed in the child as Blackstone presupposes it in early man, when he laid down the principle that first possession or first occupation was recognized as the right for an individual to own? Does the conception of proprietary right arise only through laws and restrictions imposed by a ruler, the principle laid down by Hume in the Leviathan; or is this conception a result of evolution, arising gradually in the child, as we attempted to show it did in man, by a gradually increasing intelligence, — a closer adaptation of man to his fellow-men, making finer discriminations with the increasing complexity of his surroundings?

The results of the returns in throwing light here were not very satisfactory. That the child at this early age has no such conception to start with is most clear. That out of their quarrels over articles, claimed by each, children must get some idea of a right in another to own is clear. But the fact of parents interfering in so many cases, though this interference may teach ideas of the privileges of others, vitiates the results by not letting the idea develop of itself, if it will. The cases in which children come to an agreement by themselves show that the child here recognizes some right in another; also cases where one child gives up to another more persistent. These cases, it is significant, occur among children six or seven years of age and older. Younger children do not settle in this way. This seems to give support to the view we have taken in our anthropological study, that the conception of a proprietary right is a growth. One fact shown in this material is that in children under six the desire for the article — to say, " I want it " — is sufficient reason to the child to have or own it, and it is because of this that quarrels over ownership are so common in children. Property is also one of the first things children quarrel over.

To the request to describe an instance in which a child long desired some toy or plaything, e.g., wagon, gun, doll, and very unexpectedly received it as a gift, 305 returns — 133 from females and 77 from males, ages four to fifteen years — were received.

The state of children in the first few moments is either extreme exaltation, in which the impulse is to run, dance, or shout; or all action seems to be inhibited; or there is a combination of these two, much like and often approaching hysteria. After this first shock the one idea is to have every one see it and make much of it. The child lavishes the utmost amount of care, will scarcely touch the article, will allow no one else to touch it, will not let it leave his sight. Some sentences are quoted here, taken at random from different papers:

Danced around with great glee. Could not speak one word. I laughed and cried at once. At first could not say anything but just stood and looked at it. Jumped upon the floor, shouting and clapping her hands. So pleased she could not stop laughing. Jumped up and down, clapping her hands and screaming with delight. Did nothing but jump and laugh. Did not speak for five minutes. Face was all smiles, eyes wide open. Became bashful, ran and got behind her mother. Stood as though struck dumb for one moment, then danced and fairly screamed. So overcome she could not say a word. Could not speak for joy. Burst into tears and could not be comforted for some time. Was afraid to touch it.

This naïve spontaneity of the child gives to us an insight into the effects of property on the mind. Things are never so real, never so large, as in childhood. As the individual grows older his experiences have broadened his horizon so much that it takes great events or circumstances to affect him. As Höffding says, the young man on beholding for the first time some grand and beautiful spectacle in nature, as a scene in the Alps, feels his soul swell up within him, his personality expands, embracing it all, the whole aspect of the world and life seems changed and new, while the man who has looked on the same scene many times has no such feelings. He may appreciate it more, but his personality has enlarged to that extent that he is affected but little. This is why, in studying men, the difficulty of finding the things which affect the mind is so great; not so in the child.

So it is we see that these spontaneous reactions of the child on receiving some long-desired article give evidence of not a little value in respect to the large part that ownership plays in widening the scope of the mind and in enlarging self and self-feelings.

The effect of ownership of property in which he has an exclusive right has a marked effect upon the child's attitude towards property in general. Not only do children take better care of belongings to which they have an undivided right, but they are more inclined to respect the property rights of others, especially if this be of kinds similar to their own. The growth of this property sense is conditioned by the age of the child.

140 out of 150 cases show that children take much better care of their own property than that of another, and that children are careful of their own possessions. Only 10 cases were reported where owning property made them less careful; these were cases of very young children.[1] 47 cases, or 31.3 per cent., of 150 cases show that children not only are careful of their own possessions, but, after six years of age (average eight or nine years), that possession of a certain article makes them more careful of other articles of the same kind belonging to others, and articles belonging to others in general.

These returns bring some very emphatic evidence to bear upon the question whether it is best for schools to furnish children with books. That they should not seems clear unless the books are given to children outright. An examination of all the returns, and this one in particular, shows that ownership adds a dignity to the child, expands the self and self-feelings, and stimulates feelings of pride. The things owned in childhood are very close to the child's inner being. As one little girl said, when a book was returned to her with pages turned down and leaves soiled, "I felt as though a part of myself had been injured." These things appear large to children. Their life in a large part is wrapped up in the little world of their toys, dolls, wagons, and books. So when we say it is better for a child to own its books and other school appliances, we bring not only evidence of its practicability as a saving and better keeping of these things, but we also urge it for higher reasons, claiming that the sense of possession

---

[1] Six out of ten only had ages given; four of these were four years of age or younger.

fills a gap in the child's nature, adding to his dignity and self-respect, expanding the feelings of self, giving an idea of worth and responsibility, and that these are factors of importance in the child's education, and we believe that because of these very facts the child takes more interest in his books, and that he gets more out of them.

M., 5. Tom was always careless about his books. The books were furnished by the school, and he had ruined two books since he began going to school. His teacher gave him a picture book for being regular in attendance, and he was very much pleased with it. He would not allow the other boys to look at his book or touch it unless their hands were clean. Soon after he was given this book he began to erase the pencil marks from his schoolbook, and he said, " I don't suppose teacher wants her books all dirty any more than I do."

F. Used to tear books that they gave her to look at, — tear whole leaves out and fold others over and over again. But when one Christmas she received a book of her own she was just as careful of it, and afterward she never tore the leaves of books or even turned them over.

A point of not a little interest to the writers arises from the fact that 47 cases, or 31.3 per cent., of 150 cases show that it is out of their own possessions, by making objective those feelings of care of property, love of possession, pride in ownership, or, in other words, realizing that such feelings exist in others as well as in themselves, that respect for others' property comes and some notion of a proprietary right obtains. In the question on quarrels among the young children — ages three to four and five to six — the desire or wish for the article seemed to be a sufficient reason to them to possess it. "I want it," was enough. They could not see then why they should not have it. Among the children at this age we find little care or respect for others' property. The children of the 47 cases above were, on the average, eight or nine years old, some much younger, some older. In these cases the process was purely psychological. The child reasoned from its own desires, namely, that they were as strong in others; that if they did not respect the possessions and property of others, they could not expect others to respect theirs. This corresponds to the growth of the conception of property in the mind of primitive man.

From this study it is easily seen that the relations between childhood and property are very close and very important. They throw light not only on psychological phenomena, but also bring up questions in pedagogy of interest and value. Property is a great factor in developing the mind of the child. We see its relation here to the development of the five primary senses in early childhood; its power in teaching the child about his own self; how it feeds self-consciousness, gives feelings of importance and worth, enlarges personality, develops respect for property in others by having property of one's own, quickens activity of mind. All that property has done in evolving the mind of man is repeated to some extent in the history of childhood. Above all, property getting in childhood is of prime importance because it is *anticipatory*. Adult life is largely made up of acquiring property. The child in his tenacious acquisition, his extreme selfishness, is preparing himself for this struggle. Professor Groos says: " I regard the instinct whose mandate in the struggle for life is, Keep what you can get, as very important. Men and animals must learn not only to acquire but also to defend and protect their property with tenacious energy."

PROPERTY, PERSONALITY, AND FEAR

In answer to the questions, What have you observed among children concerning the feeling of ownership in property and the influence it had over their attitude both toward the property and valuables in general, e.g., care of books, tools, or a new article of clothing? and On wearing a new dress

how did the child behave to parents, companions, strangers?
160 returns were received,— 126 females, 15 males, and 19
sex not given. Typical answers were as follows :

F., 11. With a new dress on was cold toward her companions and
not disposed to obey her parents.

M., 15. When he wears his new suit, stands straight, walks proudly,
and is more polite than usual.

F., 9. Changes her general attitude as soon as she gets on a new
article of clothing. She acts like a different person.

F., 7. When she puts on anything new always acts ashamed and tries
to keep out of sight. It makes her over self-conscious.

On wearing new garments a feeling of pride and desire to show is
almost always manifested. Have observed children on meeting to make
their new garments the first topic of conversation, i.e., before any greet-
ing, e.g., " I 've got new shoes," etc. Bashful children, however, will not
put on new-style garments, and do not like to appear in a garment until
it has been worn for some time. They imagine every one looking at
them. It increases their self-consciousness. — From a professor of
long experience.

To the questions, What effect has a new overcoat, high
hat, high heels, ribbons, plumes, bright-buttoned uniforms,
articles of jewelry, buttons, badges, etc., upon the self-confidence, self-assertiveness, and personality of the wearer?
What is your own experience in such matters? and What
have you observed about persons collecting stamps, coins,
autographs ; poems, ballads, pictures, and the like for scrapbooks ; various and sundry articles for memory books, wall
ornaments? 232 returns, cases of all ages, were received.

M., 34 (president State Normal School). Dress, plumes, buttons,
badges, increase our egotism, measure our opinion of self. I have noticed
this in myself and others.

M., 32. Usually one feels more self-confident in good clothes.
Have made many a poor recital in school and in college because I was
poorly dressed. One is much more assertive when well dressed. The
effect is especially noticeable in women.

F., 7. Had to recite in school. Asked her mother if she could wear her new dress and ribbons. "Mamma," she said, "I'm sure I can speak better if I am dressed up."

F. (supervisor to department State Normal School). Says she "can teach much better in new clothes."

F., 20. Wearing new clothes and finery does not make any difference in the treatment of my friends, still inwardly I have a great deal more confidence in myself. If I were obliged to wear an old dress to a party my whole evening's enjoyment would be spoiled, while if I could have a fine dress on I should have a grand time, should feel like suggesting new games and in general taking the lead.

The following phrases occurred most frequently in the returns, as descriptive of the effects of dress : "gives a dignified bearing"; "forgot my timidness"; "increased my self-respect"; "can never act natural in new clothes"; "feel increased in size"; "feel in better state of mind"; "felt older"; "makes me awkward, bashful, and shy"; "increased self-confidence and importance."

There were 229 returns descriptive of the effect of sudden and unexpected increase or loss in property, and the loss of relatives and friends.

M., 60. Inherited a small (to him a large) fortune. The very first thing he did was to tell all his friends and invite them to a supper. Before this he had been rather a quiet man and not given to pushing himself into anything. Now, however, he was heard from in most enterprises.

M., 30. Became suddenly rich by the death of a relative. His first act was to invite his friends to a champagne dinner, and the next day buy a fast running horse. All that he seemed to care for was a good time and to have all about him happy.

F. This young woman was quite poor ; married a young business man, who took her to a nice new home which he had built. The change made her proud ; she slighted her friends and relatives, and became generally disliked. Age improved her manner.

F., 25. Father very wealthy, she was greatly admired in all the social circles ; she gave parties, teas, etc., to which nearly every one in the small town in which she lived was invited. At the death of her father it was found that the estate was completely involved; that she and her mother owned nothing. She committed suicide in a few days.

The changes in, and fluctuations of, personality under the stimulus of property are neither peculiar nor exceptional psychoses, that appear only under the very best test conditions; they belong to the common stock of everyday experience. We therefore appeal to this common wealth of experience both for data and for justification of what follows. The observations accorded above are merely introductory and suggestive.

We have seen that the child lays claim earliest to those things that satisfy its wants in the sphere of instinct and the senses. What the child does in this instinctive and natural way the adult strives to do through the myriad devices of the intellect, but the aim is the same, i.e., to satisfy wants and enlarge the *pleasure field*. Property, then, is an instrument to avert pain and procure pleasure. Considered psychologically, property is anything which procures pleasure and satisfaction to the individual, and anything is a loss that induces want and pain. In this sense a beautiful painting, a landscape, a gorgeous sunset is property to any beholder, while the *possession* of a pair of boils is a decided loss, although the former may vanish within a few seconds, and the latter remain six weeks.

The manifold wants of dress come next after those of physical hunger and thirst. Professor James observes: "There are few of us who, if asked to choose between having a beautiful body clad in raiment perpetually shabby and unclean, and having an ugly and blemished form always spotlessly attired, would not hesitate a moment before making a decisive reply." Objectively, our clothes argue, persuade or repel, command and talk for us. They project and partially represent the social self. They are our envoys extraordinary. Subjectively, good clothes enlarge the pleasure field and increase the feelings of size, confidence, egoism, self-consciousness, courage, etc. The self-feelings among children and youth may be so intensified thereby as to create disturbances in their social strata. Lotze emphasized the fact that clothes aroused the feelings of physical extension, and that one's personality was enlarged by them through our bodily parts being enlarged as to sensation in this or that direction by the articles attached. May not this expansive, self-assertive effect of dress on personality account for the custom of warriors of all ages entering battle decked out in rich attire — with blazoned shields, glittering steel, waving plumes, and bright raiment? The slang word *fierce* is attributed to one appareled in a gorgeous costume.

The property value of one's name deserves the space of a paragraph. When Shakespeare said " What's in a name? " he propounded a question of not a little psychological interest. A man's name is a possession which is closely assimilated with his ego. As has been said, " The name has grown layer by layer." It has grown with the ego and the man. It would be an interesting study to learn from married women their feelings on losing the name with which they had grown up and coming into possession of a new one. The writer [France] finds on limited inquiry that there are very peculiar feelings of the ego having lost a part of itself, of almost shame on writing or giving the new name, and a lack of "at homeness" with one's self. Professor Sanford has defined personality as "the sum total of all the reactions that can be got from an individual at any one moment." A study of the *first reactions* of individuals who have come *suddenly* and *unexpectedly* into the possession of a large fortune, and of those who have sustained great and sudden losses, would show, perhaps, the most fundamental effect of material property on the ego. The first reactions under such conditions are most likely to be the instinctive, unconscious, flashing out of the real naked ego before the intellect can get her inhibiting machinery into working order.

Of the 229 cases on this topic 60 describe the behavior of persons made suddenly rich, 51 describe persons meeting with sudden loss, and 118 are descriptive of feelings at the sudden loss of a relative, friend, etc. Ten per cent. of the 60 cases are described as continuing in their ordinary affairs unchanged; they went about in the even tenor of their ways as though nothing had happened. Eight per cent. immediately turned spendthrifts and prodigals ; they seemed pleasure-intoxicated, bent on giving the passions the widest possible amplitude ; few of these cases ever face about and settle down to business. Twenty per cent. at once conceived some generous deed, — gathered their poor friends in for a dinner, — headed some humane and philanthropic movement, began to help a poor boy to prepare for the ministry ; they are often described as loving everybody, even becoming good to animals. Thirty-eight per cent. are described as haughty, proud, arrogant, forgetting and "cutting" their old friends, domineering, harsh and cruel to servants, unsociable ; some turn out misers. It must be stated, however, that some of this portion of the returns are seriously damaged by the evident presence of the "green-eyed monster," which, of itself, is an interesting property psychosis. There seems to be greater uniformity of behavior among those sustaining sudden loss. The majority have little to say, they avoid old friends, seek seclusion, and maintain a dogged silence to the world. They are often found in deep study, and overheard talking to themselves. Some commit suicide. And more than we are aware of spend their last days in an insane asylum. Of course some vigorous and well-poised souls begin cheerfully over again.

Disregarding a few exceptional cases, with the knowledge of new possessions personality sallies forth with the altruistic and the whole host of self-feelings wonderfully intensified. At the news of a wrecked fortune personality is timid, silent, evades society like the peafowl with lost plumage, and is at times seized with morbid fears. Wherefore does property have such transforming power on the ego? Why these cataclysms in the nature and disposition of man at an increase or decrease of things owned?

If we view conscious personality subjectively, we find that it is not a constant entity but rather a consensus of those things present at any time in the stream of consciousness. The constituent elements in the mosaic of personality are what interest us here. What are they in the main? We have observed repeatedly that personality grows in proportion as the things one recognizes as his own increase, and that it shrinks, that much of it becomes as nothing, as the things once owned are swept away. Hobbes says property is grounded internally or psychologically in the consciously apprehended capacities and requirements of human personality. Jhering, in his *Struggle after Law*, says: " In making the object my own I stamped it with my own person : whoever attacks it attacks me, the blow struck it strikes me, for I am present in it." Is not this the answer to our query? The recognition of things owned by me as mine is the material that makes up much of my personality ; and the concept *mine* is the cement to the entire mosaic mass constituting the ego. The attitude of monks, nuns, and hermits towards property is an illustration in point. The one aim of their lives is to subjugate self, annihilate their *own* personality in order that they may take on the likeness of another. To do this they dispossess themselves of everything, wear the plainest clothes, often even expel their own ideas and thoughts. Most convents and monasteries forbid their inmates to own anything.

Another illustration showing that property is the very backbone of personality is seen in general paresis. Here, under the processes of devolution, under reversionary conditions, the one great delusion present is that of vast wealth ; the idea of ownership stands out in the mind in relief amidst the crumbling and fading away of all other psychoses. Again, the prospect of great wealth, a promising scheme whereby a fabulous fortune is to be realized, for example, the South Sea Island project, the scheme for extracting gold from sea water, a trip to the Klondike, will take away the good sense, mother wit, and judgment of many people. Under these conditions their credulity runs riot ; any device, however absurd, is wholly adequate to the end in their eyes. In fact they will not attend to details, will refuse to consider ways and means, so blinded have they become in dreaming over the fabulous returns at the goal. When we consider that no one factor is so intimately associated with all of life's activities as property getting; that property has been and is the one great sessilizing agency for the human race, converting nomads to husbandmen ; that mind and civilization have developed through it and by it, it is no wonder that shattered and wrecked fortunes should be accompanied by dismembered and tottering personalities.

Probably the most general and most urgent motive prompting the acquisition of property in its many forms is fear. The absurd and outlandish practices of the miser will serve us as an introduction to this phase of the subject. The items here recorded are taken from 104 returns on this subject.

M., 52. Crabbed, dishonest, had but few friends. Had one child, a son, to whom he willed a large pile of almanacs. The son was on the point of burning them when he happened to look in an almanac and found twenty dollar bills between the leaves. By looking carefully through the file he found a large sum.

F., 60. Lived in a garret, thought to be very poor. Ate the poorest food, finally died of starvation. When her room was searched four bank books were found and deeds of a great deal of property ; the whole amounted to about half a million dollars.

F. Lived alone, dressed poorly, neighbors thought her poor. She aroused their sympathy until they practically supported her. She was found dead. While disposing of effects to defray funeral expenses three thousand dollars was found stuffed in an old clock.

M., 33. Have always felt that it would be such a disgrace to be buried at public expense.

M., 39. I have often been haunted with the fear of poverty and dying in want. It is the most distressing and depressing state of mind.

Carlyle declared that the hell English people fear most is poverty. We think the declaration might as well be made to include the rest of the human race, for in matters so fundamental there is slight room for differences.

Poverty is pain. It always has been and is ever enlarging the pain field. Its areas include ignorance, bondage, human slavery, cruelty, and misery in its divers forms. Fear is the dread of pain or of the possibilities of pain. The fear of poverty arises in anticipation or dread of the pain that it may cause. The fear is as deep seated as the suffering thereby has been great. There is no cause for wonder at those nameless feelings of dread that steal over one at the thought of being left defenseless in the world without a cent, of being suddenly cut off from the pleasures that delight us, and of being assimilated with outcasts, charges, and irresponsibles, of spending one's last days in the poorhouse, of being buried at public expense and taking one's eternal rest in the potter's field. All those feelings of distrust of man for man in the business world, the always more or less strained relations between creditor and debtor, and the constant over-anxiety about the safe-keeping of property are further expressions of the property-fear psychosis. It crops out among those people who put their money out at small interest in some safe place instead of putting it where pleasure and benefit in a large revenue could be derived. The extreme form of this fear leads some persons to hide their valuables in ridiculous and out-of-the-way places, for instance, in the hems of a garment, in a bundle of carpet rags, underneath a stone, in hair combings, etc. Every one has seen or heard many incidents of this nature. One usually ascribes the hiding of money to misers, which is usually the case ; but all misers do not hide money, nor are all money-hiders misers. Fear and distrust may cause even a liberal man to keep his money in his own peculiar way. Money-hiding, however, is one of the things of minor interest about the miser.

Science lacks a psycho-sociological treatment of the miser. It is true that numerous descriptions of his nature, disposition, and appearance are found in certain species of ethical literature. These descriptions attempt nothing at his origin, and are inadequate in showing his relations to society. The plan of this paper permits only a brief statement of the theories relating to his *origin* and *nature*. The subject deserves a separate monograph. The miser belongs more particularly to the climacteric and post-climacteric periods of life. He has lost interest in his species, — the instinct feelings of parenthood are dead within him, for he evades and shirks her holy ordinances. The dynamic push up of life's forces, the progress of all life, is a concatenation of forces that he avoids. He steps aside when they move in his direction. He will not be caught up by them. Although the most sessilized form of the human race, his sessile apparatus is of the very crudest sort — a miserable hut or cave. He will not beautify a home. Even if given one, the marks of time soon begin to show on it. He reverses every principle of hygiene, every sentiment of home, and a better part of the customs of society. Whence this anomalous sociological element ? Is he a product of a morbid passion to get money plus a morbid fear of poverty, both having become fixed ideas ? or is he an individual whose nature the altruistic wand of adolescence never touched ? Was he truant to life's school while nature was teaching her one great lesson of self-sacrifice ? Is the miser a man with a child's notion of property, i.e., that property is an *end* and not a means ? or may he have resulted from an enforced unselfishness and altruism in childhood, not allowing the instinct of selfish acquisition to play itself out ? or may he have resulted from some mental shock as disappointment in love,[1] loss of friends, thereby aborting that instinct of providing for one's children, which, we have shown, is so fundamental in the normal individual? This latter theory appeals strongly to the writers as one which accounts, at least, for not a few misers. Sweep away from a man his friends, by some evil blow destroy his faith in his own kind, and leave him thus without a purpose, with no one to care for — what will be the result? Silas Marner was such a man. We quote the opinion of George Eliot : " Have not men shut up in solitary imprisonment found an interest in marking the moments by straight strokes of a certain length on the wall until the growth of the sum of straight strokes, arranged in triangles, has become a mastering purpose? Do we not while away moments of inanity or fatigued waiting by repeating some trivial movement or sound until the repetition has bred a want, which is incipient habit? That will help us to understand how the love of accumulating money grows into an absorbing passion in men whose imaginations, even in the very beginning of their hoard, showed them no purpose beyond it. Marner wanted the heaps of tens to grow into a square ; and every added guinea, while it was itself a satisfaction, bred a new desire. In this strange world, made a riddle to him, he might, if he had had a less intense nature, have sat a-weaving, looking toward the end of his pattern or toward the end of his web, till he forgot the riddle and everything else but his immediate sensation, but the money had come to mark off his weaving into periods, and the money not only grew, but it remained with him. He began to think it was conscious of him as his loom was, and he would on no account have exchanged these coins, which had become his familiars, for others with unknown faces. He handled them, he counted them till their form and color were like the satisfaction of a thirst to him, but it was only in the night when his

---

[1] R. L. Stevenson, in his novel *Kidnapped*, gives disappointment in love as the cause of David Balfour's uncle becoming such a cruel miser.

work was done that he drew them out to enjoy their companionship." [1]

Every human being must have something in the world upon which to lavish affection and solicitude, something to which he can turn for companionship in his hour of leisure, some end in which his labor finds reward. And if through some mishap in the economy of nature, some abortion of his own instincts, he be deprived of such of these as his own human kind afford, he must turn elsewhere, and that iron-handed master, habit, may well determine that his fate be turned into a rut of money hoarding. It was the entrance of a little child into the life of Silas Marner that transformed the old crabbed miser into the tenderest of fathers. If the child had entered his life first and passed again from it, he might in turn have become the miser. Such is the "expulsive power of a new affection," but affection there must be in every breast, — an end in every life. We do not attempt to choose among these several theories on account of the small number of facts in hand. To study the miser with any degree of satisfaction, both his life history and that of his ancestors should be well in hand.

Linus W. Kline
C. J. France

BIBLIOGRAPHY

Allen, Grant. Flash Lights on Nature. Doubleday, Page & Co., New York, 1898.

Bolton, Frederic E. "Hydropsychoses," *American Journal of Psychology*, Vol. X, pp. 169–227, January, 1899.

Dawson, George E. "Psychic Rudiments of Morality," *American Journal of Psychology*, Vol. II, pp. 181–224, January, 1900.

Groos, Karl. The Play of Animals (translated by E. L. Baldwin). D. Appleton & Co., New York, 1898. 341 pages.

Hall, G. Stanley. "Moral and Religious Training of Adolescents," *Princeton Review*, Vol. X, pp. 26–48, January, 1882; also *Pedagogical Seminary*, Vol. I. pp. 196–210, June, 1891.

[1] *Silas Marner*, by George Eliot, p. 19.

Hall, G. Stanley. "Some Aspects of the Early Sense of Self," *American Journal of Psychology*, Vol. IX, pp. 351–395, April, 1898.

James, William. Principles of Psychology, Vol. I, p. 292, New York, 1890. 2 vols.

La Fargue, Paul. Evolution of Property. Scribner, London and New York, 1890. 174 pages.

Lancaster, Ellsworth G. "The Psychology and Pedagogy of Adolescence," *Pedagogical Seminary*, Vol. V, pp. 61–128, July, 1897.

Letourneau, Charles. Property, its Origin and Development (Contemporary Science Series). Scribner, London, 1892. 401 pages.

Mason, Otis T. Women's Share in Primitive Culture. D. Appleton & Co., New York, 1899. 295 pages.

Monroe, Will S. "The Money Sense of Children," *Pedagogical Seminary*, Vol. VI, pp. 152–158, March, 1899.

Moore, Mrs. Kathleen C. Mental Development of a Child. Macmillan, New York, 1896 (150 pages) ; also *Psychological Review, Monograph Supplements*, Vol. I, No. 3, 1896 (150 pages).

Morgan, C. Lloyd. Habits and Instinct. E. Arnold, London and New York, 1896. 351 pages.

Newcomb, Professor G. B. "Theories of Property," *Political Science Quarterly*, Vol. I, p. 595, 1886.

Oberholtzer, S. L. School Savings Banks. Published by American Academy of Social and Political Science, Philadelphia, 1893.

Starr, Frederick. "Dress and Adornment," *Popular Science Monthly*, Vol. XXXIX, pp. 488–502; Vol. XL, pp. 44–57, 194–206, August, November, and December, 1891.

Sully, James. Human Mind, Vol. I, p. 476; Vol. II, p. 106. D. Appleton & Co., New York, 1892.

Tassin, Wirt. "Descriptive Catalogue of the Collections of Gems in the United States National Museum," *Report of the United States National Museum for 1900*, pp. 473–670, Washington, 1902. (Special reference is called to the mystical properties of gems, pp. 558–587; also to the exhaustive bibliography.)

Tylor, Edward B. Researches into the Early History of Mankind and the Development of Civilization. H. Holt & Co., New York, 1878. 388 pages.

Weir, James, Jr. "The Herds of the Yellow Ant," *Popular Science Monthly*, Vol. LIV, pp. 75–81, November, 1898.

FETICHISM IN CHILDREN [1]

Use of the Terms "Fetich" and "Fetichism"

The words *fetich* and *fetichism* are commonly used as blanket terms for all forms of savage religion, whether worship of sticks, stones, trees, rivers, mountains, fire, animals, or the heavenly bodies, but following Major A. B. Ellis, who has spent many years as an officer in West Africa, I here restrict the terms to their original significance.

When the Portuguese began explorations in West Africa some four hundred years ago, Christian Europe was full of relics and images of saints, charmed rosaries, crosses, etc., which were supposed to give protection and success, and when worn gave still greater protection. Such charms were called *feitiços*, and when the Portuguese saw the negroes paying the same reverence to charmed stones they applied the same word to the savage charms.

As to this significance of fetiches there is much diversity of opinion. To Brinton the fetich is something more than the mere object. That the savage beats his fetich when it does not bring him success proves the contrary, nor have we evidence that primitive man was ever able to distinguish between the body and spirit.

Fetichism at first confounded the spirit and the object; later, when man became more cultured, he thought of the fetich as the place where the spirit chose to manifest itself, and finally came to consider the fetich as a symbol, an aid to devotion, or even came to rise above its use. With growing

[1] Reprinted in abridged form from *Pedagogical Seminary*, Vol. IX, pp. 205–220, June, 1902.

culture came a growth in æsthetic sense, and the fetich is improved by a gradual conformity to the human figure or some animal form. There is no line of demarcation between the rough unhewn stone fetich and the Aphrodite of Melos.

Primitive man worshiped where it paid him to do so, and naturally enough, under the influence of his needs and the environment, certain things that ministered to those needs were worshiped and all others fell into disfavor. Fetichistic practices also form part of the outer worship of Lamaite Buddhism and Taoism, and they are not only tolerated but prescribed by other universal religions. I need but mention the amulets, talismans, scapularies, miracle working relics, etc., among Mohammedans and Christians.

Stone worship exists to-day in England, Scotland, Wales, and France as widely as ever.

"Modern folklore is full of fetichism, and it is a development of the religious sentiment which flourishes in all times and climes. Amulets, charms, lucky stones, everything that we call by the familiar term of *mascot*, partakes of the nature of a fetich. Through some fancied potency not to be found among its physical qualities it is believed to bring us good fortune."

RECAPITULATION OF THE RACE IN THE CHILD

The old saying that parents live again in their children is no less true than that the child lives again the history of the race.

Biologically the child passes through a series of types ranging from protozoan to man. At conception the organism is a minute unicellular structure, by the second week it suggests an invertebrate type, at three weeks it has fishlike gill pouches, by the fifth week it has developed amphibian traces and the limbs have become differentiated from the body; thence on to the middle of the third month reptilian characters are found. Gradually the fœtus assumes an anthropoidal character, and from about the fifth to the seventh month the body is covered with short downy hair, without pigment.

Any interference with the course of nature may cause arrest at any of these stages and result in monsters at birth.

The atavisms of young children are suggestive. The infant sits with the soles of the feet together, as do the apes. Some newborn children can sustain themselves for one minute by clinging to a stick. This is not so strange when we remember that the young of apes have to cling to their mother. There are a large number of rudimentary organs in the body, which, like the vermiform appendix, were useful at some stage of the organic evolution.

Psychologically there are many things explained only by the recapitulation theory. In dreams, the old racial fears often make nights miserable. Kissing has developed as evidence of faith that the person would not be eaten, a fear which, so common in our animal ancestors, must be taken to account for the strange fear many have for teeth, fur, etc. Blushing is perhaps a survival of the sex fear. Distrust of strangers and neighbors, so common in sparsely settled communities, is a survival of the fear that primitive man, always at war for existence, had for his fellow-men. The suddenness with which the fear of disease and death may spring up to overmastering power " shows a deep hereditary root copiously watered by superstition."

The tendency of children to run away is an echo of the migratory impulse of our ancestors, which has become abnormally developed in the tramp and " globe trotter."

The fascination which water has for children and even adults has been taken by Bolton as "abundant proof of man's pelagic ancestry."

FETICHISM IN CHILDREN

Mrs. Burk in her study of the collecting instinct saw there was something yet to be explained, but did not offer a solution.

"When we consider its universality, its widespread affection; when we consider its intensity, the number of collections children make and the interest they take in them; when we consider the variety of the things collected, showing that the mania seizes upon any and practically every outlet imaginable, and showing, too, that to collect is more important than what is collected; when we consider, moreover, that the phenomenon has a definite progress, — a rise, a growth, and a decline, an age development, — we are inclined not to hesitate in calling it an instinct " (p. 238 of this volume).

The psychological explanation of this instinct seems to be that the child has in it the survival of the savage impulse to collect the strange and beautiful in the hope that some good will come thereby. This vague, unanalyzed feeling in the child was the philosophy of its savage ancestors. Just as nameless fears and mysterious impulses are echoes of ancient psychoses, so is this collecting impulse a dim reminder of the fetichism of our ancestors. Evidence of this is seen in Mrs. Burk's study, in the fact that even "a comparatively few " reported collections made for " luck " (p. 230 of this volume).

CHILDREN'S ANIMISTIC CONCEPTIONS OF INANIMATE OBJECTS

It is hard for the child to distinguish between the self and not-self. This is seen in the way in which things are regarded as a part of the personality or family.

F., 18. I want to keep forever everything I ever worked and played with. Toys and even schoolbooks seem a part of me and I would not part with them.

F. At home they have a large brass match box, 200 years old, which has always been in the family. She feels that it is a part of her ancestry.

F.'s brother has an old kitchen clock which used to be in her home. She regards this as one of the family.

Playthings are regarded as persons.

M., 5. Was strongly attached to a small, rude, chair-shaped block of wood ; called it "boy block," took it everywhere, hugged it, cried when it was lost, etc.

F., 17. My brother, aged three, has a bit of an old strap, which he always keeps and talks to and takes to bed with him. We cannot find out why.

F., 19. I wore a star and crescent badge of our club. I felt it was somehow like a man.

M., 9. Played pretty stones were people.

The rudiments of a philosophy are found in the child's explanation of the origin of things.

M., 23. As a boy, I saw lime slaked and immediately conceived great awe of it. I got and cherished a piece and fancied many things about it.

M., 23. Wondered where stones came from but was ashamed to ask.

F., 19. Thought stones came up out of the earth.

M., 7. Thought stones were made of ground when it got hot; clouds of dust turned into stones. Wondered if they turned back.

Here we have speculations on ancient history and attempts to solve the problem of nature. The last example quoted is remarkable as closely approximating Heraclitus' theory that all is a flux, and also suggests the ancient Greek theory of physics, that material phenomena are different condensations of a primal substance.

F. I had certain places where imaginary friends lived, and I did n't want other people to go there.

F. I remember I used to make collections of different kinds of buttons and imagine them as men and women and make them act as if they were alive. Sometimes I thought they were an army and I would make them have a fight by shaking them up, and all those that turned over I thought of as dead.

Such conceptions as these give the foundation for a mythology that only needs time to develop it.

Stones are regarded as having feeling, as knowing what is going on, as sympathizing in trouble.

F., 16. Stones have feelings. She fell on one and struck it back to make it feel bad too.

F. When angry vented her anger upon the object which caused it.

F. Vents anger upon the thing that bothers her; if algebra, she pounds it; if a door, she slams it.

F. When angry would go to her room and throw and tear things. She did this to show that she could conquer *something*. She would then try to mend the broken article.

F. Feels that stones have sympathy; that the one in her ring knows what is going on. Seems pathetic to her to throw a pretty stone into water.

F. Would not throw a pretty stone into water because she would not want to part with it. She regards stones as friends.

F., 8. Threw stones into deep water and cried because she was sorry for them. She thought stones stuck to the bottom of ponds and pails, and wondered if they were hurt, or if it was cold, dark, smothery.

F. Thought a certain rock saw all she did and would sometime tell.

Human relationships are conceived of as existing between large and small stones, and distinctions between animate and inanimate objects are not made.

F., 19. Large rocks are the fathers of the little ones.

F., 18. Thought sand was alive and grew. Sand was young stones that would grow up to be rocks.

F. In the country, said, " Stones grow larger here than at home."

F., 17. Thought a big black stone in the forest must be very old.

One of the most fascinating diversions of the child is to trace forms in the figures of the wall paper, or anything else.

F. Used to look at the cracks in the walls and imagine them to be forms of animals or plants.

F. Used to imagine pictures of people, etc., in the wall paper of a certain room.

These last two examples show an instinct that is very common in adults who delight to sit in the dark and trace in the glowing embers of the open hearth or the flickering shadows on the wall the forms of men and fairies or grotesque animals. This instinct to people the darkness or an unfrequented wood with nameless monsters is especially noticeable when fear has aroused it. One of the things that helped primitive man to fill the world with spirits must have been the fantasies of his mind, which seemed to appear and dissolve into the natural objects to appear elsewhere. Under such a frame of mind primitive man came to think of the spirits as dissociated with natural objects but manifesting themselves through them as caprice prompted.

The savage to-day sees a knotted piece of wood which happens to suggest something to his mind, and at once the piece of wood becomes to him the abode of a spirit and is taken home to give protection to him and his property.

In the child there is the combination of the mother instinct with the fetich.

The child's plaything may suggest the features of a person disliked.

F. I had one doll which I never liked, because it resembled a very disagreeable person. We used to hang this doll on the clothesline and take turns throwing stones at it.

This may appear a meaningless matter, but it is what is very common among savages and survives in parts of England and elsewhere. To the savage mind anything that looks like a person is supposed to contain a part of the personality of that person. Anthropologists have nearly lost their lives in making drawings of natives, because the drawing was supposed to contain the " shadow " of the person it resembled, and if any ill should befall it, or any indignity be given it, the evil results would fall on the original of the picture. In England it even now occasionally happens that a doll dressed to resemble an enemy is taken and filled with pins with the purpose of causing the death of the person it resembles. Salem witch-craft days were full of such tales. It has not passed away in America, as the hanging in effigy, occasionally practiced, re-echoes the old belief that such an act would cause the death of the person.

CHILD MAGIC

To the savage mind the powers of nature were sometimes friendly and sometimes not. In the child's mind either of these views may be dominant, or the one or the other may be dominant as the child feels it has done right or wrong.

F. Feels that a large rock near her home would protect her, and she often goes there to cry.

M., 6. Rocks suggested strong soldiers.

M. Rocks made men strong. It was pleasant to sit on them and talk to them. Always felt safe near them.

Probably very large rocks cause the sense of fear, while the smaller ones give the sense of protection. The writer well remembers his childhood terror of large rocks and cliffs, but took keen delight in playing near small bowlders. Even with more mature years, he feels *more comfortable* when there are no large rocks or cliffs near.

Two of the most remarkable returns are given here.

—. Wishes on a stone and spits on it to make things come true.

F., 10. Visits a white flat stone, wishes over it, and throws it over her shoulder to make things come true.

Spitting on the fetich is common among savages and has great potency among the people of northern England.

Throwing stones over the shoulder recalls the myths of Deucalion and Pyrrha. Whether this myth had been told the child and her acts had been imitative matters not, for the fact that such things could appeal to the child's mind shows that it is in the same condition as that of the savage.

Stones are worn as charms and any harm to them may bring bad luck.

F. Carried a little red stone for protection.

F. Has a lucky stone that she thinks brings luck.

F., 16. Lost a game because the stone was broken and could not win.

When the child vents anger upon any object it is due to the idea, however vague, that it is to blame for all the trouble or should exert some restraining influence, as the following shows:

F., 16. Got mad one day and knocked a piece off a big stone with a hammer, "so it would remember and not let me get mad again."

Other objects than stones are used for luck.

F. I remember picking up pins and thinking at the time of the say-ing that they would bring good luck. I also have stopped when riding or driving to pick up a horseshoe.

A primitive faith cure or Shamanism is found in children.

F., 17. A boy of five emptied his pockets for me. In them were . . . a pill box with imaginary salve to cure your finger if it got hurt, some pretty stones carried " because," etc.

Instances of this kind might be multiplied indefinitely. In Vermont horse-chestnuts are carried to keep off rheumatism, " sulphur bags " are worn to keep away colds, etc.

" Making believe " is a universal occurrence among children, and exists in countless forms. One common thing is to turn work into play.

F. When I washed dishes I used to call the knives men, the forks women, and spoons children. The steel knives and forks used in the kitchen were servants. I always arranged them in families. This form continued until I was thirteen or fourteen years old I think.

F. When I used to be tired of practicing on the piano I made believe that my hands or fingers were children chasing each other up and down the scales. The other instance was when I was wiping dishes. I called the knives men, the forks women, and the spoons children.

Jewels especially have a very warm place near the heart of man, and are almost a language of feeling. They are loved and feared and have strange power over human life. For some pearls bring tears, opals are worst of all, and diamonds are best.

F. Thinks she could not get along without her birth stone, an opal, but would not wear one unless it had been her birth stone.

F. Has always felt that opals were bad luck, and that pearls bring tears. She would not wear either.

F. Made a collection of pretty stones because they seemed so like gems. She wears a lucky pin and carries lucky bones.

Single coins of silver and especially gold are often made fetiches of by adults.

F. Knows a distinguished attorney who has for years carried a penny given him by an old lady, who assured him that he would not lose any cases while he carried it.

Often one charm has not virtue enough, and as many kinds of lucky articles as possible are worn.

F. Carries a rabbit's foot for good luck, has a four-leaved clover in her watch, also she carries a lucky penny. She cried when she lost her four-leafed clover.

FETICHES OF ASSOCIATION

One form of fetichism that is extremely common is the souvenir craze. It takes every possible phase from the Colonial Dame who prides herself on her collection of teapots, to the college student who decorates his room with things " swiped " on many a midnight lark. This collecting instinct is due to the psychological law of association in which the familiar object serves as a stimulus to set off the original mental state connected with it. This, in the savage mind, amounts to the law that whatever suggests a thing *is* that thing. This is the psychological basis of the " make-believe " plays of children.

M., 18. When about five I had a passion for mementoes and would bring a stone from every place I went, to remember it by. I kept my relics to bring up past experiences.

F., 29. I lately came across a box of things that were very precious to me as a child. It contained a blue cuff button, two jacks, a glass stopper, an ivory umbrella handle, an empty perfume bottle, shells, a bit of coral, funny letters, many bits of cloth and ribbons, tissue paper, etc. All of my girl friends had such things and we traded much, but allowed no one to touch our treasures.

F., 23. Thirteen years ago we went from the East to Chicago. Just as we were leaving, my bosom friend, Nellie, and I were walking arm in arm ; we each picked up a stone and gave the other. Later, in Chicago, I would talk to my stone as if it were Nellie. Each of us still cherish our stones, and I feel if anything happened to it, something would be wrong with her.

F., 16. My uncle I never saw, for he died in the war ; but I took great pleasure in and felt great awe over the things kept sacred in his trunk, — a spoon, knife, a notebook, a pack of cards, an arrowhead, etc.

These illustrate what has just been said of the law of association as recalling past experiences. This is paralleled in the scalps which the American Indian proudly exhibits, and in the thousand and one incidents of savage life where abstraction is impossible and every thought clings to concrete forms, and also brings out the fact that one cannot love in the abstract. There must be something to keep memory fresh and the heart tender. It is natural to keep the things that remind one of dear friends removed from earthly life, and where it does not occur we feel something is lacking in one's nature. The tenderest, best emotions of life are wrapped up in a faded flower or some seemingly meaningless and worthless object. This is nowhere better seen than in love fetiches. Everything that the mistress has worn or touched, be it ever so humble, is sacred to the ardent lover ; the perfume she prefers recalls her with overwhelming emotions ; souvenirs collected on strolls together are dearer than gold ; the ring that acknowledges their engagement is sacred above all else to the maiden's heart from its associations and, perhaps, from a superstitious regard of it. Photographs well show how a savage can look at an image. The lover kisses the photograph and speaks to it as tenderly as if it were the original. Nice distinctions as to appearance and reality never trouble him, unless with the consciousness that the photograph is not as satisfactory as the original.

Others smile at the lovers, but "all the world loves a lover," and never is man so close to the past history of the race as when he is a lover.

Articles of food are often regarded mystically. Friends keep half of a cracker each, curious candies, fruit, bits of wedding cake.

Conclusion

While the arrangement of material has been arbitrary, the fact nevertheless remains that in the child can be found all the elements that, united, made man a religious being.

As a suggestion in race pedagogy, it is well to remember that two millenniums of Christianity has not removed but only modified the old savage traits. Intellectually we have risen above the savage, but in the emotional nature we are about the same as ever. We have but to scratch the skin of the American soldier to find the Tartar, and we have only to go among the most refined American homes and schools to find the old race superstitions surviving in about their pristine strength. A man cannot make himself over in one day, much less a race.

This would be a dismal world indeed if every one were confined to cold facts in speech. This survival of animistic ideas in children is proof of its necessity in the development of the race and individual.

Cases like those reported by Dr. Gould often cause parents no little alarm, but the child will certainly come out safely if left to himself.

Thanks are due to Dr. Hall for suggestions and material; also to Miss Power of the Home School for collecting much of the data upon which this paper is based.

G. HAROLD ELLIS

BIBLIOGRAPHY

Black, William G. Folk Medicine. Folklore Society Publications, London, 1883. 228 pages.

Brinton, Daniel G. Religion of Primitive Peoples. G. P. Putnam's Sons, New York, 1898. 264 pages.

Chamberlain, Alexander F. The Child: A Study in the Evolution of Man (Contemporary Science Series). W. Scott, Ltd., London, 1903. 498 pages.

Deniker, Joseph. The Races of Man (Contemporary Science Series), London, 1900. 611 pages.

Ellis, Alfred B. The Tshi-Speaking Peoples of the Gold Coast of West Africa. Chapman & Hall, London, 1887. 343 pages.

Gould, George M. "Child Fetiches," *Pedagogical Seminary*, Vol. V, pp. 421–425, January, 1895.

Gregor, Waller. Folklore of the North-East of Scotland. Folklore Society Publications, London, 1881. 238 pages.

Grimm, Jakob. Teutonic Mythology. G. Bell & Sons, London, 1882–1888. 4 vols.

Guillet, Cephas. "Recapitulation and Education," *Pedagogical Seminary*, Vol. VII, pp. 397–445, October, 1900.

Hall, G. Stanley. "A Study of Fears," *American Journal of Psychology*, Vol. VIII, pp. 147–249, January, 1897.

Henderson, William. Folklore of the Northern Counties of England and the Borders. Folklore Society Publications, London. 391 pages.

Johnson, John H. Rudimentary Society among Boys. McDonogh, Maryland, 1893. 66 pages.

Kline, Linus W. "The Migratory Impulse versus the Love of Home," *American Journal of Psychology*, Vol. X, pp. 1–81, October, 1898.

Sebillot, Paul. "The Worship of Stones in France," *American Anthropologist*, N.S., Vol. IV, pp. 76–107, 1902.

Sikes, William. British Goblins. Osgood, Boston, 1881. 412 pages.

Spencer, Herbert. Principles of Sociology, Vol. I. D. Appleton & Co., New York, 1882. 838 pages.

Tylor, Edward B. Primitive Culture. Henry Holt & Co., New York, 1888. 2 vols.

BOY LIFE IN A MASSACHUSETTS COUNTRY TOWN FORTY YEARS AGO [1]

Between the ages of nine and fourteen my parents, who then lived in a distant town, very wisely permitted me to spend most of the schoolless part of these five years, so critical for a boy's development, with a large family on a large farm in Ashfield of this state. Although this joyous period ended long ago, the life, modes of thought and feeling, industries, dress, etc., were very old-fashioned for that date, and were tenaciously and proudly kept so. In more recent years, as I have come to believe that nowhere does the old New England life still persist more strongly or can be studied more objectively, I have spent portions of several summers, with the aid of a small fund placed in my hands for the purpose, in collecting old farm tools, household utensils, furniture, articles of dress, and hundreds of miscellaneous old objects into a local museum, a little after the fashion of the museums of Plymouth, Salem, and Deerfield. I have interviewed all the oldest inhabitants for details of customs, industries, persons, become interested in a map of the original farms, verified in part by old walls and cellar holes and apple trees, and compiled a brief history of the town. My vacation interest grew into a record, partly because so many facts of the early life and thoughts of old New England are still unrecorded and are now so fast passing beyond the reach of record, with the lamented decay of these little old towns, partly because despite certain evils this life at its best appears to me to have constituted about the best educational environment for boys at a certain

[1] Reprinted from *Proceedings of the American Antiquarian Society*, N.S., Vol. VII, pp. 107–128, 1891.

stage of their development ever realized in history, combining physical, industrial, technical with civil and religious elements in wise proportions and pedagogic objectivity. Again, this mode of life is the one and the only one that represents the ideal basis of a state of citizen voters as contemplated by the framers of our institutions. Finally, it is more and more refreshing in our age, and especially in the vacation mood, to go back to sources, to the fresh primary thoughts, feelings, beliefs, modes of life of simple, homely, genuine men. Our higher anthropology labors to start afresh from the common vulgar standpoint as Socrates did, from what Maurice calls the *Ethos* and Grote the *Nomos* of common people, and of a just preceding and a vanishing type of civilization, to be warmed with its experience and saturated with its local color.

I have freely eked out the boyish memory of those five years with that of older persons, but everything that follows was in Ashfield within the memory of people living there a few years ago. Time allows me to present here but a small part of the entire record, to sample here and there, and to show a few obvious lessons.

I begin with winter, when men's industries were most diversified, and were largely in *wood*. Lumber, or timber, trees were chopped down and cut by two men working a crosscut saw, which was always getting stuck fast, in a pinch which took the set out of it, unless the whole trunk was pried up by skids. Sometimes the fallen trees were cut into logs, snaked together, and piled with the aid of cant hooks, to be drawn across the frozen pond to the sawmill for some contemplated building, or, if of spruce, of straight grain and few knots, or of good rift, they were cut in bolts, or cross sections, of fifteen inches long, which was the legal length for shingles. These were taken home in a pung, split with beetle and wedge, and then with a frow, and finished off with a drawshave on a shaving horse, itself homemade. These rive shingles were thought far more durable than those cut into shape by the buzz saw, which does not follow the grain. To be of prime quality these must be made of heart and not sap wood, nor of second-growth trees. The shavings were in wide demand for kindling fires. Ax helves, too, were sawed, split, hewed, whittled, and scraped into shape with bits of broken glass, and the forms peculiar to each local maker were as characteristic as the style of painter or poet, and were widely known, compared, and criticised. Butter paddles were commonly made of red cherry, while sugar lap paddles were made by merely barking whistlewood or bass and whittling down one end for a handle. Mauls and beetles were made of ash knots, oxbows of walnut, held in 'shape till seasoned by withes of yellow birch, from which also birch brushes and brooms were manufactured on winter evenings by stripping down seams of wood in the green. There were salt mortars and pig troughs made from solid logs with tools hardly more effective than those the Indian uses for his dugout. Flails for next year's threshing ; cheese hoops and cheese ladders ; bread troughs, and yokes for hogs and sheep, and pokes for jumping cattle, horses and unruly geese, and stanchions for cows. Some took this season for cutting next summer's bean and hop poles, pea bush, cart and sled stakes, with an eye always out for a straight clean whipstock or fish pole. Repairs were made during this season, and a new cat hole beside the door, with a laterally working drop lid, which the cat operated with ease, was made one winter. New sled neaps, and fingers for the grain cradle, handles for shovels and dungforks, pitchforks, spades, spuds, hoes, and, a little earlier, for rakes ; scythes and brooms were homemade, and machines and men of special trades were so far uncalled for. Nearly all these forms of domestic woodwork I saw, and even helped in as a boy of ten might, or imitated them in play in those thrice-happy days ; while in elder popguns, with a ringing report, that were almost dangerous indoors ; hemlock bows and arrows, or crossbows with arrow-heads run on with melted lead (for which every scrap of lead pipe or antique pewter dish was in great demand), often fatal for very small game ; box and figure-4 traps for rats and squirrels ; windmills ; weathervanes in the form of fish, roosters, or even ships ; an actual sawmill that went in the brook, and cut planks with Marino and black and white Carter potatoes for logs ; and many whittled tools, toys, and orna-mental forms and puppets ; in making all these and many more I even became in a short time a fairly average expert as compared with other boys, at least so I then thought. How much all this has served me since, in the laboratory, in daily life, and even in the study, it would be hard to estimate.

The home industry in woolen is a good instance of one which survives in occasional families to this day. Sheep, as I remem-ber, could thrive on the poorest hay or oats, the leavings of the neat cattle. In summer they could eat brakes and poly-pods, if not even hardhack and tansy, and would browse down berry briers and underbrush, while their teeth cut the grass so close that cows could hardly survive in the same pasture with them. The spring lambs were raised in the shed by hand, sometimes as cossets by the children, who often derived their first savings therefrom. Sheep-washing day was a gala day, when, if at no other time, liquor was used against exposure ; and shearing, which came a week or two later, was hardly less interesting. A good shearer, who had done his twenty-five head a day, commanded good wages, — seventy-five cents or a dollar a day ; while the boys must pull the dead sheep, even though they were only found after being some weeks defunct. Fleeces for home use were looked over, all burrs and shives picked out, and they were then oiled with poor lard. " Bees " were often held to do this. Carding early became specialized, and carders were in every town, but the implements were in each family, some members of which could not only card but could even use the fine, long-toothed worsted combs in an emergency. The rolls were spun at home, novices doing the woof or filling, and the older girls the warp, which must be of better quality. It was taken from the spindle sometimes on a niddy-noddy held in the hand, at two rounds per yard, but more commonly on a reel, in rounds of two yards each. Every forty rounds was signalized on a reel by the snap of a wooden spring or the fall of a hammer, and constituted a knot, four, five, seven, or ten of which (in different families and for different purposes) constituted a skein and twenty knots made a run. Four seven-knotted skeins of filling or six of warp was a day's work, though now, I am told, few young women can accomplish so much without excessive fatigue. The yarn, doubled if for stocking, after being washed clean of grease, next went to the great dye tub in the chimney corner. Butternut bark for everyday suits, indigo for Sunday suits, and madder for shirting was the rule. There were also fancy dyes and fancy dyeing, braiding, binding tightly or twisting in a white thread to get the favorite hit or miss, or pepper-and-salt effect, a now almost incredible ingenuity in making up figures and fancy color effects for loom patterns in girls' dresses. Next the filling was quilled and the warp spooled, the former ready for the shuttle and the latter for the warping bars (both of these latter being often homemade), to which it goes from the scarn or spool frame. In warping, the leese must be taken with care, for if the order of the threads is lost they cannot be properly thumbed through the harnesses and hooked through the reed, and are good for nothing but to make into clotheslines and the piece is lost. A raddle also acts in keeping the warp disentangled and of proper width before the lathe and tenters can hold it. Some-times blue and white shirt-formed frock cloth was woven, sometimes kerseys and plaid dress patterns of many colors, or woolen sheets and even woolen pillowcases, which were as warm and heavy, although coarser, than those the olfactorial zoölogist, Jäger, advises and sells to his followers. The complication of harnesses and treadles required to weave some of the more complicated carpet, and especially coverlid, patterns evinced great ingenuity and long study, and is probably now, although the combinations were carefully written down, in most communities a forever lost art. On coming from the loom the cloth was wet for shrinkage and the nap picked up with cards of home-grown teasels and sheared smooth on one side, although in those days this process had already gone to the local fuller. Coarse yarn was also spun from taglocks, which were, of course, home carded. Knitting was easy, pretty, visiting work. Girls earned from two to three York shillings a pair for men's stockings, paid in trade from the store, which put out such work if desired. Shag mittens were knit from thrums or the left-over ends of warp. Nubias and sontags were knit with large wooden needles, and men's gloves, tidies, and clock stockings with ornamental openwork in the sides were knit with one hook, and the tape loom, held between the knees, was kept going evenings.

Domestic flax industry still lingers in a few families. The seed was sown broadcast and grew till the bolls were ripe, when it was pulled and laid in rows by the boys and whipped, in a few days, to get the seed for meal. After lying out of doors for some weeks till the shives were rotten, it was put through the process of breaking on the ponderous flax-brake. It was then swingled, hatcheled, and finally hanked. It was then wound on the distaff made of a young spruce top, and drawn out for spinning. Grasshopper years, when the fiber was short, this was hard, and though ticking, meal bags, and scratchy tow shirts could be made, finer linen products were impossible. After weaving it must be bleached in a good quality of air.

However it was with adults, child life was full of amusements. Children were numerous in every neighborhood, and though they were each required to be useful, they were in early years left much to themselves and were at home in every house, barn, or shed within a mile or more. There was, of course, coasting, skating, swimming, goal, fox and hounds, and snowballing, with choosing of sides, lasting for a whole school term, with elaborate forts ; cart wheel and men o' morn's in the snow ; collar and elbow, or square-hold wrestling, with its many different trips, locks, and play-ups, — side and back hold being unscientific ; round ball ; two and four old cat, with soft yarn balls thrown at the runner. The older "girl-boys" spent the hour's nooning in the schoolhouse and either paired off for small games or talks, or played "Here we stand all round this ring," "Needle's eye," "Kitty corners," or "Who's got the button." As in the age of Shakespeare the queen's maids of honor played tag, so here all children and even adults often played children's games with gusto. In the family, as they gathered about the stove, or sometimes about the grand old fireplace in the back kitchen, with its backlog, crane, pothooks, and trammels, there were stories of the old fort, of bears, wild cats, Indians and Bloody Brook, and other probably unprinted tales perhaps many generations old. There were some who could sing old English ballads that had come down by tradition, and which had never been in print in America, and more who could sing a comic song or pathetic negro melody. Lord Lovel, Irving, Bunyan, *The Youth's Companion*, and many Sunday-school books were read aloud. A pair of skates was earned by a boy friend one winter by reading the entire Bible through, and another bought an accordion with money earned by braiding for the women the plain sides of palm-leaf hats where no splicing was needed, at a cent per side. All families allowed the game of fox and geese, a few permitted checkers, and one, backgammon, which was generally thought to be almost gambling ; dominoes were barely tolerated, but riddles, rebuses, and charades were in high favor by old and young, and were published in all the local weekly papers. It was here that I learned that card playing, which I had often seen before but did not much understand nor care for, was very wrong, and a boy friend was taught old sledge and euchre up over the horse sheds on Sundays between services by an older son of the officiating minister. There were "hull gull," cat's cradle with two series of changes, string and knot puzzles, odd and even, and most of the games and many more than those in Mr. Newell's charming and largely original book entitled, *The Games and Songs of American Children*, connecting many of them conclusively with the sports and pastimes of the English people in the merry olden time of Brand. One maiden lady, whom we all loved, could spell "the abominable bumblebee with his head cut off" in an inverse house-that-Jack-built fashion, with a most side-splitting effect. There was the charming story of the big, little, and middle-sized bear, and I recall the thrill when at the turn of the story, "the dog began to worry the cat, the cat began to kill the rat, the rat began to eat the corn," etc. There were beechnutting and chestnutting parties, raisings, and days set apart for all the men in the district being warned out by the surveyor to gather and work on the roads with teams. Work was easy, as it was for the town, and stories were plenty. There were huskings, with cider and pumpkin pie, and games on the barn floor when it was cleared of corn ; paring bees, with bobbing, swinging a whole paring thrice around the head, thence to fall on the floor in the form of the fancied initial of some person of the other sex ; and counting seeds to the familiar doggerel, "one I love, two I love, three I love I say, four I love with all my heart, and five I cast away, etc." Here the apples were quartered and strung, and hung in festoons to dry all over the kitchen. There were quilting bees for girls about to marry, where the men came in the evening and partook of the new species of rice popcorn, served in two large milk pans, with perhaps the most delicious homemade spruce and wintergreen beer. Spelling schools in which the parents took part, and where the champion spellers of rural districts, after exhausting several spelling books, agreed to spell each other down on an abridged Worcester's dictionary. There were weekly evening singing schools in winter, and several of us taught ourselves or each other to play the accordion and fiddle by rote, to dance single and double shuffle on a board and the steps of waltz, polka, and schottische. Even square dances were attempted to our own music, if we could get a " caller-off." This latter was here a stolen sweet, as was the furtive reading of the thrilling tales of the *New York Ledger*, especially those of Sylvanus Cobb, sets of which were smuggled around among the boys and read after retiring, or in sheep shed, haymow, or attic on rainy days. I must not forget the rage for trapping and hunting, by which we learned much of the habits of crows, hawks, musk-rats, woodchucks, squirrels, partridges, and even foxes, and which made us acquainted with wide areas of territory. In a regular squirrel hunt, organized by choosing sides, and a din-ner to the victors paid for by the vanquished party, as deter-mined by counting tails, boys of my age were not old enough to participate. We made collections, however, for whole sea-sons, of heads, legs, wings, and tails, as well as of woods, leaves, flowers, stones, bugs, butterflies, etc.

The dull days in haying time brought another sort of educa-tion. The men of the vicinity strolled together in a shed, and, sitting on tool bench, grindstone, manger, wagons, chopping blocks, and hog spouts, discussed crop prices, ditching, wall-ing, salting cattle, finding springs with witch-hazel, taxes, the preaching, the next selectmen, fence viewer, constable, and, I suppose a little earlier, wardens, leather sealers, deer reeves, surveyors of shingles and clapboards and of wheat, field drivers, tithing men, clerk of the market, and pound keepers, as well as the good brooks and ponds for trouting or snaring pickerel with brass-wire loops and a white-birch-bark light at night, and every sort of gossip. The old uncles who came to be the heroes of current stories, and who were, in a sense, ideal men, were shrewd and sharp, of exceeding few words, but these oracular, of most unpromising exteriors and mode of speech, with quaint and eccentric ways which made their quintessential wisdom very surprising by the contrast ; while in weather signs and in drugs the old Indian was sometimes the sage. At the opposite extreme was the unseasoned fellow who can be fooled and not get the best of it if he was "run" or played some practical joke. Absurd exaggerations told with a serious air, to test the hearer's knowledge or credulity, were the chief ingredients of this lowery-day wit. Thus the ass's head was not unfrequently clapped on some poor rich fellow, green from the city or some larger town, suspected of the unpardonable sin of being "stuck up."

In this air a good "nag" has great viability. As a boy here, e.g., I often played hunt, snapping a disabled old flintlock musket at every live thing in field and forest, for which an adult neighbor used to "run" me unmercifully before the whole shed. Years after, when I was at home on a college outing, he had not forgotten it, and for perhaps a dozen summers since I have met it. On a recent evening, when walking with a dignified city friend, he met me with the same old grind, "Hello, huntin' much this summer with Philander's old gun ?" as he slapped his thighs and laughed till the hills rang, and, though I did not hear him, I am no less certain that he said to the neighbor with him, when they had ridden well by, that I was always a pretty middlin' good sort of a fellow after all, and was n't stuck up. The joke will no doubt keep fresh another quarter of a century if my friend lives, and there are many more of the same kind. Another grind at my expense illustrates the inventive cleverness of this old Yankee type. As one of the speakers at an annual dinner in honor of the old town academy, I had been several times introduced as a specimen of the former students of the academy. One night, at the crowded post office, this shrewd old farmer told, in my presence and for my benefit, the story of old Joe W., who went on the road as a drummer for the old tannery. He said Joe had just experienced religion, and was just then so all-fired honest that he selected, as the samples he was to sell from, pieces of sole leather a trifle below the average quality, instead of above, as an honest drummer should do. He was afraid to hope that Professor N., who presided at the dinner, had experienced religion, but leastways he was so all-fired honest that he leaned over backwards worse than old Joe in calling me out as a sample academy boy, for although I was middling smart there was not a boy of them who was n't a plaguy sight smarter than I was. Another of his stories was of Stephen and Ann. They were courting, and she had sat in his lap in the kitchen one Sunday evening for some hours, when she suddenly asked if he was not tired. He gallantly replied, " Not a mite, Ann ; keep right on settin'. I was awful tired an hour ago, but now I am numb." That is the way, he said, it was probably with my hearers and pupils.

Then there was the story of old Deacon S., who sold home-made cider brandy, or twisted cider, at the rate of twenty-five cents per gallon, but who always used to get his big thumb into the quart measure, which had lost its handle, displacing its cubic contents of brandy. There was another tale of Captain A., who, being cheated in a horse trade by Mr. B., called all his sons and grandsons together solemnly, as if for family prayers, told them the circumstances, and enjoined them to cheat B. back to the amount of six dollars, and if they did not live to do it, to teach their children and grandchildren to cheat his descendants to the end of time; but a few months later, after another trade with B., the captain convened his family again to say that the score had been paid with interest, and to release them from the covenant. There was the story of Uncle G., who began his courtship by "creepin' in, all unbeknown," behind his best girl, stealing up close behind her as she was washing dishes, hat on and chair in hand, with the salute, "Well, Sal, feel kind'er sparky to-night?" to which she coquettishly but encouragingly replied, "Well, I reckon p'r'aps a *leetle* more sorter than sorter not"; and how at last, the minister being away, they rode together on one horse twenty miles alone, and were married. There was the legend of old Squire V., who used to be a great favorite with the girls. Driving up to the town clerk's door one day he told him to have him "published" the next Sunday with Miss B., and drove off. Soon he returned and desired the name changed to Miss C., and finally, after several changes and some minutes of profound deliberation, settled on Miss H., whom he married. There was the tale of the turning of the Deerfield River by the two great but mystic ancestors of one family in town. It once flowed down the gap in Mr. P.'s pasture, through the pond and over the plain of the village, and was stipulated as the northern boundary of the possessions of these pioneers. They were ambitious, and had noticed that new settlers and their depredations followed rivers, so they hired hundreds of Indians to dig with sharpened sticks, day and night, one entire summer, till the stream at length washed down over a more northerly valley so suddenly as to sweep away the dusky maiden beloved by one of the pioneers; with many other romantic incidents. There was the story of the old horse-jockey G., who in his travels found a negro of great strength, but so simple as to agree to work for him a hundred years, on the expiration of which time the old jockey was to give him all the property and serve him a century; and who cured him of the inveterate habit of sucking eggs by showing him a dozen, apparently freshly laid, in his bed one morning just after he had risen, and frightening him out of the practice by convincing him that he had laid the eggs while he slept. There was the story of the old cat ground up in the mill, with dreadful caterwaulings, and of the two bushels of good rye required to grind the mill-stones clean again. Another was of the case, famous in history, of the nonconforming Baptist deacon who would not pay his town tax to support the Congregational preaching, and whose apple trees were dug up by the constable and sold for payment; of the deacon's going to Boston to the General Court, and of his return with a barrel of cider brandy drawn on two poles strapped together, one end of each in the hold-backs and the other end dragging on the ground. There were stories of a noted lady pioneer in the cause of female education, who solicited domestic utensils and produce of every kind for a young ladies' seminary, following the men into stable and around haymow in her quest; of old Heeper, suspected of witchcraft, who lived apart and was buried outside the cemetery; of old Sloper, who had no friends, and vanished so mysteriously that gradually a detailed story of his murder by a prominent but not beloved citizen was evolved; of the old church, stone cold in winter, with two services and sermons from ten to four, and in summer with the rocks black at nooning with people, mostly members in close communion, eating their Sunday dinner and picking caraway or meetin' seed; of the waste of timber or the greed of individuals in shacking hogs on the then extensive undivided land, or common, and even of the secular variations of the compass to account for the disparity between the old surveys of boundary lines and new ones.

Evenings in the kitchen were spent in light work and gossip unremitting. Candles, in olden times before cotton, it is said, were made by loosely spinning tow wicking. Candle rods were then whittled out or cut from cat-tails, on which wicking for a dozen candles was put, and they were hung over the back of an old, high, straight-backed chair tipped down, and dipped every few minutes in beef, or, better, mutton tallow melted in the tin boiler. Of course candles grew faster on cold days, but were more likely to crack. Good iron candlesticks were rare, and at balls and parties potatoes and wooden blocks were used. The evolution, I have heard, was first a "slut," or linen rag in fat, or a bowl of woodchuck's oil with a floating wick through a wooden button. Later came a square strip of fat pork with a thin sliver of wood thrust through to stiffen it and serve as a wick. Fire could still be made by friction of wood in an emergency. The best-raked fire would sometimes go out, and then fire must be borrowed from a neighbor. Those who wished to be independent obtained tinder boxes with flint and iron, smudged tow, and punk. Homemade matches, with brimstone and saltpeter, would catch readily, but friction matches were a great novelty. One of these friction matches, also homemade, of spruce lumber, by the boys, was "drawed" by their incredulous father, who, when he found it would really go, put it carefully in his pocket for future use.

The ideal hearth and fireplace of olden times (restored at Plymouth, and especially at Deerfield, Massachusetts, by George Sheldon) was indeed the center about which the whole family system revolved. On the swinging crane, evolved from the earlier wooden lug pole, hung from pothooks, chains, and trammels several species of iron pots and brass kettles, in front of a green backlog so big and long that it was sometimes snaked in by a horse. Below, attached to the upright part of the andirons, was the turnspit dog, revolved by hand, and sometimes, at a later date, by clockwork, for fancy roasts. There were roasters and dripping pans, and the three-legged spider in which bread was baked, first on the bottom and then tipped up to the coals, or else the top was done by a heavy, red-hot iron cover. Here rye used to be roasted and mortared for coffee, which was later boiled in water and maple molasses. On the shelf or beam above the fire stood the foot stove, a horn of long and another of short paper lamplighters ; a sausage stuffer ; tin lanthorn ; mortar; chafing dish ; runlet ; noggin ; flatirons, perhaps of new fashion, hollowed for hot iron chunks ; tinder box ; tankard ; and coffee pots ; and high above all a bayoneted flint gun or two, with belt, bayonet sheath, brush, and primer. Overhead on the pole hung always a hat or cap on the end, and perhaps a haunch of dried beef, with possibly a ham, a calf's rennet stretched with a springy willow stick inside ; pumpkins cut into long ringlets ; bundles of red peppers ; braided seed corn and dried apples, the latter also perhaps half covering the roof and south side of the house. About the fireplace stood or hung the bed warmer, the tongs, and long " slice," a hollow gourd or crooked-necked squash ; candle holders with long tin reflectors ; bellows ; woolen holders ; toasting irons ; smoking tongs ; pewter porringer ; spoon molds ; trivet ; skillet and piggin ; a tin kitchen ; a tin baker and steamer ; a flip iron ; the big dye tub always in the corner, and the high-backed settle in front. Near by stood the cupboard, displaying the best blue crockery, and the pewter, kept bright by scouring with horsetails (equisetum) ; sealed measures and a few liquids, and perhaps near by a pumpkin Jack-o'-lantern, with an expression, when it was lighted in the dark, as hideous as that of the head of an Alaskan totem post.

The grandma was both nurse and doctor, and the children had to gather for her each year a supply of herbs. Chief among these were pennyroyal, tansy, spearmint, peppermint, catnip, thoroughwort, motherwort, liverwort, mugwort, elecampane, burdock, mayweed, dogweed, fireweed, ragweed, pokeweed, aconite, arnica, scratch grass, valerian, lobelia, larkspur, mullein, mallow, plaintain, foxglove or nightshade, osier, fennel, sorrel, comfrey, rue, saffron, flag, anise, snakeroot yarrow, balmony, tag alder, witch-hazel, and bloodroot. Each of these, and many more, had specific medicinal properties, and hung in rows of dried bunches in the attic, and all grew in Ashfield. In Mr. Cockayne's *Leechdoms, Wortcunning, and Starcraft*, a remarkable collection of Anglo-Saxon medical prescriptions, I have identified the same symptoms for which the same herb was the specific, showing how this unwritten medical lore, as Mr. Mooney calls it in his interesting pamphlet, survives and persists unchanged.

The attic floor was covered a foot deep with corn on the ear, to be shelled winter evenings by scraping across the back of a knife driven into a board, the cobs being fed out to stock or used for baking and smoking fires. Here too were tins and boxes, and barrels of rye and barley, and later oats, wheat, and buckwheat. In the corner stood or hung, perhaps, a hand winnower, a tub of frozen cider apple sauce, an old hat and wig block, a few woodchucks' skins to be made into whip-lashes, a coon skin for a cap, a hand still for making cider brandy or twisted cider. So, too, the cellar, shed, hog house, barn, sheep and horse barn, sugar house and corn house were stored with objects of perennial interest to boys.

The " sense of progress," which a recent psychological writer calls a special though lately evolved sense, was by no means undeveloped. Men loved to tell of old times, when maple sap was caught in rough troughs made with an ax, and stored by being simply turned in their places ; to show the marks on old maple trees, where their grandfathers tapped by chipping with a hatchet and driving in a basswood spout made at a blow with the same iron gouge that prepared for its insertion, and to describe how, later, the rough unpainted tubs with unbarked hoops, and, because smaller at the top, so hard to store and carry, and so liable to burst by the expansion of the ice on freezing, were superseded by the Shaker pails. The old days when sap was gathered by hand with a sap yoke, and stored in long troughs and boiled out of doors in a row of kettles on a pole or crotches, were talked over, with complacent pity, perhaps, while modern pans on a new arch and in a new sugar house were kept going all night during a big run which had filled every tun and hogshead, while the best trees were running over.

Hour glasses, especially to spin by, and dials were sometimes used, and there were many noon marks at intervals over the farm. In many families, even where coal and kerosene stoves are used, along with wood, oven wood is still cut for the old brick oven, which Christmas time, at least, if not once every week or two through the winter, is heated and then swept out with a wet birch broom. First, the rye and Indian bread is made up in a bread trough and then put on the broad, meal-sprinkled peel, with hands dipped in water to avoid sticking, and very dexterously thrown in haycock and windrow shapes, perhaps on cabbage leaves, on to the bottom of the oven. When this was done it was still so hot that pies could be baked, and, last of all, a bushel of apples was thrown in and the week's baking was over. Many could then tell of the time when, with pudding or mashed potatoes and milk for the meal, no table was set, but each took a bowl of milk and helped himself from the kettle on the stone ; or again, the family gathered about the well-scoured table, with no individual plates or butter knives, or waiting on the table, but each took a slice of bread and helped himself from the meat dish, or dipped the brown bread into the pork fat with forks. Wooden, pewter, then earthen plates, was the order of evolution. So, in the dairy, milk used to be set in wooden trays, then in thick, brown earthen bowls, before the modern milk pans came into vogue. The evolution of the skimmer from the clam shell, through a rough wooden skimmer ; of churning, from a bowl and paddle on to the old dasher churn ; of straining milk, from the linen rag strainer up ; of bails, from the ear and peg

fashion on; the history of the artistic forms of butter balls
and the stamps used; the very gradual development of the
scythe snath, which no artist ever represents correctly, to the
present highly physiological and very sharply discriminated
forms, as well as of the hoe and pitchfork; why are not these
and the growth of the cornsheller, hencoop, plow, mop;
the story of the penstock; the broom, from a bush or bundle of
twigs up through the birch broom with fibers stripped both
up and down; of window transparencies, from the whole and
oiled paper, etc., as scientific anthropological themes as the
evolution of the fishhook, arrowhead, and spear? Why is not
the old soap-making process, with the lye, strong enough to
support an egg, dripping from the ash barrel on the circularly
grooved board or stone, and the out-of-doors boiling and basket
straining, etc.; why is not the old-fashioned semiannual geese-
picking day, with the big apron, great, vase-shaped goose basket,
and the baby's stocking drawn over the goose's head to keep
it from biting; why is not cheese making, when the milk from
three families was gathered in a big tub, coagulated with a
calf's rennet, broken up into curds and whey by the fingers,
scalded, chopped, salted, perhaps saged, hooped, turned, and
pared of those delicious curds, and daily greased all summer;
why is not the high festivity of road breaking in winter, when
all the men and oxen in the neighborhood, often twenty yokes
of oxen in one team, turned out after a long storm and blow to
break out the roads, which the town had not discontinued for
the winter, to church, stores, doctor, and school, when steers
were broken in, sandwiched between the yokes of old cattle,
where, often up to their backs in a drift, with a sled to which
plows were chained to each side and a dozen men and boys
on it, they could only wait, frightened and with lolling tongue,
to be shoveled out; why are not the antique ceremonies and
sequelæ of butchering day, and the fun and games with pluck
and lights and sausages, which city-bred boys were told, and

said to believe, were caught like fish; the process of making pearl ash and birch vinegar; cider making; the manifold summer beers and other domestic drinks, etc., quite as worthy of investigation, of illustration in museums, as the no more rapidly vanishing customs of savage tribes?

At the place and time of which I write many domestic industries were more or less specialized. Farmers' sons often went away to learn trades. Broom making, e.g., was the evening occupation of one member of the family I knew, and I saw the process of planting, breaking, tabling, hatcheling, for the seed was worth about the price of oats, bleaching with brimstone in a big "down cellar," etc. Tying was the most interesting process. It included arranging the hurls, braiding down the stalks on the handle with wire, pressing in the great vise, and sewing with a six-inch needle, thimbled through by leather palms. I was allowed to sandpaper the handles, and once, in a time of stress, when a man was making forty plain Shaker brooms per day, even to put on the gold leaf. The local tanner allowed us to run among his vats and see the hides salted, pickled, washed, and limed, and, best of all, skived over the big beam. Last summer this tanner told me he believed his eighteen months in tanning an ox hide and the six weeks required by modern chemical methods represented about the relative durability of the two leathers. His trade has lasted on, despite such competition, because his townsmen have something the same idea. Within boy range, too, was a cooper's shop, a gunsmith, a family who made baskets, a small carding mill, turning shops where wooden spoons, bowls, sieve rims, pen handles, plain broom handles, etc., were made, a general tinker and solderer, besides carpenters, blacksmiths, shoe and harness makers. Some farmers specialized more or less in sheep; others in young cattle, or pigs and horses. Some were always lucky with corn, others with rye or wheat, buckwheat, potatoes, grass, etc., to which they had mainly settled after much experiment, or to which the traditions of the farm or family inclined them. Thus, in fine, there were many grades of progress and versatility. Many of these old home industries I can still practice and have added to them by "lessons" in Germany. All come handy in the laboratory. I know I could make soap, maple sugar, a pair of shoes, braid a palm-leaf hat, spin, put in and weave a piece of frocking or a rag carpet, do crude carpentry, farm and dairy work, and I envy the pupils at Tuskegee who can do more of these things and better than I.

I have alluded to but few of the occupations of these people. Their commonest industries — planting, fertilizing, gathering each crop — have been revolutionized by machinery and artificial fertilization within twenty-five years. These, together with their religion and beliefs, domestic social customs, and methods of doing their small business, are all fast changing. The women are haggard and worn with their work, the men are sometimes shiftless, and children are very rare. The heart of these communities has left it, and only the shell remains. The quaint, eccentric characters that abound in these towns, types of which may be found faithfully depicted by Mary E. Wilkins or in Mary B. Claflin's *Brampton Sketches*, or in a few of the sketches in *Profitable Tales*, by Eugene Field, are for the most part types of degeneration well recognized by alienists and characterized by Morel. These are quite different from the no less rustic characters in De Gaspé's *Canadians of Old, or the Work of Du Pray's School*. Life then and there, although perhaps a century or more later than that described in the books of Alice Morse Earle, did not differ much from it. Did the earlier generations work too hard in digging stumps and stones, and laying the hundreds of miles of heavy stone wall and clearing the timber? Were the conditions of life too severe? Is our race not adapted to the new conditions of climate, soil, water, and, as Dr. Jarvis said, is it still a problem whether the Anglo-Saxon race can thrive in its new American home, or is this but an incident, an eddy in the great onward current of progress? I have no answer, but I know nothing more sad in our American life than the decay of these townlets.

Nowhere has the great middle class been so all-controlling, furnished so large a proportion of scientific and business leaders, been so respectable, so well combined industry with wealth, bred patriotism, conservatism, and independence. The farm was a great laboratory, tending, perhaps, rather more to develop scientific than literary tastes, cultivating persistency, in which country boys excel, if at the expense of versatility. It is, says Professor Brewer, the question with city parents what useful thing the children can do; while in the country, where they are in great demand on the farm, they are, in a sense, members of the firm. Evenings are not dangerous to morality, but are turned to good account, while during the rowdy or adolescent age the boy tendency to revert to savagery can find harmless vent in hunting, trapping, and other ways less injurious to morals than the customs of city life.

Some such training the heroes of '76 had; the independent conditions of communities like this was just the reverse of that of the South at the outbreak of the Rebellion; such a people cannot be conquered, for war and blockade would only drive them back to more primitive conditions, and restore the old independence of foreign and even domestic markets. Again, should we ever have occasion to educate colonists, as England is now attempting, we could not do so better than by reviving conditions of life like these.

I close by mentioning an interesting new educational experiment as a bright spot in this somber present, which was somewhat feebly but happily tried in Ashfield, as a result of the recently awakened interest in its own antiquities. A prominent citizen, once a teacher, has studied from sources largely unprinted the history of the town, which connects it with the Revolution, and even the French and Indian wars, and, on the lines of old maps he has made of the original town surveys, gave an hour per week during part of a winter to teaching history from a local standpoint in the little academy, with its score of pupils, and adding many of the antiquities such as this paper has referred to, with free use of the museum, and all with excellent results. A village pastor, who is an excellent botanist, took the class a few times each year on excursions, and the older girls have gathered and pressed for him in a school museum all the Ashfield plants and grasses, on the basis of which he taught a little botany gratuitously. The doctor coöperated with them and talked on physiology and hygiene, and brought his microscope and other instruments. A student of an agricultural college has gathered all the Ashfield rocks and minerals and taught geology. He has gathered cabinets of the local animals, birds, eggs, butterflies, and insects, which a summer resident makes a basis of some instruction. A summer boarder was drafted in to teach drawing to all comers half a day per week. This experiment, in what I consider coöperative education, begins at home, with what is nearest and often despised. The local Faculty about the teacher give but little time, but their teaching is full of interest and stimulus. They strengthen the teacher whom they really guide, and bring home and school nearer together. This new curriculum is without expense, and altogether may prove a suggestive novelty. To-day old domestic industries of the age of the tinder box and stone milk pan and niddy-noddy are taught by a specialist, Miss H. B. Merrill, to history classes from the city schools in turn in a central museum of American antiquities in Milwaukee.

G. STANLEY HALL

BIBLIOGRAPHY

Brand, John. Observations on the Popular Antiquities of Great Britain. G. Bell & Sons, London, 1882. 3 vols.

Claflin, Mary B. Brampton Sketches: Old-Time New England Life. T. Y. Crowell & Co., New York, 1890. 158 pages.

Cockayne, Oswald. Leechdoms, Wortcunning, and Starcraft (published under direction of the Master of the Rolls). Longmans (and others), London, 1864–1866. 3 vols.

De Gaspé, P. A. Canadians of Old (translated by Georgiana M. Pennée). G. and G. E. Desbarats, 1864. 331 pages.

Earle, Alice Morse. Child Life in Colonial Days. Macmillan, New York, 1899. 418 pages.

Earle, Alice Morse. Customs and Fashions in Old New England. Scribner, 1893. 387 pages.

Earle, Alice Morse. Home Life in Colonial Days. Macmillan, New York, 1898. 470 pages.

Field, Eugene. A Little Book of Profitable Tales. Scribner, New York, 1890. 286 pages.

Mooney, James. "The Sacred Formulas of the Cherokees," *Annual Report of the Bureau of Ethnology, 1885–1886*. Government Printing Office, Washington, 1891.

Newell, William Welles. The Games and Songs of American Children. New and enlarged edition. Harper & Brothers, New York, 1903. 242 pages.

Wilkins, Mary E. A Humble Romance and Other Stories. Harper & Brothers, New York, 1887. 436 pages.

Wilkins, Mary E. In Colonial Times: the Adventures of Ann the Bound Girl of Samuel Wales of Braintree in the Province of Massachusetts Bay. Lothrop Publishing Company, Boston, 1899. 115 pages.

INDEX

Classics In
Child Development

An Arno Press Collection

Baldwin, James Mark. **Thought and Things.** Four vols. in two. 1906-1915

Blatz, W[illiam] E[met], et al. **Collected Studies on the Dionne Quintuplets.** 1937

Bühler, Charlotte. **The First Year of Life.** 1930

Bühler, Karl. **The Mental Development of the Child.** 1930

Claparède, Ed[ouard]. **Experimental Pedagogy and the Psychology of the Child.** 1911

Factors Determining Intellectual Attainment. 1975

First Notes by Observant Parents. 1975

Freud, Anna. **Introduction to the Technic of Child Analysis.** 1928

Gesell, Arnold, et al. **Biographies of Child Development.** 1939

Goodenough, Florence L. **Measurement of Intelligence By Drawings.** 1926

Griffiths, Ruth. **A Study of Imagination in Early Childhood and Its Function in Mental Development.** 1918

Hall, G. Stanley and Some of His Pupils. **Aspects of Child Life and Education.** 1907

Hartshorne, Hugh and Mark May. **Studies in the Nature of Character. Vol. I: Studies in Deceit; Book One, General Methods and Results.** 1928

Hogan, Louise E. **A Study of a Child.** 1898

Hollingworth, Leta S. **Children Above** 180 **IQ, Stanford Binet:** Origins and Development. 1942

Kluver, Heinrich. **An Experimental Study of the Eidetic Type.** 1926

Lamson, Mary Swift. **Life and Education of Laura Dewey Bridgman, the Deaf, Dumb and Blind Girl.** 1881

Lewis, M[orris] M[ichael]. **Infant Speech:** A Study of the Beginnings of Language. 1936

McGraw, Myrtle B. **Growth: A Study of Johnny and Jimmy.** 1935

Monographs on Infancy. 1975

O'Shea, M. V., editor. **The Child: His Nature and His Needs.** 1925

Perez, Bernard. **The First Three Years of Childhood.** 1888

Romanes, George John. **Mental Evolution in Man:** Origin of Human Faculty. 1889

Shinn, Milicent Washburn. **The Biography of a Baby.** 1900

Stern, William. **Psychology of Early Childhood Up to the Sixth Year of Age.** 1924

Studies of Play. 1975

Terman, Lewis M. **Genius and Stupidity:** A Study of Some of the Intellectual Processes of Seven "Bright" and Seven "Stupid" Boys. 1906

Terman, Lewis M. **The Measurement of Intelligence.** 1916

Thorndike, Edward Lee. **Notes on Child Study.** 1901

Wilson, Louis N., compiler. **Bibliography of Child Study.** 1898-1912

[Witte, Karl Heinrich Gottfried]. **The Education of Karl Witte,** Or the Training of the Child. 1914